IMAGES
of America

HOPE CEMETERY

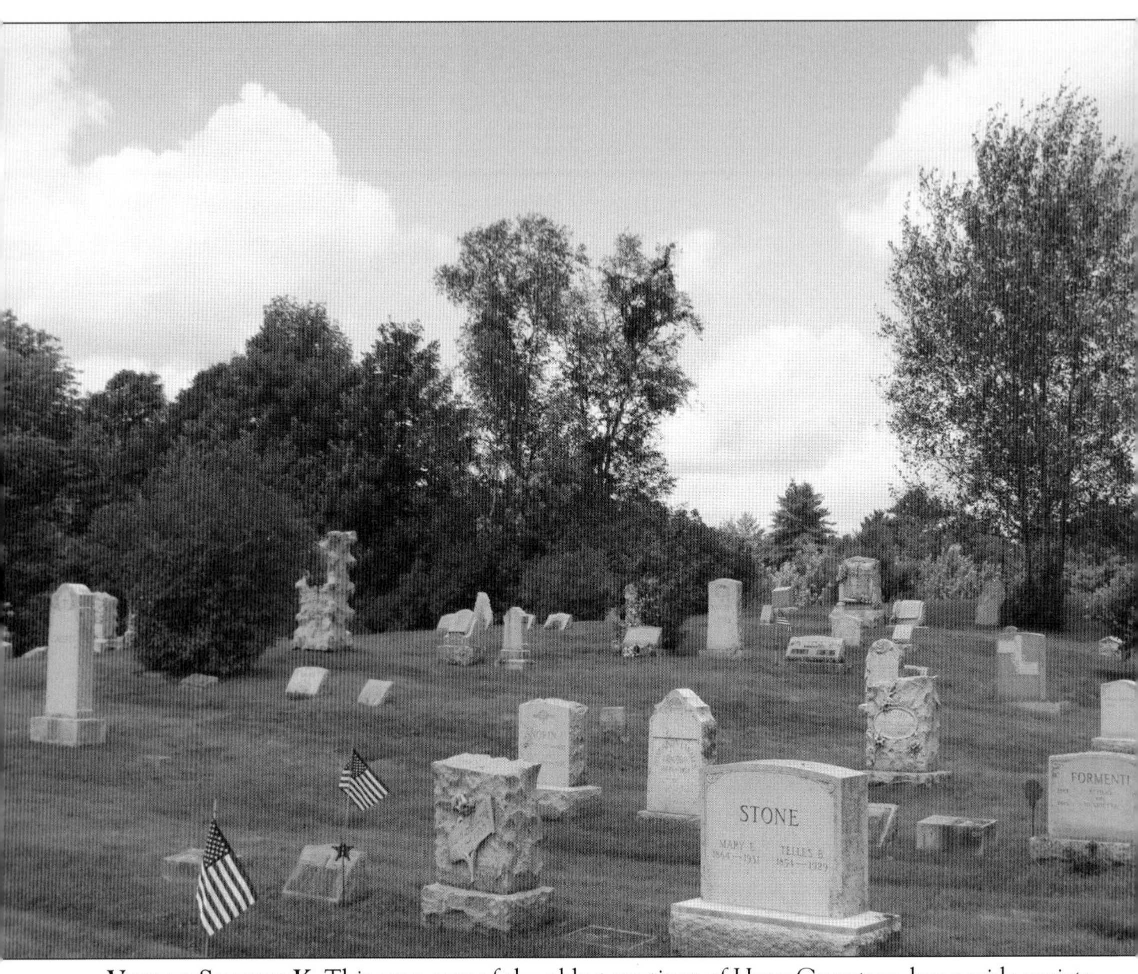

VIEW OF SECTION K. This area, one of the oldest portions of Hope Cemetery, has a wide variety of monuments that highlight the skills of Barre's earliest immigrant stonecutters. Also note the terraced effect of the landscape, an early planned feature so that each row of monuments would be easily visible from the cemetery's roadways. (Author's collection.)

ON THE COVER: ELIA CORTI. Stonecutter Elia Corti (1869–1903) was killed during a political rally at the Socialist Labor Party Hall in Barre. (Author's collection.)

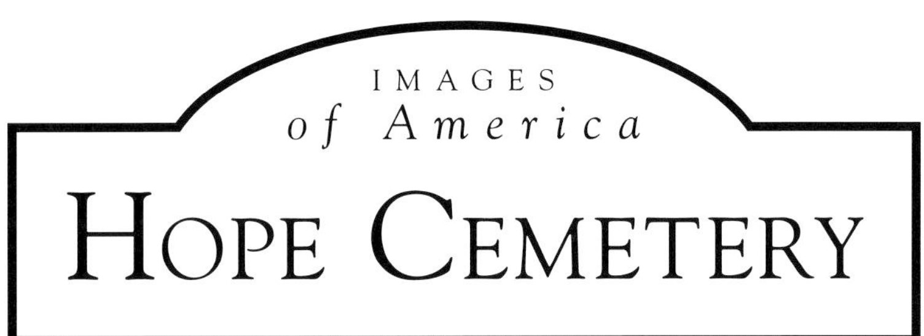

Glenn A. Knoblock

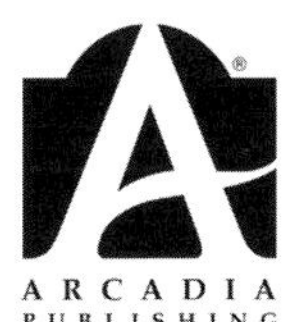

ISBN 978-1-4671-2847-6

Published by Arcadia Publishing
Charleston, South Carolina

Printed in the United States of America

Library of Congress Control Number: 2017953968

For all general information, please contact Arcadia Publishing:
Telephone 843-853-2070
Fax 843-853-0044
E-mail sales@arcadiapublishing.com
For customer service and orders:
Toll-Free 1-888-313-2665

Visit us on the Internet at www.arcadiapublishing.com

To Giuliano Cecchinelli, the last of the old-time stonecutters and the dedicated men and women who maintain and manage Hope Cemetery to the highest degree

Contents

ACKNOWLEDGMENTS

Writing this book has long been a goal of mine, which started with the first visit made some years ago with my wife, Terry, who, like me, fell in love with Hope Cemetery. For their help in making this dream a reality, I have a number of people to thank; first and foremost is Terry Knoblock, who has been my companion on nearly all the trips I have made to Barre and has provided excellent editorial feedback. We also had a lot of enjoyable time spent during our trips back and forth. I also thank Ashley Steinkopf and Delina Bickford, who rearranged their schedules and so ably cared for our daughter Anna during our extra time away from home. Other individuals that have rendered valuable assistance include Scott McLaughlin, executive director, Vermont Granite Museum; Stephanie Quaranta, City of Barre, assistant director, Buildings & Community Services–Recreation; Jeff Bergeron, City of Barre, director, Buildings & Community Services; Todd Paton, director of Visitor Services, Rock of Ages; Amanda Pittsley, marketing manager, Rock of Ages; Jeanne McCool, network technician, Aldrich Public Library; and Sarah Costa, library director, Aldrich Public Library. Special thanks are extended to Giuliano Cecchinelli, both father and son—the latter for agreeing to arrange a meeting in Hope Cemetery with his father, and the former for the extended tour he gave me of Hope Cemetery, which resulted in many valuable insights.

Included at the end of this work is an index to many of the monuments discussed herein, which should serve as a helpful guide for those visiting Hope. In regard to records, burial records for the earliest years are incomplete. Later records are computerized and offer plot and interment information, but the dates for the placement of monuments are not recorded. For the census, immigration, and vital record information given, I have consulted federal and state records via Ancestry.com. While I do offer some personal history for many individuals, space constraints limit the amount presented. Causes of death are given for some individuals, but where these deaths are recent, I have refrained from doing so out of respect for their families.

Unless otherwise noted, all images in this work are from the author's collection.

INTRODUCTION

Hope Cemetery was established out of a simple need to accommodate a growing population that would soon require more burial spaces than the earlier established town cemetery, Elmwood Cemetery, could provide. However, it was the confluence of two related events in this rural Vermont community that would soon establish Hope Cemetery as one of the finest cemeteries, a virtual open-air museum, in all of New England. The first of these was the discovery of the great granite deposits that were present in the area, soon to be renowned as Barre granite, a light-grey, finely grained granite composed of quartz, mica, and feldspar known for its texture and superior weather-resistant properties. Barre's rise to prominence as the center of the granite industry would come in 1875, when a branch rail line was constructed linking Barre to the state capital, Montpelier. Along with the great increase in the granite trade that came with this development, there came the influx of the men with the required skills to work the raw granite into its finished form as statues and monuments. The most skilled of these men were immigrants from Italy—many from northern towns, such as Carrara, known for their stone sculptors and artisans—as well as Scotland and Spain. While the finished works of granite art made by Barre's immigrant artisans, including commemorative statuary and cemetery monuments, were shipped all over the United States, it was only natural that these craftsmen would also supply the monuments for family and friends, and, in many cases, craft the monuments that would eventually mark their own graves, in Hope Cemetery. Interestingly, oral traditions in Barre state that some 75 percent of Hope's early monuments were crafted by stonecutters for use on their own graves or for those of their family members. Within a decade or so from its establishment in 1895, following the purchase of 53 acres of land from a local farmer, Hope Cemetery in effect became a showroom highlighting the talents of Barre's stonecutters. Indeed, in 1895, few could have imagined that in less than 50 years, Hope Cemetery would become one of New England's most renowned burial places and that, by the 1980s, it would become an established Vermont tourist attraction.

First and foremost, Hope Cemetery is distinctive for the wide range of monuments that are found here, showing in full spectrum and at the highest skill level the evolution of American monument design and traditions from the beginning of the 20th century down to the present time. Hope's early monuments offer a combination of traditional American forms then in vogue, such as tree-stump monuments and those crafted in the traditions of the late Victorian era using floral and architectural elements, but also offer up some fine examples of European-influenced monuments of classical-religious design that are reflective of the immigrant stonecutters who crafted them. As American tastes in monuments changed through the 20th century, so too did Barre's stonecutters strive to meet that demand; while classic religious themes would always remain popular, Art Deco– and Art Moderne–influenced designs would come into vogue by the 1930s and 1940s, and by the late 1950s, distinctively modern monuments, ones with a greater degree of personalization than ever seen before, would begin to emerge and have become bolder in design down to the present day. No matter what types of monuments may be found in Hope Cemetery, one thing is certain: even many of the less publicized monuments found within its confines, those that are not featured in cemetery tours, are excellent examples of the monument maker's art that would stand out in almost any other New England graveyard.

Much of the change for the types of monuments found in Hope Cemetery has been driven by technological advancements within the stonecutting business; at first, monuments were crafted by hand by artisans using air hammers and chisels. In these early times, from the 1890s and into the 1950s, monuments were created in the town's numerous granite sheds by teams of craftsmen as the hunk of granite chosen for a given monument made its way through the shed in almost assembly-line fashion; one man would specialize in carving a monument's floral components, others were known for their lettering skills, and so on, each portion often taking hours to complete. Though they are regarded as works of art today, very seldom was one of these early hand-worked monuments signed by an artist, for the simple reason that more than one artist had created it. Later on, however, other methods of making monuments were developed that utilized modern artistic skills resulting in personalized monuments that, in many cases, were more affordable and took less time to create. Sandblasting—whereby a silicone or rubber design pattern is produced by an artist and adhered on the granite to be worked, the design etched in stone by means of air blasting grains of sand against the stone—gained in popularity by the 1940s and would remain a mainstay, but in 1989, laser technology was introduced in the monument-making business and is dominant today for the versatility in design the systems offer. Despite these changes, one artisan stonecutter, Giuliano Cecchinelli, remains in Barre today, crafting handmade monuments using the traditional methods used by Barre's first immigrant stonecutters.

Just as the types of monuments found in Hope Cemetery were influenced by the local granite and stonecutting business, so too did the layout of the cemetery itself have its important influences. The cemetery was eventually laid out in the form that became popular with the advent of the rural cemetery movement in America, beginning in the 1830s. The rural, or garden, cemetery, as it is often termed, developed by this movement was well landscaped, designed to have a parklike setting that would be attractive to the public—in contrast to earlier New England burial grounds, which were rather forlorn places without any planned aesthetics. These garden cemeteries were first popular in larger cities like Boston and Philadelphia but later came to be used in smaller towns too. When the land for Hope was first purchased, burials began by 1896 in random fashion. The town took its first steps toward development in 1899, when it hired civil engineer Edward P. Adams of Medford, Massachusetts, to draft plans for a fully developed garden cemetery. The plan he formulated was ambitious in design, and while it would never be fully realized, its importance lay in the fact that it served as a conceptual guide for later development that would result in a beautiful garden-style cemetery that was more fitting (and less costly) for its rural location. One of the most interesting aspects of the older portions of Hope Cemetery is its tiered level approach, well developed by the 1920s, making it such that even monuments located some distance from the network of roads within are visible to visitors. This was a unique approach for the town planners to take, as in most cemeteries at this time, it was customary to separate sections of monuments with plantings in order to offer a background view. However, in Hope, it was considered critical that all monuments be visible as they themselves offered a unique background and served to highlight the work of local Barre stonecutters. The approach was a practical one, as Hope Cemetery was a virtual showroom that was visited almost daily by monument dealers from near and far in order to view the types of monuments that were produced here. Additions to the cemetery over the years are the Woodside and Hillside sections, followed by the most recent additions—Evergreen, Morningside, and Hillcrest. The Woodside section was developed beginning in 1957 and provided the model for the modern sections by utilizing a compartmentalized design principle, whereby the large area was divided into parts using boxed hedge plantings. This offered a degree of "intimacy and seclusion," in direct contrast to the older sections of the cemetery. That this principle was well-accepted by the public is indicated by the fact that the 1,800 interment plots in the Woodside section were completely sold out in less than 10 years.

Today, Hope Cemetery continues to be a place of serenity and beauty, with more incredible monuments being added every year—most crafted by local artisans who carry on the traditions of Barre monument-making. And Hope Cemetery is not done growing; expansion plans are under way for several new sections to accommodate the heavy demand for burials, thus making for an even larger "open-air museum" in the years to come.

One

The Beginning of Hope

The land for Hope Cemetery was originally the site of the farm of C.N. Benedict; the 53 acres were acquired in May 1895 in a trade that cost $7,000 according to town records, though the transaction would not be finalized until 1897. Benedict occupied the land until the fall of 1895, but the farmhouse and buildings would continue in use as the city farm. Burials commenced here by early 1896, and in 1899, civil engineer Edward Adams was contracted to draw up plans for the cemetery and provide a layout for immediate use. However, in the early years, development was slow, and even by 1906, it was noted that improvements to the cemetery were still needed. "Great improvement" was made in 1909 with the laying out of new lots, as "heretofore the commissioners have been a little backward" in their planning. However, the cemetery commissioners would not gain full control of Hope's land until the city farm was abandoned after June 1914. Interestingly, it is this part of Hope Cemetery, previously untouched, that is now under development after all these years. The Hope Cemetery of today is vastly different than it was 100 years ago; part of the cemetery in the beginning was used as a park, and in keeping with the traditions of the garden-style cemetery of the times, there once were cast-iron settees placed throughout; the settees were initially purchased from the Stewart Iron Works in Kentucky at a cost of $8.25 apiece in 1912. The view from Maple Avenue, too, is vastly changed due to expansion, this area, including the entrance driveway, once being heavily wooded and shielding Hope from view. Having been added in the early 1930s, the beautiful granite entrance gates were not an original part of Hope Cemetery. While Hope Cemetery would gradually expand in its early years, growing to 65 acres, the deadly outbreak of Spanish influenza from August 1918 through early 1919 quickened the pace out of sheer necessity.

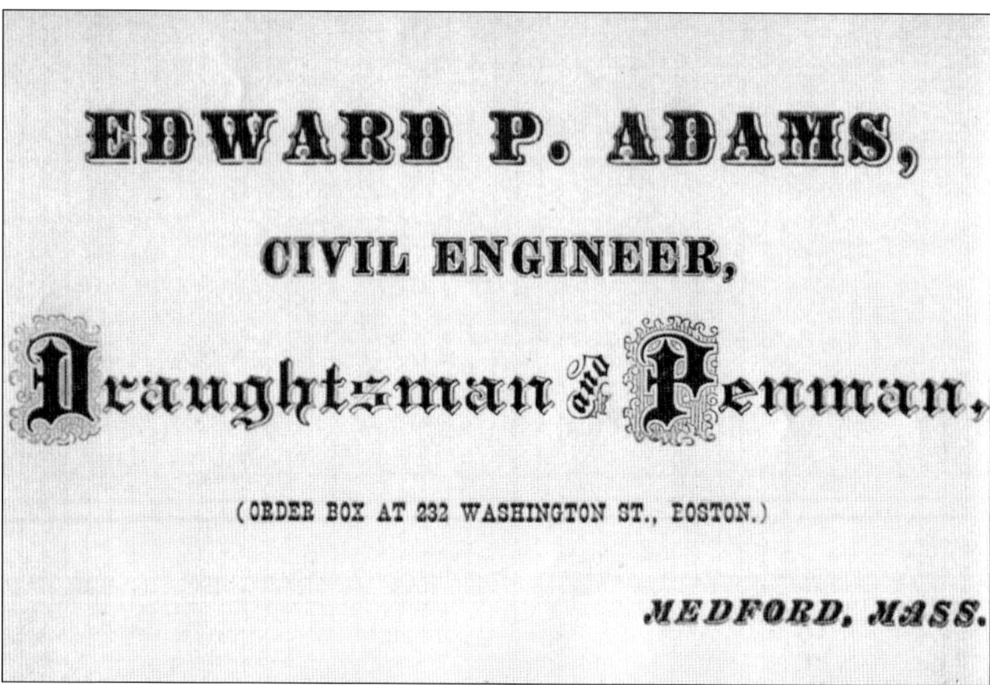

Edward P. Adams Business Card. This 1876 Worcester Polytechnic Institute graduate was hired by the town of Barre in 1899 to provide the garden-style cemetery design for Hope Cemetery. While Adams had a long career as a civil architect, he is best known for his design work for Hope Cemetery.

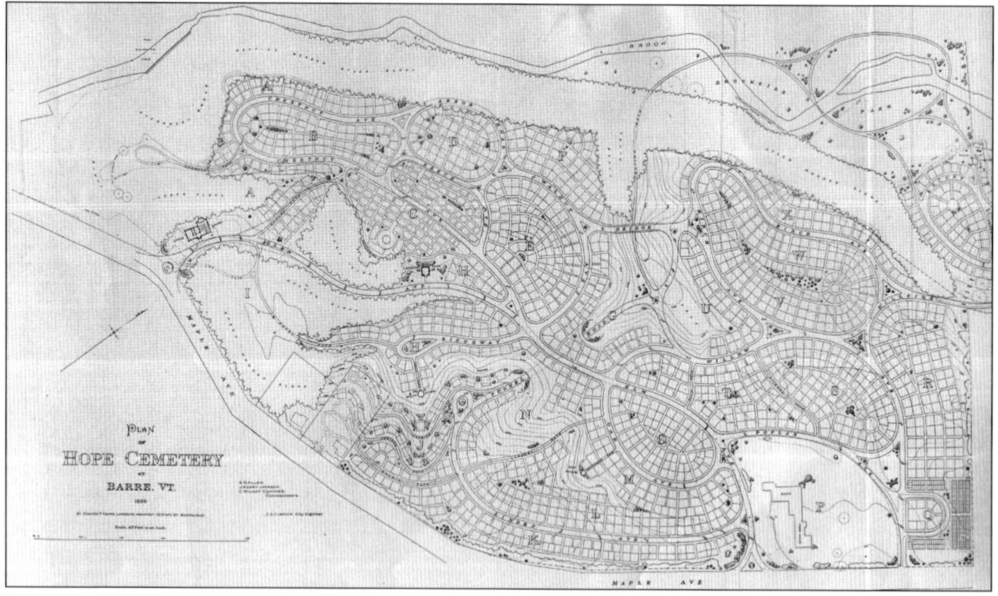

Plan of Hope Cemetery, 1899. The original design for Hope Cemetery was an ambitious one filled with many features, including a bridge, a tunnel road, a receiving tomb, a chapel, and several outdoor shelters, as well as many floral-themed pathways. While the full design by Adams would never be realized, it nonetheless served as a guide for the town and later landscape architects. (Courtesy of the City of Barre.)

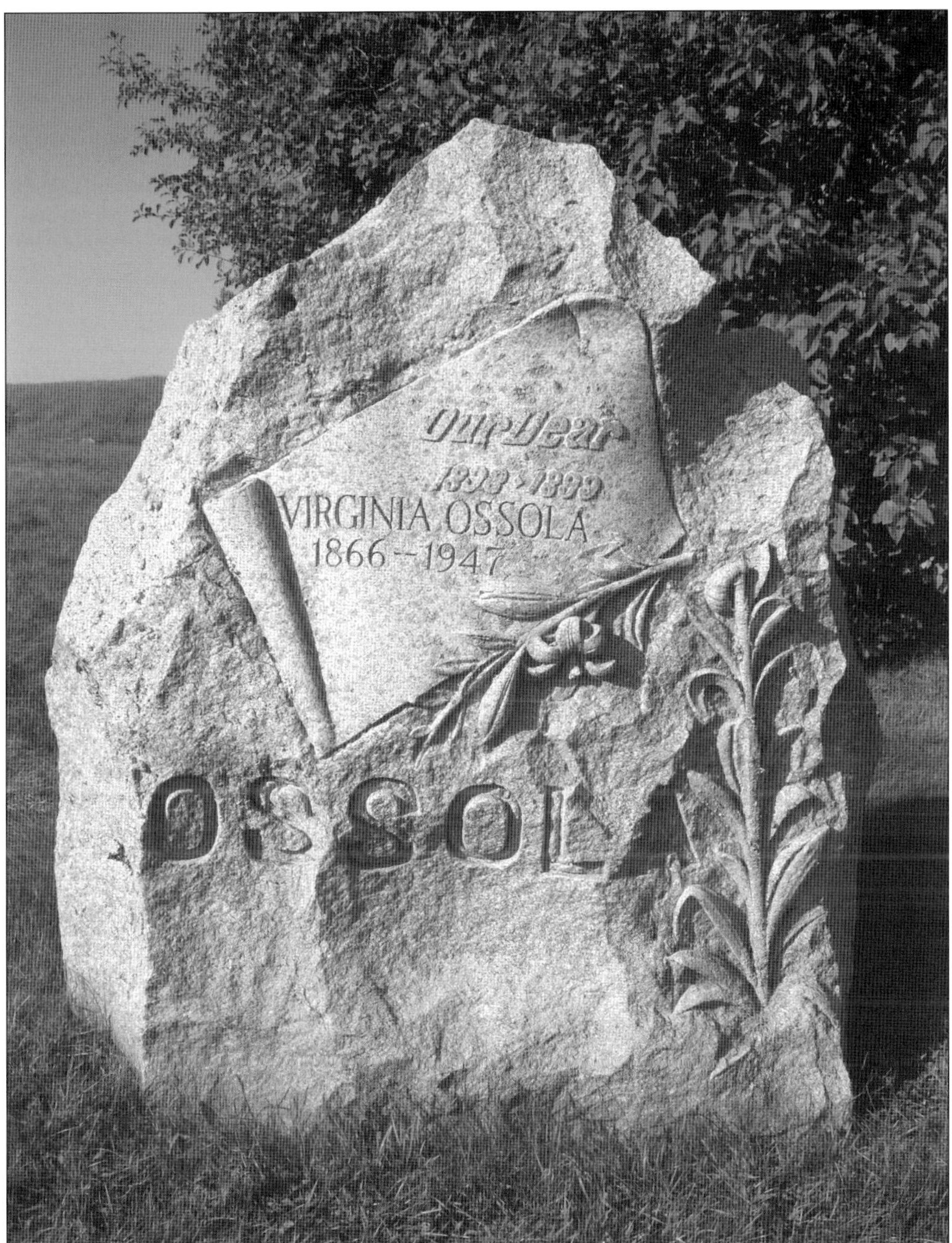

Ossola Family Monument. This naturalistic monument was placed in Section K in 1899. Note the flower, a lily, cut in two by a caterpillar, symbolic of a young life cut short. The lily itself is a Christian symbol of purity and innocence, and thus wholly appropriate for an infant. Daniel Ossola died from the croup at 10 months old, while Virginia, a native of Italy, was his grandmother. This stone is an example of the skill of Barre's stonecutters; the scroll where the names and dates are inscribed is almost paper thin where exposed at the ends, chiseled out of the block of granite, as is the raised "Our Dear" lettering. Virginia's name, added in 1947, was added by the sandblasting technique.

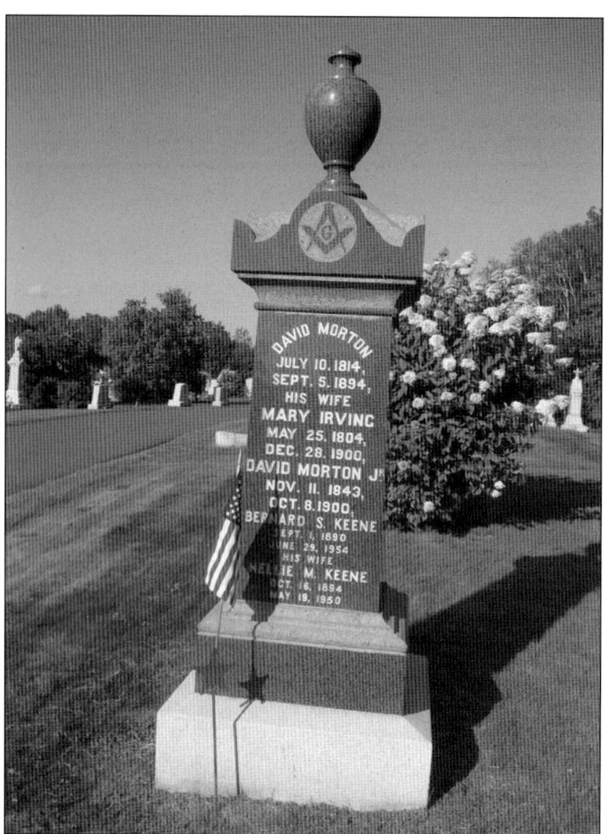

Morton Family Monument. Made of black granite from Quincy, Massachusetts, this monument is thought to be the oldest in Hope Cemetery. The tall column topped off by a funerary urn was a style that first became popular in New England in the 1830s. Note the compass and set square emblem below the urn—an indicator that David Morton was a Mason.

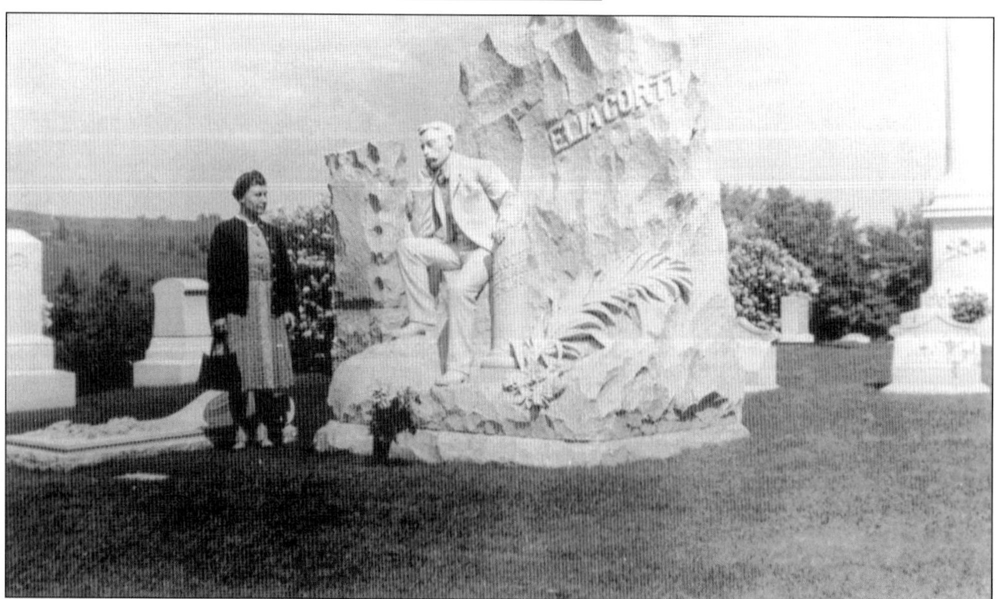

Lelia Corti Comolli (1897–1982). Shown here in this 1950s view is the daughter of the slain stonecutter Elia Corti. Just six years old at the time of her father's death, Lelia would grow up to be a teacher in Barre. In 1922, she married Armando Comolli, the owner of a granite manufacturing company. (Courtesy of the Barre Historical Society.)

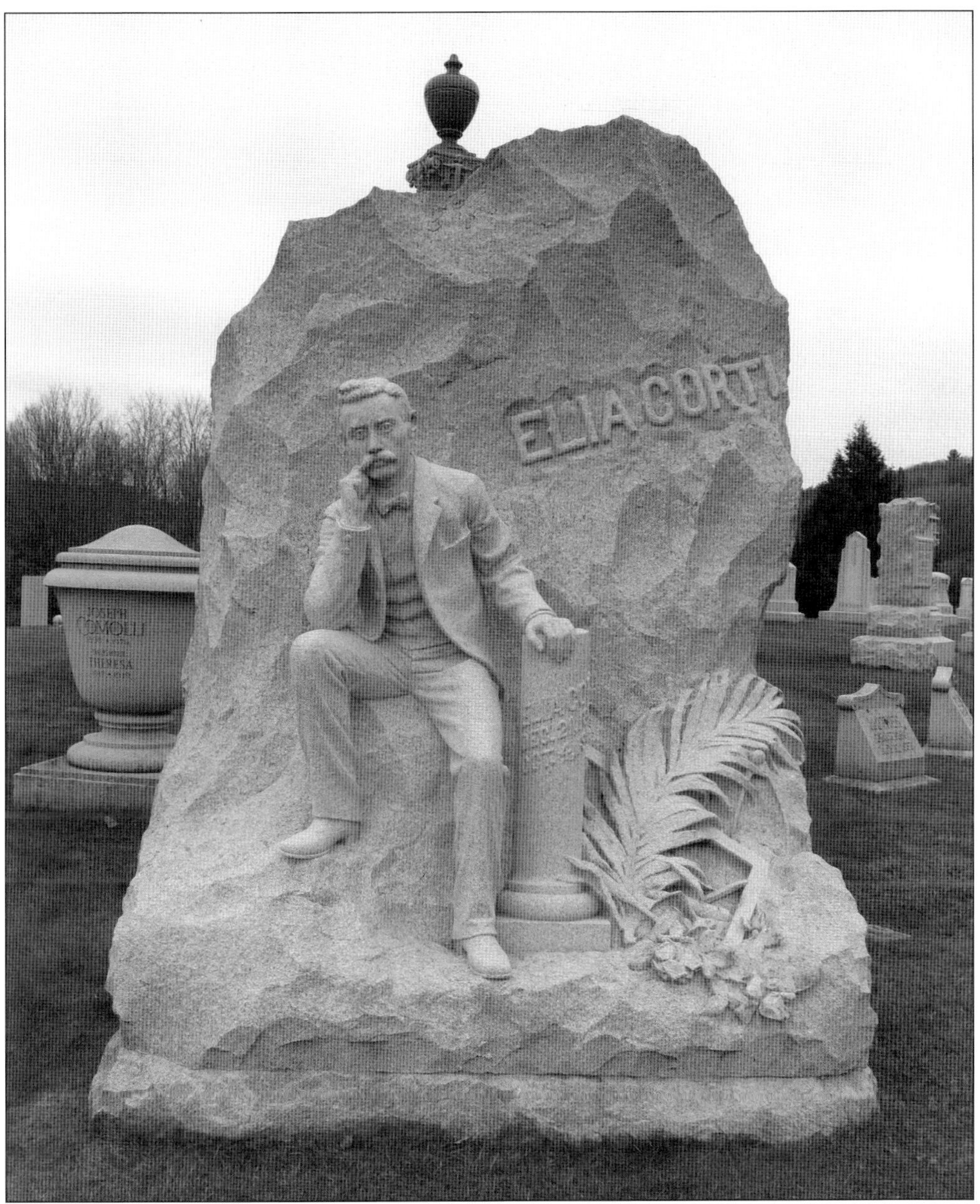

Elia Corti Monument (1903). Probably the most famous monument in Hope Cemetery, Corti's monument is also important for being the first sculpture of its kind here and set the standard for future artistic monuments. The naturalistic monument depicts Elia Corti (1869–1903) in full size with lifelike accuracy and detail. Note the tools of the stonecutter's trade scattered amongst the flowers at his feet, including calipers, a set square, pneumatic hammer, and a mallet, while the broken column his hand rests on is symbolic of a life cut tragically short. Corti was shot at the Barre Labor Hall when a fight broke out between anarchists and socialists during a political rally. At the time of his death, he was one of the most renowned sculptors of his time. The Corti monument was crafted by his brother, William Corti, brother-in-law John Comi, and likely others of his firm, making it a collective tribute by members of both his family and the firm of Novelli and Corti.

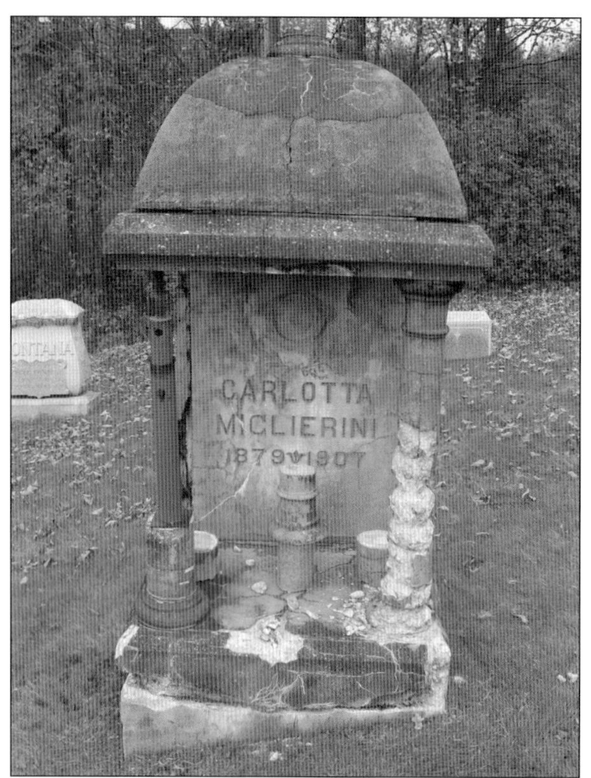

Carlotta Miclierini Monument. This monument for the young wife, who likely died from complications as the result of a miscarriage, of concrete dealer Giulio Miclierini was the only broken and damaged one in all of Hope Cemetery for years. The view at left shows how it had deteriorated, having one column replaced by a hydraulic jack. The condition of the original resulted because it was made not of Barre granite, but of concrete produced by her husband's firm and was paid no attention when Giulio moved to California permanently by World War I. The new monument (below) was placed in 2015 thanks to the volunteer efforts of local Barre citizens and businesses.

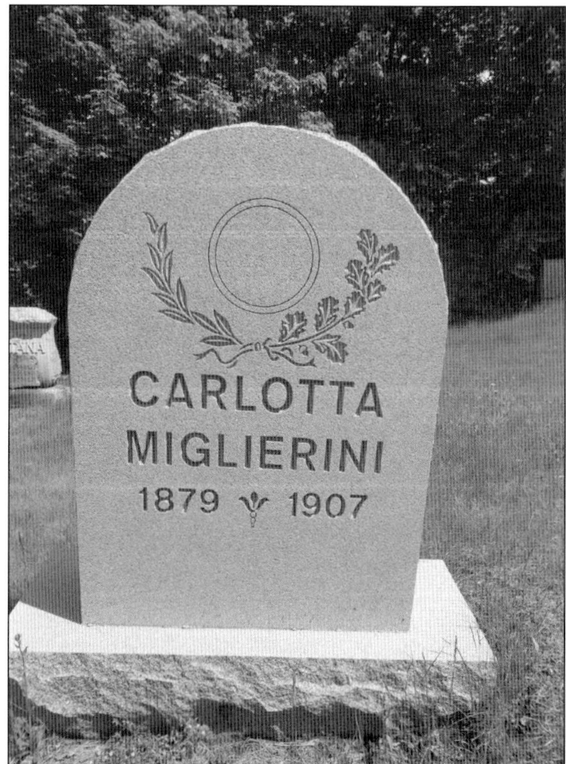

William Kelman Monument (1897). Kelman was a Scotsman from Aberdeen who worked as a granite cutter. He died from consumption, a disease affecting the lungs due to the inhalation of granite dust. This tree-stump monument was a form that first became popular by the 1880s due to the rise of the Rustic movement. With its depiction of a tree without branches, it was also symbolic of a life cut short.

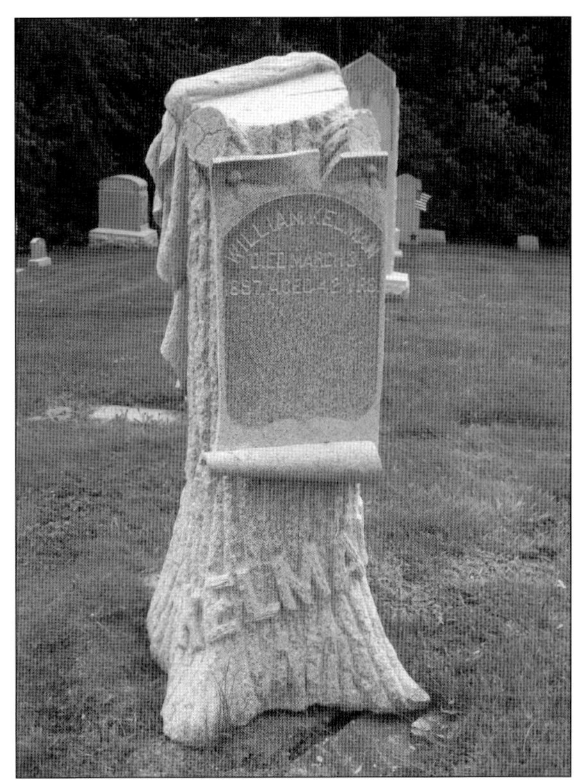

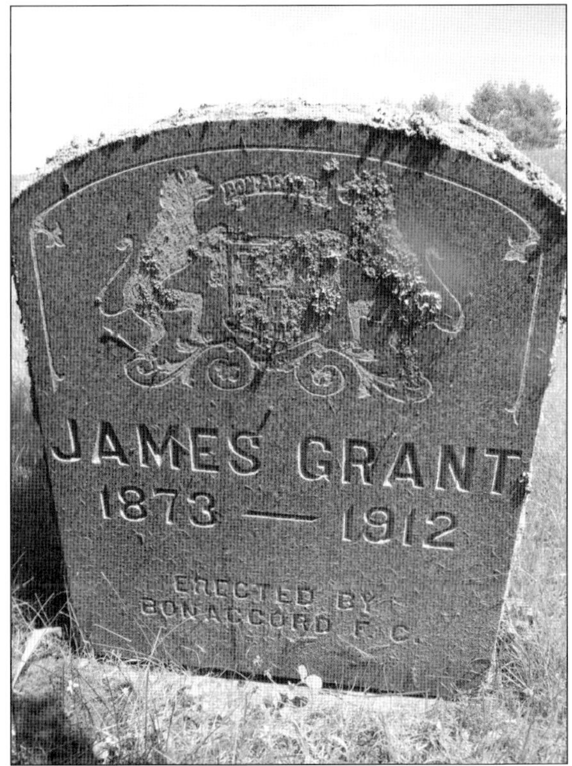

James Grant Monument (1912). The Scottish influence in Barre is evident on this marker that was erected by the Bonaccord Football Club, from Aberdeen, Scotland, and founded in 1890. Grant was a stonecutter from Aberdeen who likely played for the team. He died from shock after being run over by a freight train and having his arm amputated.

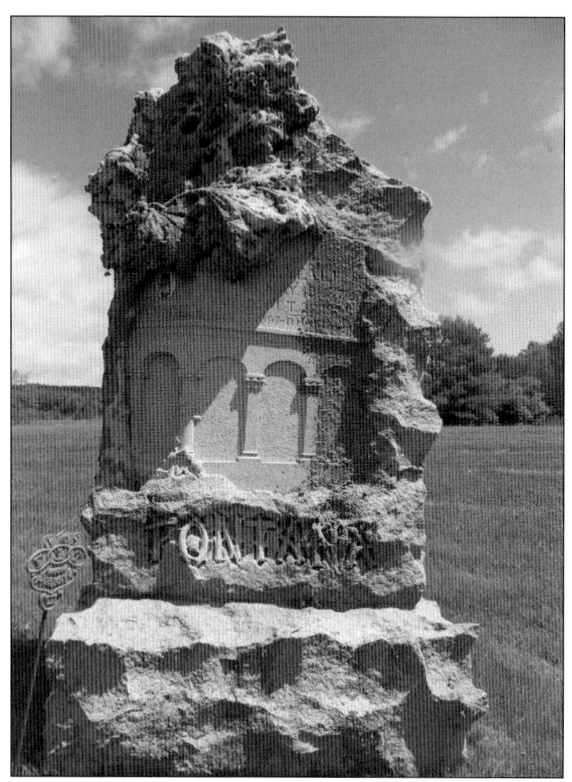

Fontana Family Monument (1900). This naturalistic and architecturally themed monument was crafted by Barre stonecutter Natali Fontana for his daughter Annie (1897–1900). Located in Section K, this finely carved stone is not only an excellent example of the work done by Barre's immigrant carvers, but also features an early example of a porcelain portrait inset (below) of the deceased. Her father, Natali Fontana (1872–1908), later a resident of Williamstown, would not long survive her, dying of tuberculosis due to inhaling granite dust, leaving behind his wife, Santonio, and five children. His portrait may also have once been placed on this stone (see the oval inset above his name).

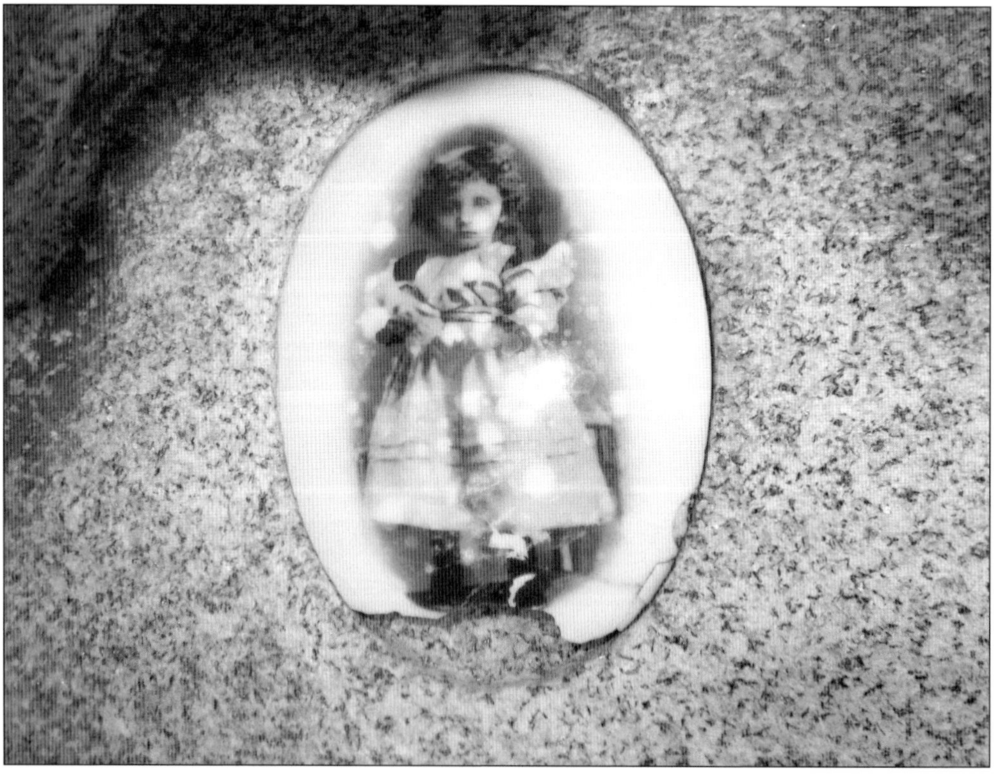

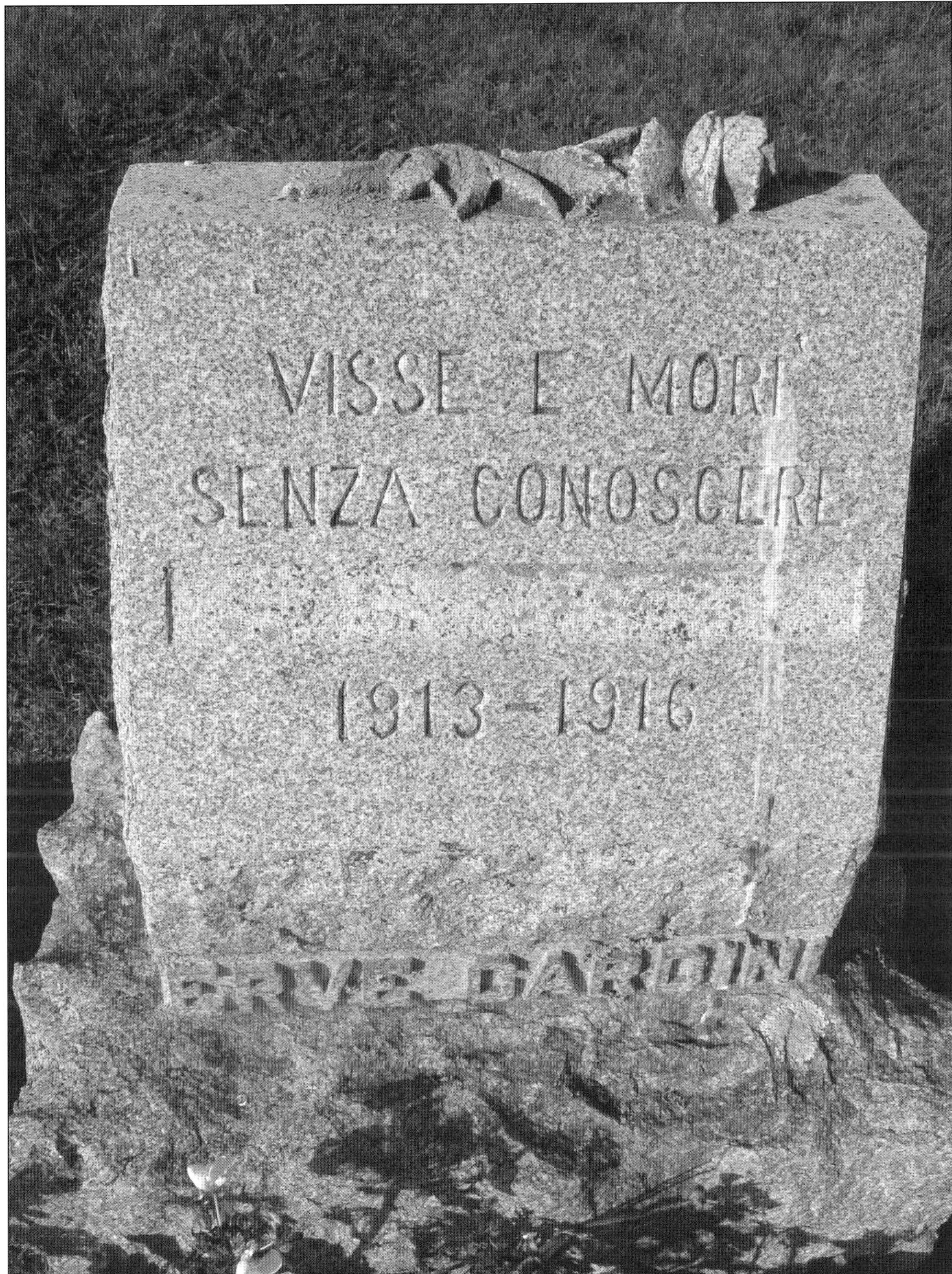

Erve Cardini Monument (1916). The daughter of stonecutter Natale Cardini, this girl died from burns suffered when her clothing caught fire. The translated partial inscription reads "Lived and Died Without Knowing," with the last line chiseled out. It originally read "Ne Dio Ne Padron," a reference to God, but was later removed (by whom is unclear) after the era of socialist and anarchist politics during the early 20th century in Barre had ended. The declaration that the child lived and died without knowing God, an indication of her father's strongly held Socialist beliefs, was considered offensive.

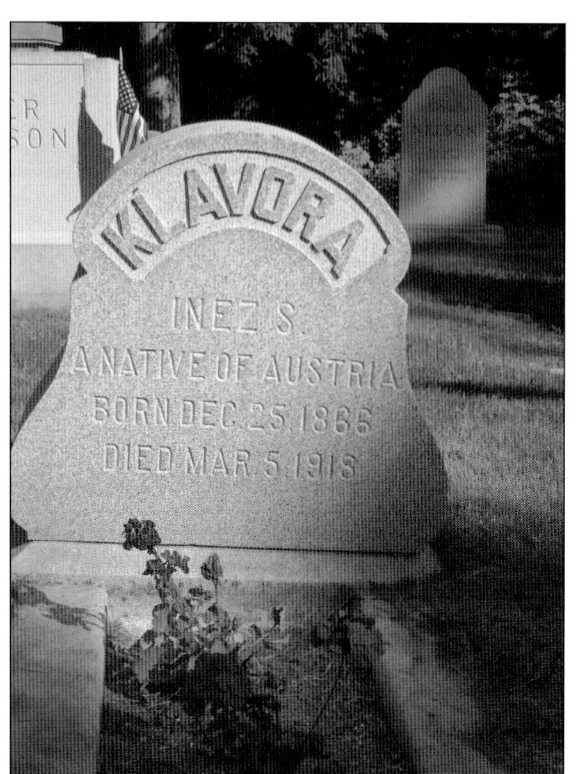

INEZ KLAVORA MONUMENT (1916). The gravesite of this native of Austria is interesting because it is outlined in granite—one of the few such plots like this in all of Hope Cemetery. Such stone outlines, however, were common practice in German and Austrian churchyards.

SPANISH INFLUENZA VICTIMS (1918). The rear portion of Section K is the burial site of many of the flu victims, including members of the Gutierrez, Danisi, and Guidali families, all of whom died in a two-day span in October 1918. Barre was hit hard by this pandemic, suffering nearly 300 deaths among 2,649 influenza cases from August 1918 to January 1919. Of these victims, 139 were buried in Hope Cemetery.

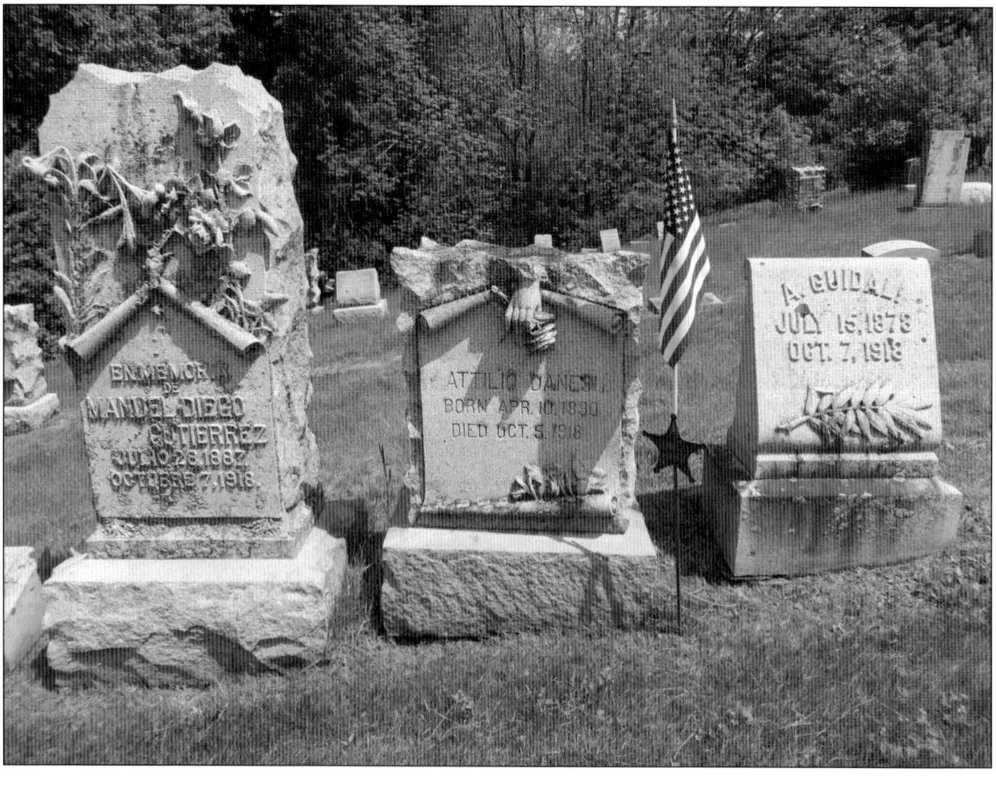

Robert Campbell Brown Monument (1918). Symbols abound on this grave marker for a World War I soldier who died from the Spanish flu. Brown (1890–1918) was a native of Barre; note the Masonic compass and set square and the three-link chain of the Odd Fellows flanking the cross, both symbols of organizations to which this popular young man, who left "a wide circle of friends," belonged.

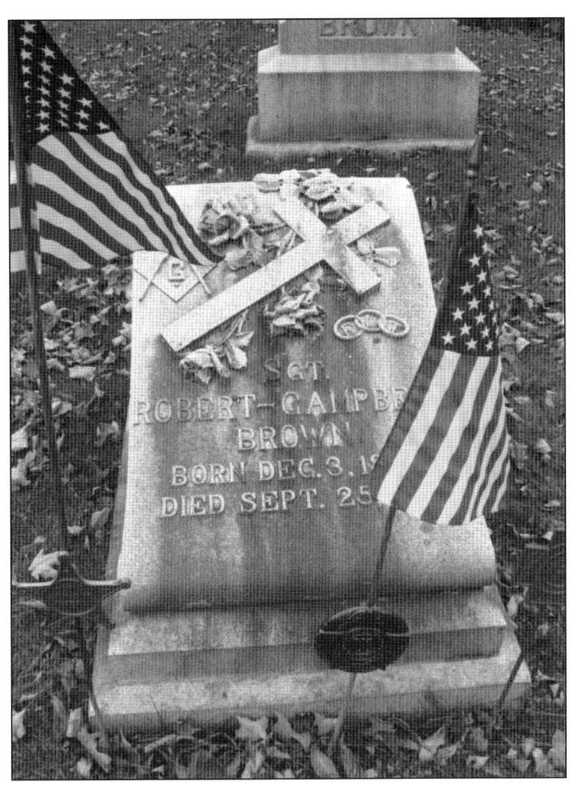

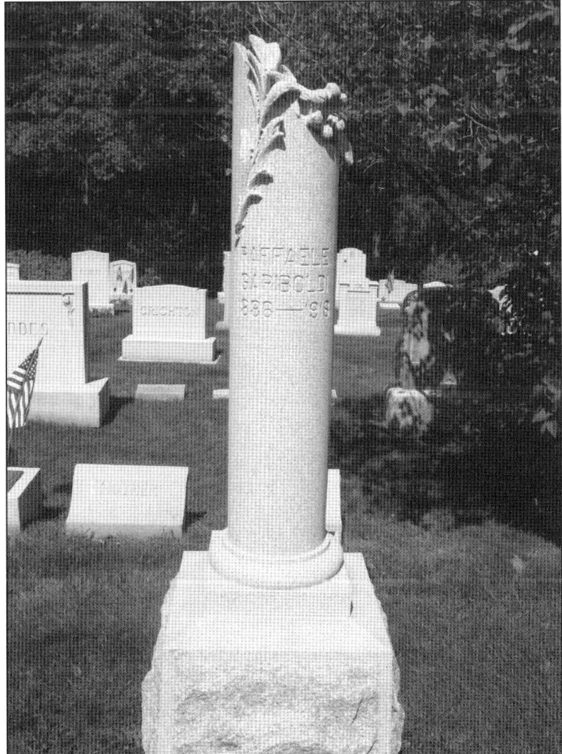

Raffaele Gariboldi Monument (1918). This stonecutter, a native of Bisuchio, Italy, and employed by the Vanetti Granite Company, was yet another victim of the Spanish flu. The broken column, topped off with a lily, is symbolic of a young man cut down in the prime of life. He left behind his wife, Armida, whom he had married in 1914.

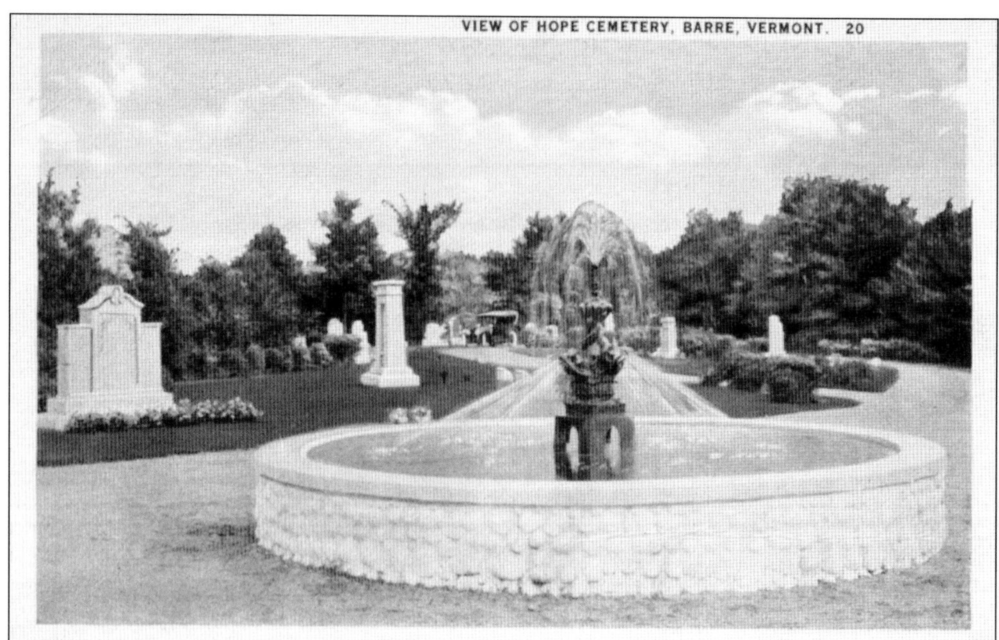

POSTCARD FOUNTAIN (c. 1910). The original fountain depicted here was quite elegant in its day. Though a fountain remains, it has been inoperable for many years due to a lack of power to operate its water circulation pump. The restoration of this unique feature has been the focus of renewed efforts by the cemetery committee since 2016.

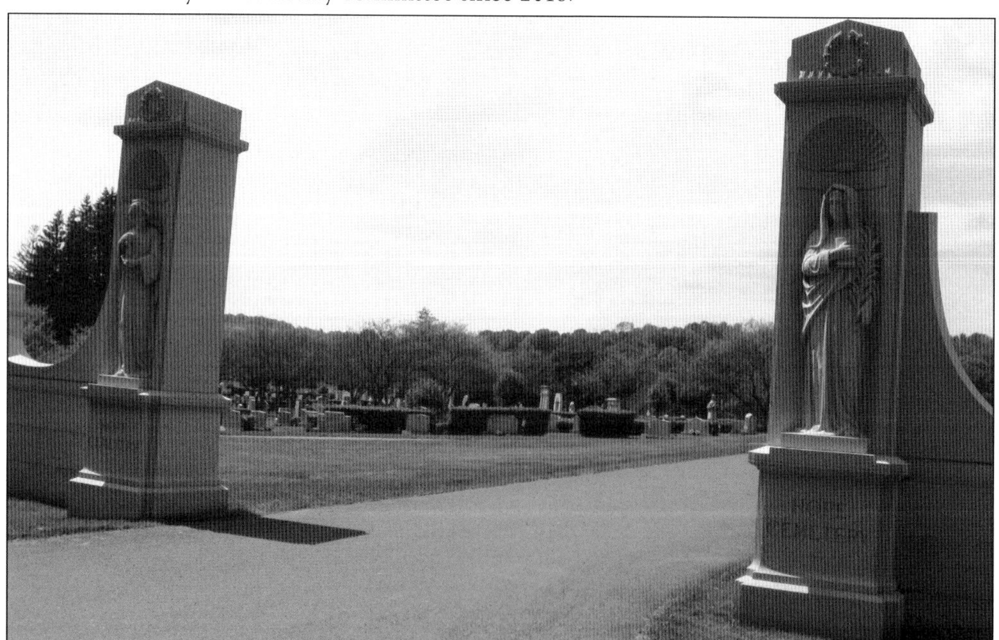

HOPE CEMETERY ENTRANCE. The entryway for Hope Cemetery, unlike most garden cemeteries, was unadorned in the beginning, but that changed by the 1930s, with the addition of these sculpted granite gates. The right side here shows the Virgin Mary holding a Bible and a lily, the symbol of Christian purity and innocence. The gates were designed by Carlo Abate and carved by Enrico Mori and Gino Tosi.

Hope Cemetery Entrance (Left Detail). This portion of the gate shows the Virgin Mary holding an anchor, the Christian symbol for hope. The model for the entrance gates was Louisa Liberty Ambrosini Fuller (1917–2003), the daughter of stonecutter Angelo Ambrosini and his wife, Maria, both natives of Varese Como, Italy.

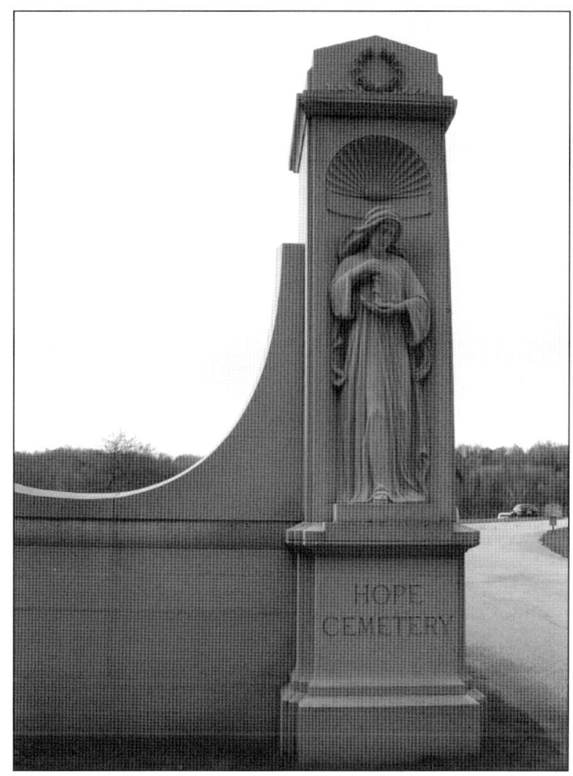

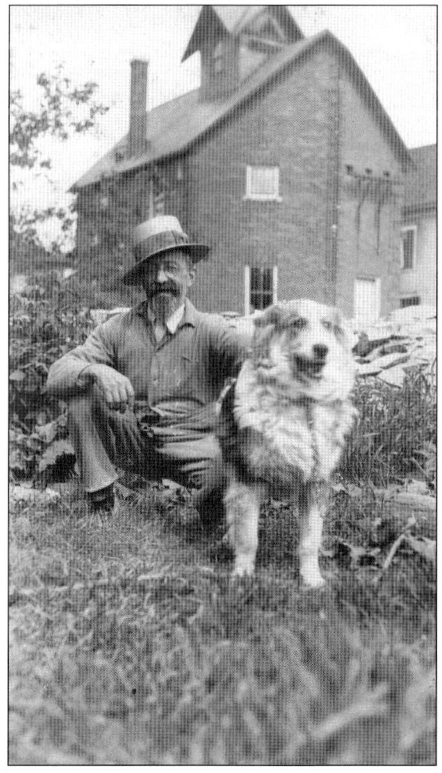

Carlo Abate (c. 1934). Abate (1859–1941), shown here with his pet collie, was one of Barre's most highly renowned citizens. Not only was he a sculptor and designer of the Hope Cemetery entrance gates, but he was also a newspaper editor, Socialist Party activist, and the beloved instructor of decorative drawing and modeling at the Barre Evening Art School for many years. (Courtesy of Vermont Granite Museum.)

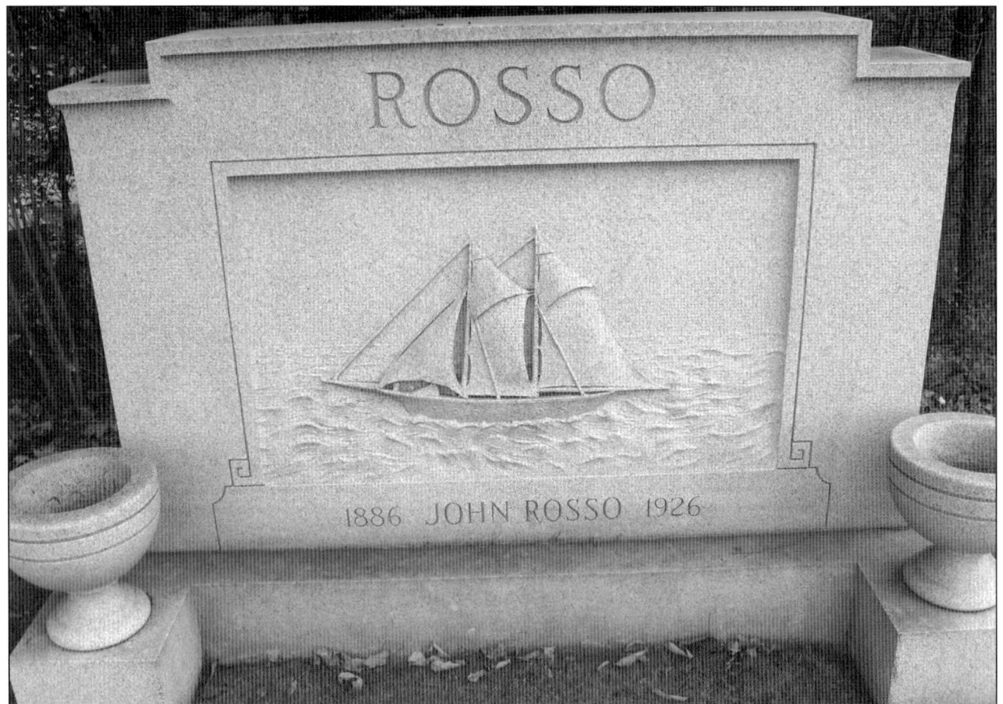

John Rosso Monument (1926). The son of Camerio and Anna Rosso, Giovanni Rosso was an immigrant, arriving in America from his hometown of Modica, Sicily, in 1909 and a naturalized citizen in 1910, Americanizing his given name to John. A single man who worked as barber, he died in an automobile accident. Rosso's stone is an exquisite one that offers a sense of tranquility.

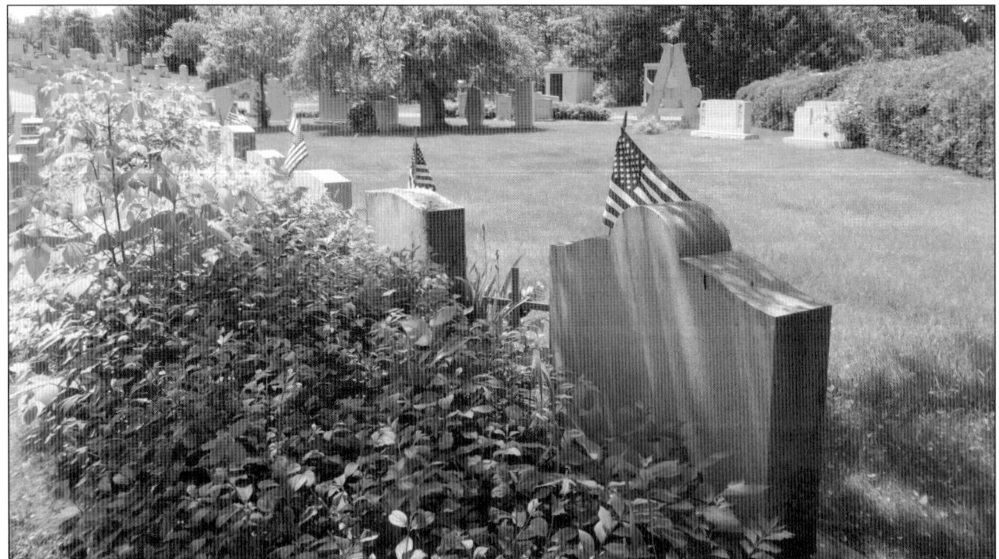

Woodside Section. Depicted here are the hedge plantings utilized in this section when designed in 1957 by landscape architect Earl Grever of East Aurora, New York. The hedges were a marked change from the older part of the cemetery, used "so that there is a degree of intimacy and seclusion within the individual parts" of Woodside. The concept was well received and has been used in subsequent parts of the cemetery.

Two

The Religion of Hope

The most prominent and numerous monuments found in Hope Cemetery feature religious themes, perhaps with a simple cross and scriptural verse, while others are of sculptured figures, such as a variety of angels, the Virgin Mary, and Jesus Christ, many carved in classical forms for which Barre's Italian immigrant stonecutters were renowned. No matter how simple or detailed these monuments are, they are indicative of the deep Catholic faith practiced in the Italian community. The Virgin Mary is the most venerated woman in the Catholic Church for the ideals of salvation and redemption she represents, so it is not surprising that images of her predominate; indeed, the cemetery's own entrance gate provide a preview of what may be found within. Angels, many of them quite striking, are also found in different forms, from the traditional to the modern, and are found on monuments at ground level all the way to the top of the cemetery's tallest monument. The most predominant of the angel forms, not surprisingly, is the angel Gabriel, depicted in both male and female form, with a trumpet to call the deceased to their Maker. Images of Jesus Christ—some alone, some with the Virgin Mary—are also very popular and are some of the most vivid monuments to be found here. Many other religious themes may also be found in Hope, including monuments that feature the Bible, as well as some that depict other figures important in the Catholic faith, including saints, monks, and Joseph, the father of Jesus, as well animals like the dove and lamb symbolizing peace and innocence. On many of these monuments, there are additional images that serve to augment messages of faith, including the Sacred Heart of Jesus, sunburst and floral designs, as well as grapes or grape leaves symbolic of the blood of Christ.

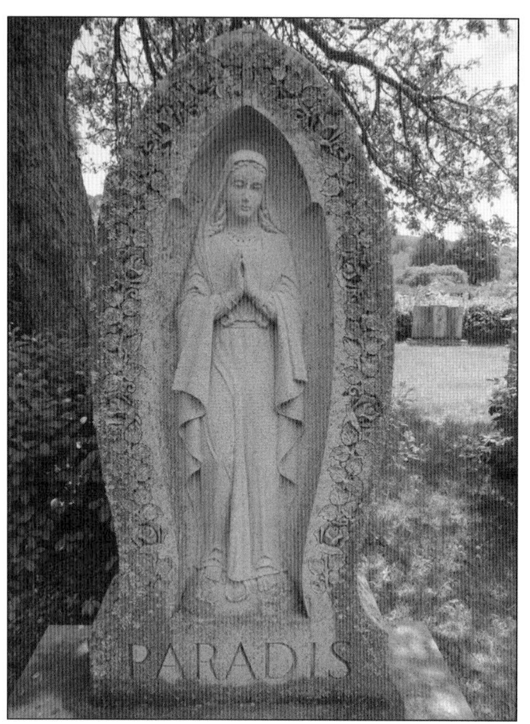

PARADIS FAMILY MONUMENT (1970). The Virgin Mary is depicted here in a half shell or grotto. This image of Mary is based on verse from the second or third century AD, which states that Jesus was born within a cave near Bethlehem. Joseph and Elvira Paradis lived in Barre; he was a Canadian immigrant and stonecutter.

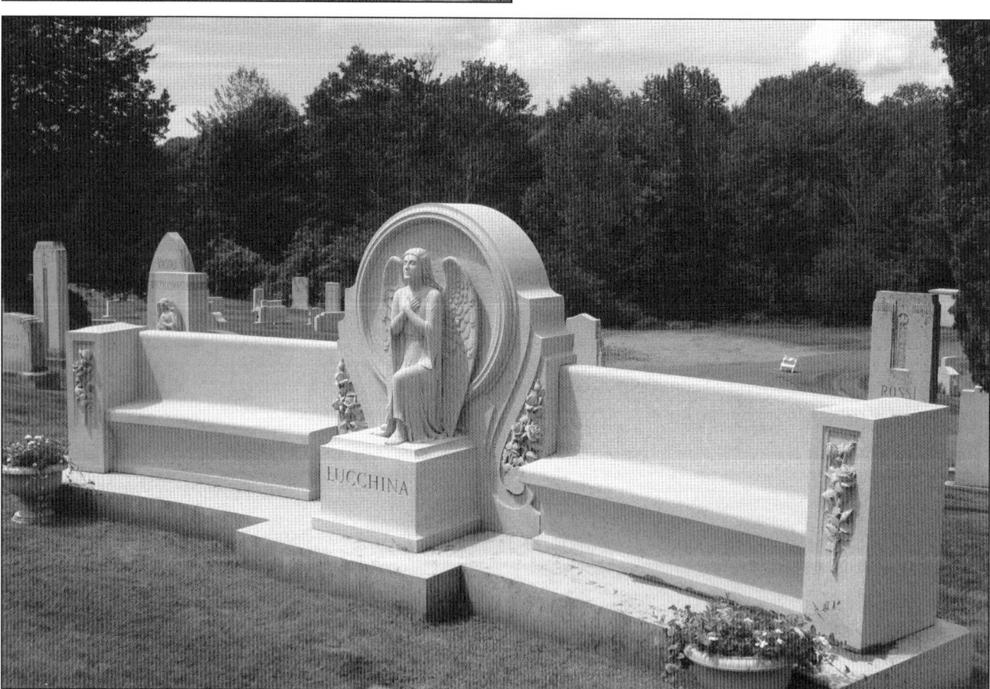

LUCCHINA FAMILY MONUMENT. This memorial offers visitors a space for quiet contemplation. Memorialized are Battista Lucchina (1870–1936), his wife, Josephine Bianchi Lucchina (1874–1978), and their children Josephine, George, Lucy, and Inez. Battista was an Italian immigrant who arrived in America in 1895 and subsequently built a successful granite firm in Barre, which was later operated by his son as the North Barre Granite Company.

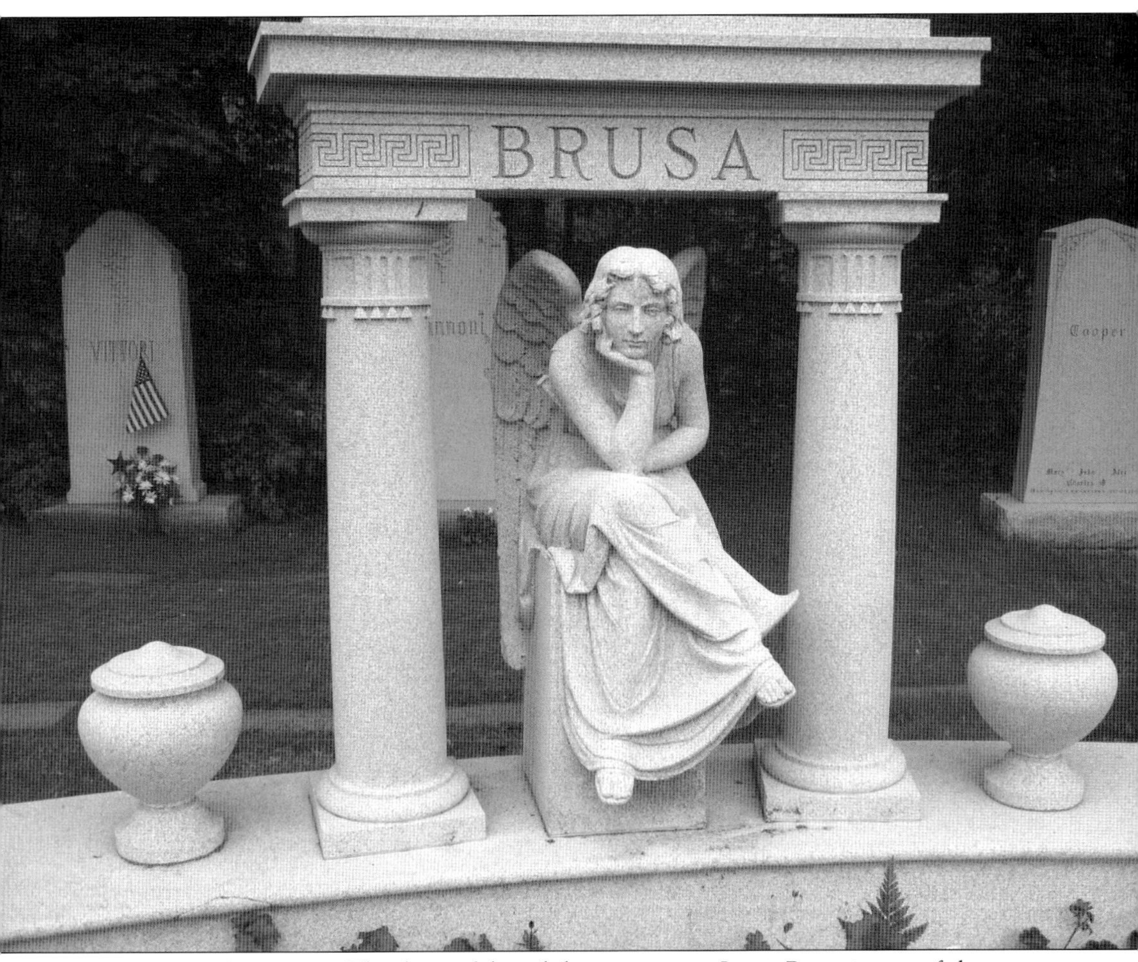

Brusa Family Monument. This beautiful work by stonecutter Louis Brusa is one of the most intriguing found here. Variously termed "the sitting angel" or "the bored angel," the monument was created for the family of stonecutter Ernesto Brusa (1851–1920) and his wife, Maria Brusa (1856–1934), and depicts a female angel Gabriel with a trumpet in her lap, clearly waiting to call the deceased to their Maker. Crafted in the 1920s, this decidedly modern angel sports a hairstyle more representative of the short flapper styles of the 1920s than the long flowing hair displayed in typical Christian images. She is the only sitting angel to be found here.

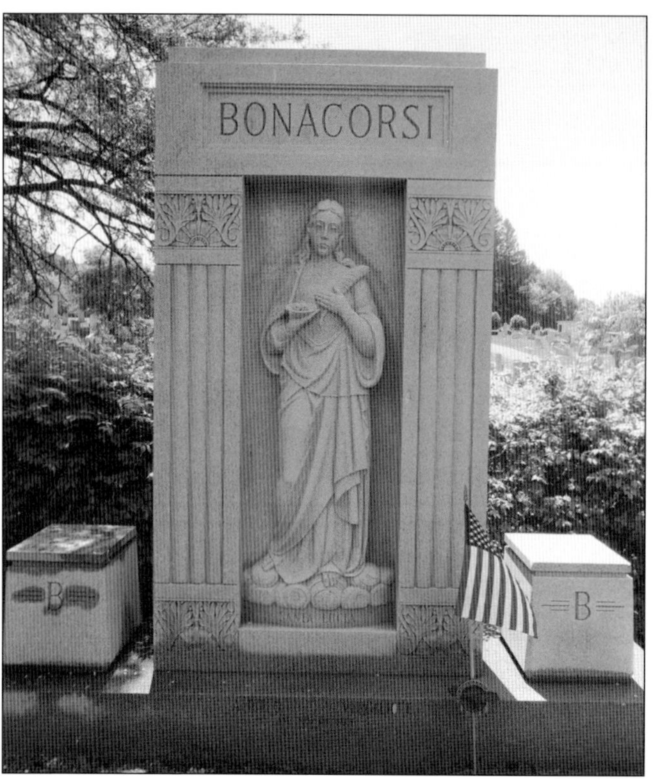

Bonacorsi Family Monument. This monument is unusual for featuring a specific saint. St. Lucia is the patron saint of the blind or those with eye trouble, but also of salesmen, which occupation Vergilio Bonacorsi (1926–2010) worked at before opening the Venetian Restaurant and later operating the Bonacorsi and Sons wholesale food-service business. This carving of St. Lucia is detailed (right); the palm branch she is holding is a symbol of the victory of Good over Evil, and the bowl containing two eyeballs is reflective of her devotion to the blind (the name *Lucia* has as its root the Latin word *lux*, which means "light"), but also the legend that her eyes were gouged out before she was murdered during an era of Christian persecution.

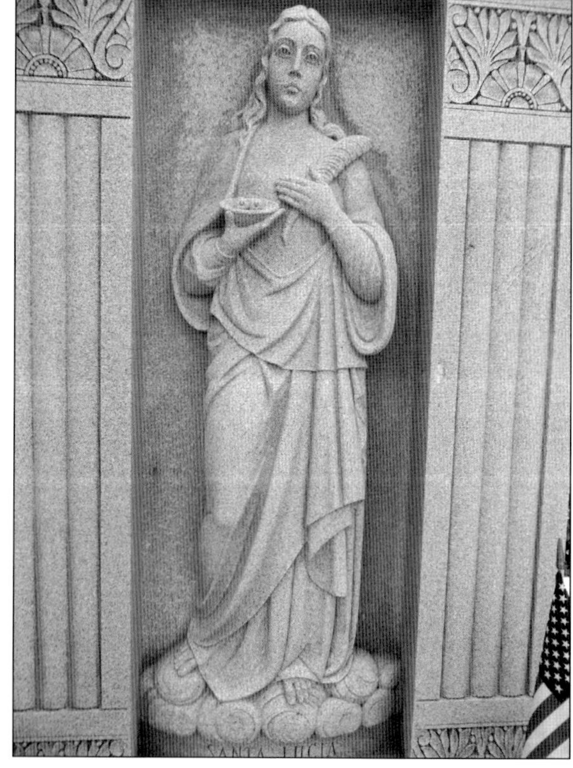

EUGENE CARUSI ADVERTISEMENT (1905). This leading Barre carver was known for his religious statuary, his firm cutting some 52 statues in the year 1897 alone. Quite fittingly, Carusi is buried in Hope Cemetery (see page 87).

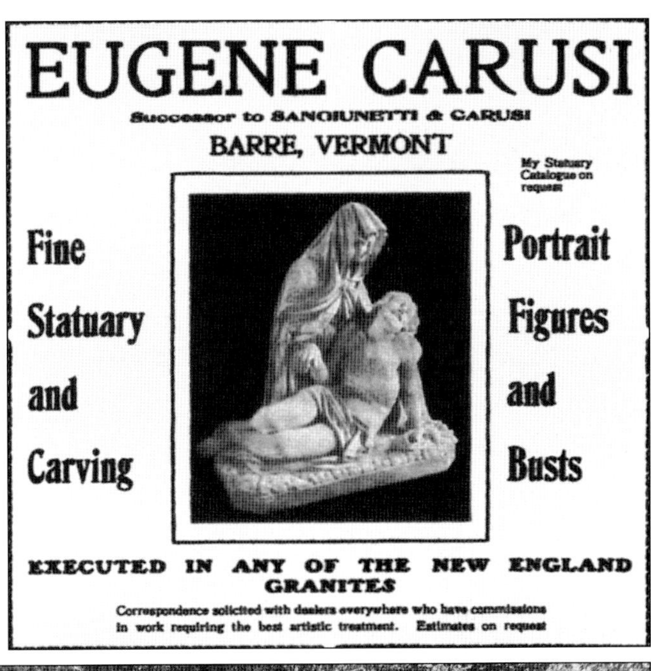

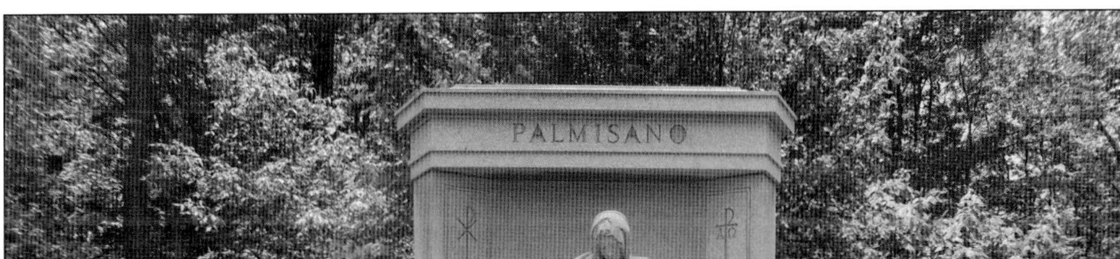

PALMISANO FAMILY MONUMENT (C. 1970). One of the most visited monuments, this work was crafted by stonecutter Alcide Fantoni. It is a replica of Michelangelo's *Pietà*, depicting Jesus after the Crucifixion on the lap of his mother Mary. The alpha and omega letters on the column at right, the first and last letters in the Greek alphabet, signify the beginning and the end and are symbolic of Christ.

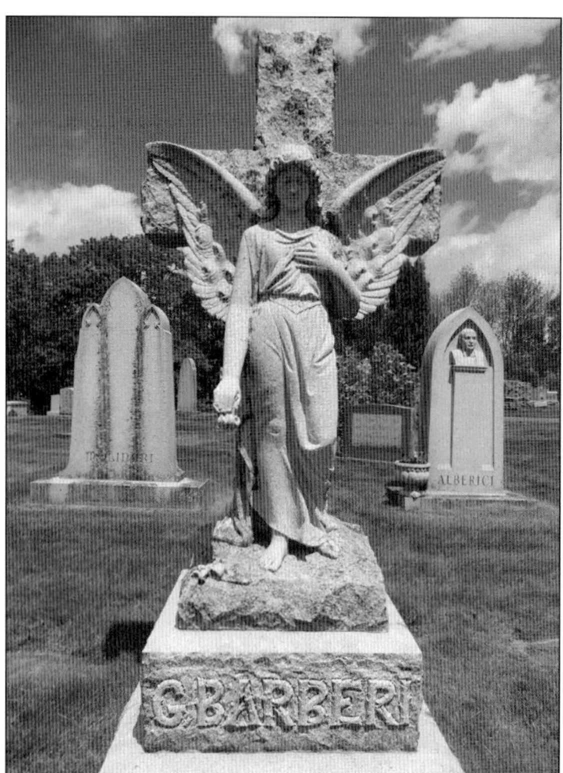

Giuseppi Barberi Monument (1933). This life-sized angelic statue is one of the most beautiful of the religious monuments to be found in Hope Cemetery. It marks the grave of an Italian immigrant from Casteletto Ticino who worked as a stonecutter in Barre from 1899 to 1929. Barberi (1875–1933), like other stonecutters, died from tuberculosis of the lungs.

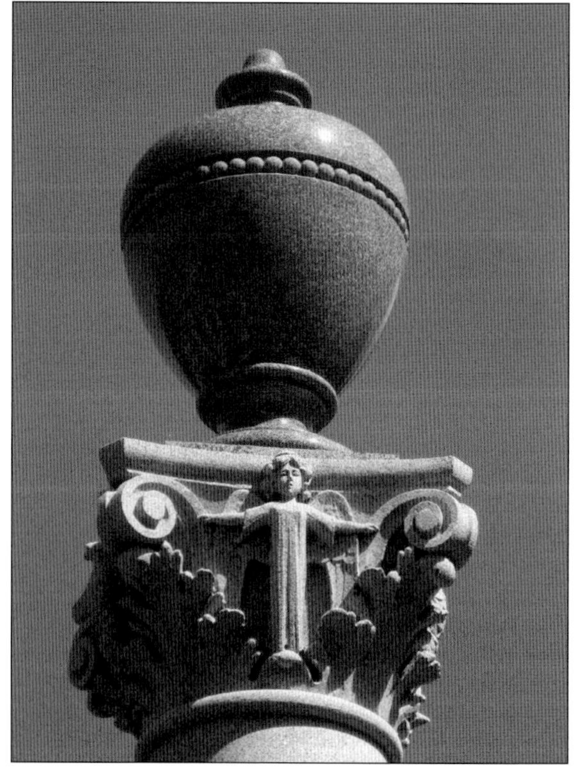

Comolli Family Monument Detail (1916). The tallest monument in Hope (see front cover) is topped off with a funerary urn, below which is a Corinthian capital featuring a tiny hand-carved angel. The patriarch of this branch of the family, Giovanni "John" Comolli (1852–1916) was a prominent stonecutter who worked as a foreman in his family's granite business before dying of pulmonary tuberculosis.

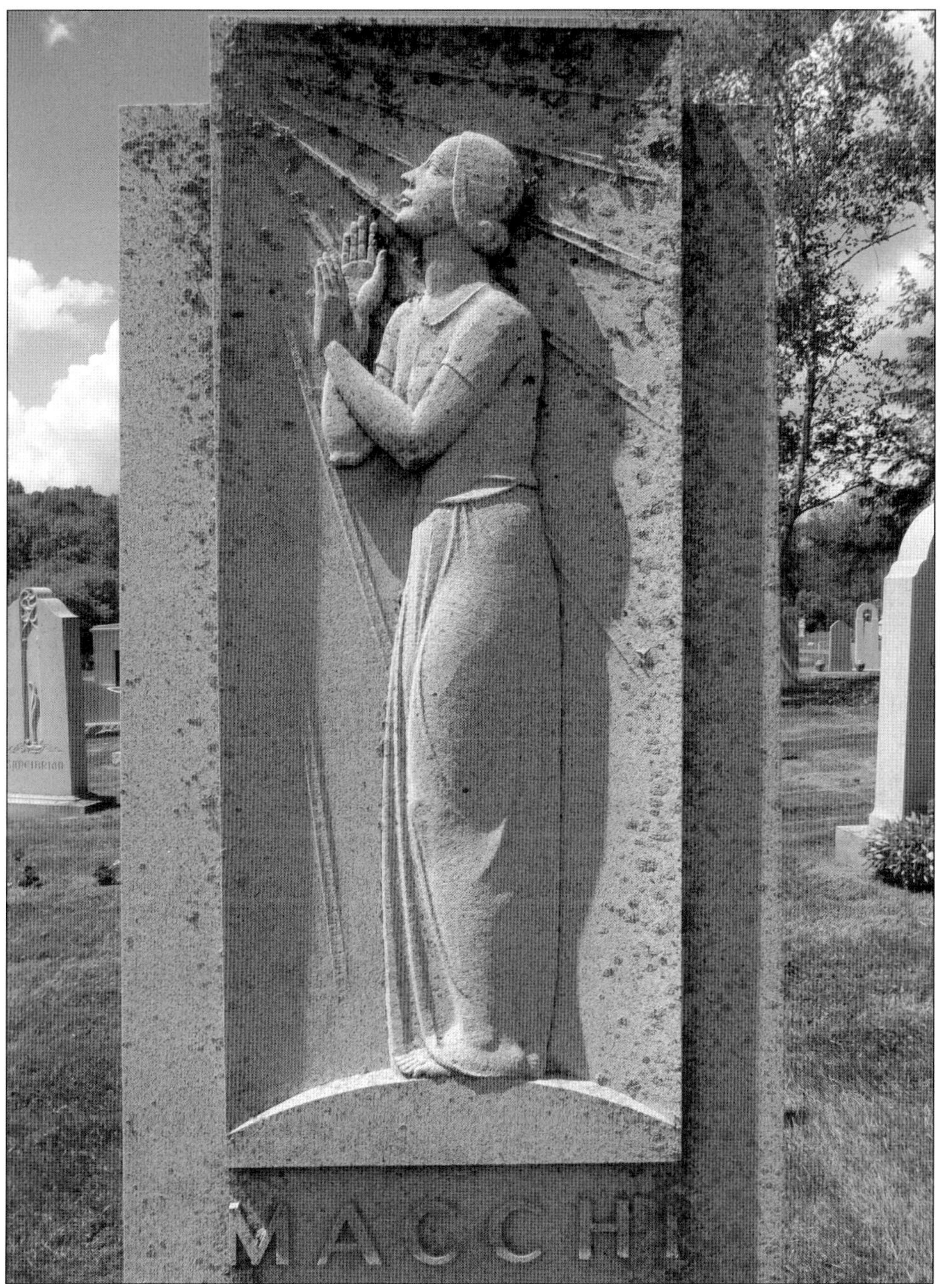

MACCHI FAMILY MONUMENT (C. 1938). This beautiful monument, done in a bas-relief style that has an Art Deco look, depicts a female, perhaps the Virgin Mary or maybe even a representation of Irene Lidia Macchi (1911–1938) or her mother, Maria Emma Macchi (1890–1940), looking skyward, bathed in beams of sunlight. It is notable for featuring the woman in profile and is so artfully carved that the form of her leg is visible beneath her flowing garment. The stone was carved by stonecutter Emilio Macchi (1875–1945), a native of Italy who arrived in this country in 1897. After the death of their daughter, Maria committed suicide by the use of illuminating gas two years later, while Emilio died due to the occupational effects of inhaling granite dust just five years later, completing a cycle of tragedy for the family.

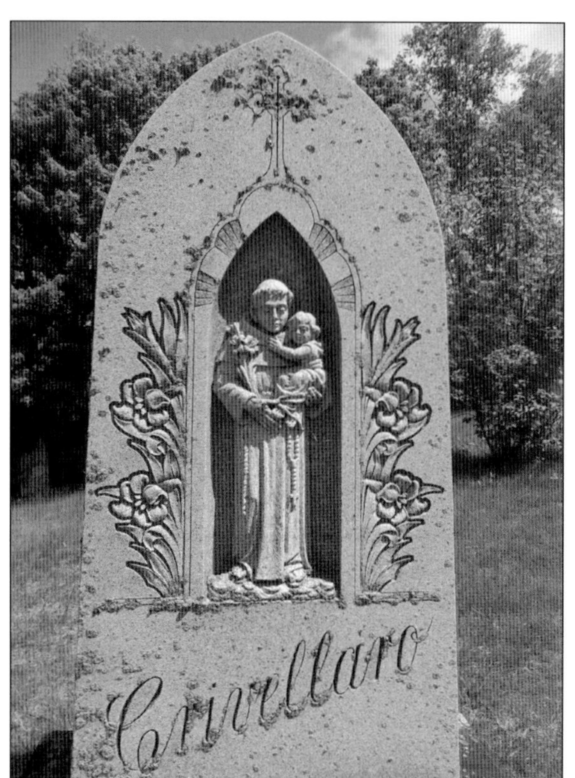

Crivellaro Family Monument (c. 1953). This monument for Napoleon, Emelia, and Ezio Crivellaro was carved by their son and brother (respectively) Louis Crivellaro (1902–1978). He was a stonecutter who followed in his father's footsteps. Depicted here is an image of St. Anthony of Padua, a Franciscan friar canonized in 1232, a year after his death, holding the Christ Child, a popular image in the Catholic faith since the 16th century.

Borne Family Monument. The modern monument shown here depicts many elements of the Catholic faith. The Virgin Mary is holding the Christ Child, both of them wearing a crown and Mary with a halo, familiar images dating back to the Middle Ages. Note also the words *Ave Maria* (Hail Mary), indicating the prayer associated with the rosary beads that are held by the baby Jesus and Mary.

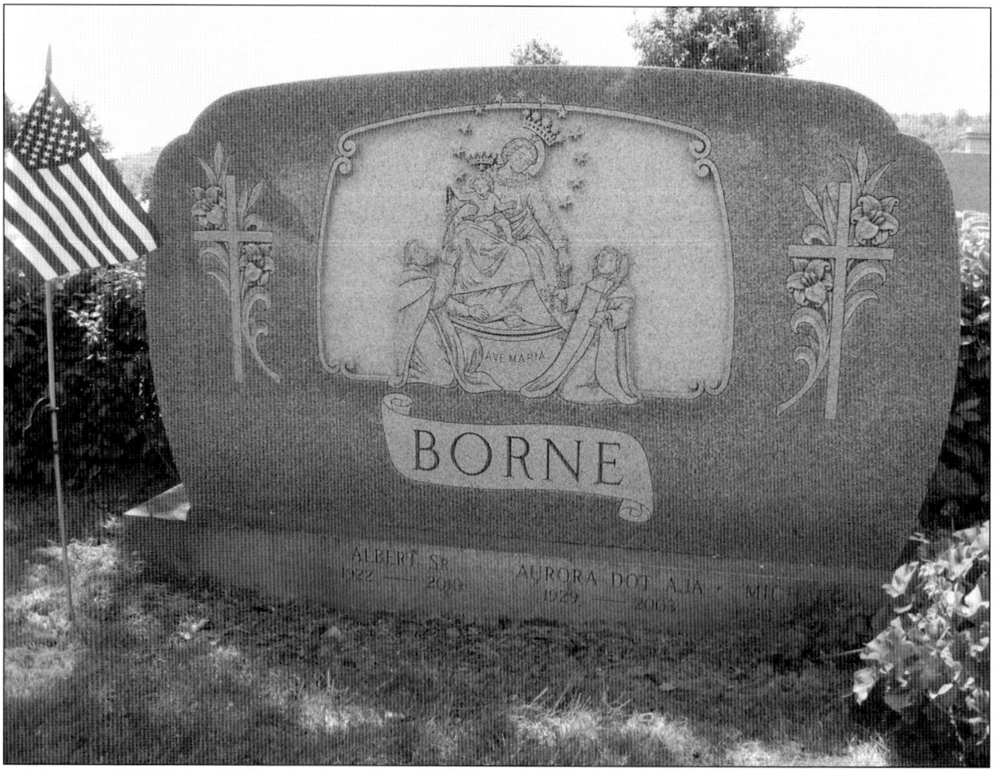

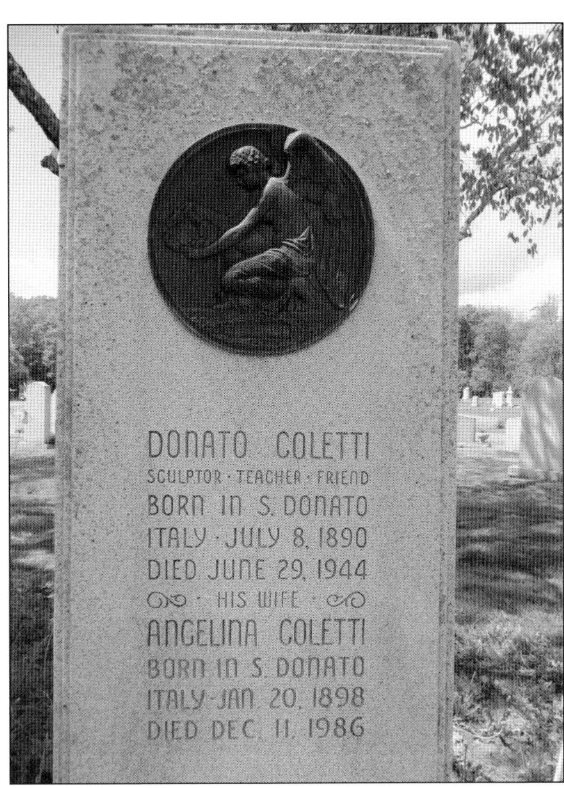

Coletti Family Monument (1944). Mixed media monuments are less common in Hope Cemetery, so this granite stone with a bronze inset medallion offers an excellent example of the versatility of Barre's stonecutters. Arriving in America in 1903, Donato Coletti was one of the most skilled of the immigrant artisans. Not only was he a teacher at the Barre Evening Art School for many years, but he also carved a number of other monuments (see page 123). The bronze medallion (below) on this monument was created by Coletti himself and is a representation of a medal he earned as an art school student many years before.

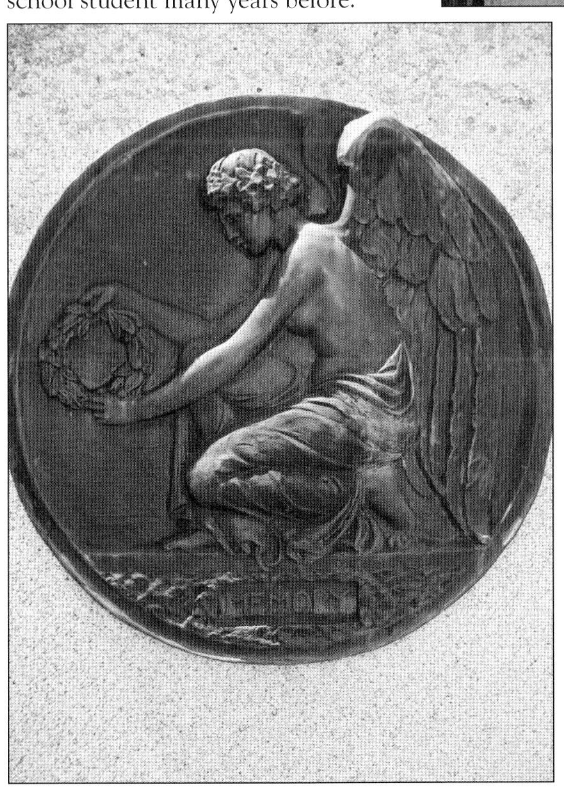

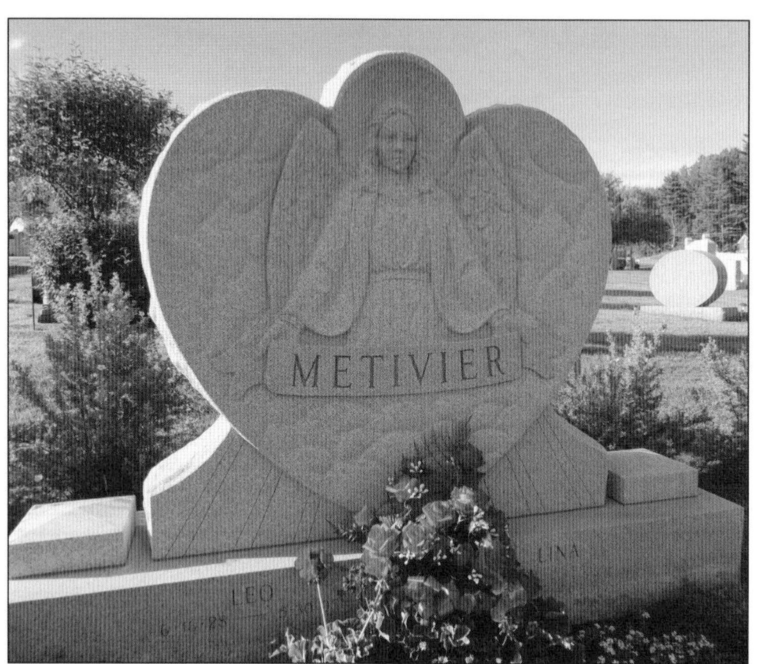

Metivier Family Monument (2005). This large modern monument is a beautiful example of the work produced by area stonecutters today. The sculptured angel with a halo and heart-shaped background adorned with clouds is pleasing to the eye. Leo Metivier (1928–2005), like his wife, Lena Gagne Metivier, was a native of Canada, hailing from Québec, and worked in the granite trade.

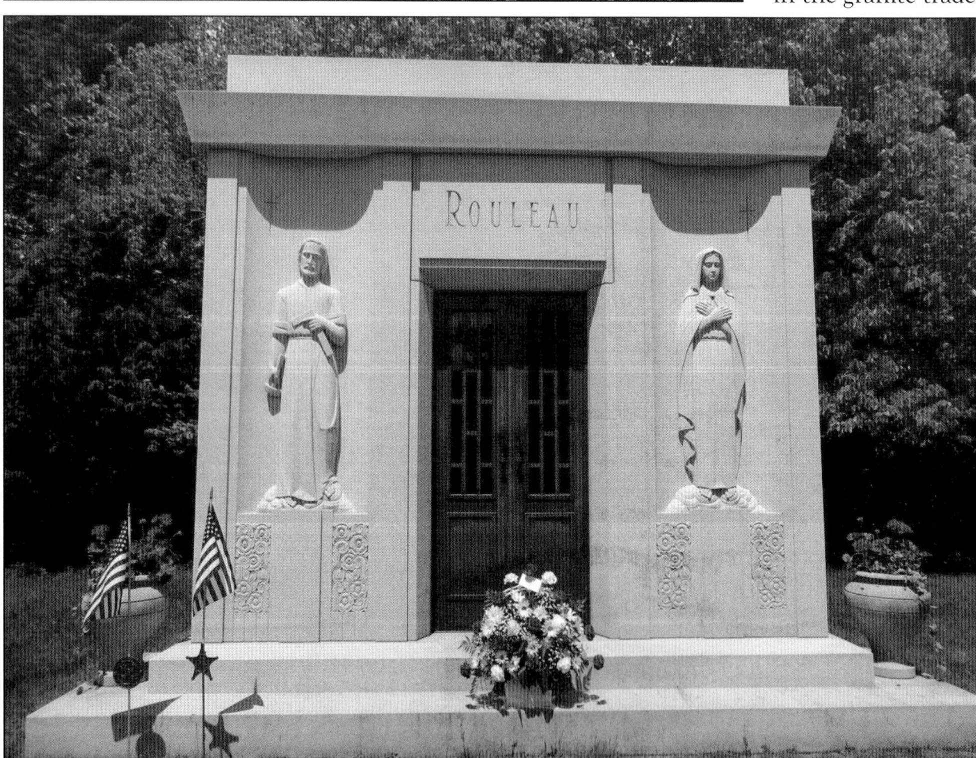

Rouleau Mausoleum (2000). Of the religious-themed mausoleums found here, this one is amongst the most impressive. It features the parents of Jesus, Joseph and Mary. Note that Joseph is depicted carrying the tools of the carpenter's trade. The remains of Lucien Paul Rouleau (1930–2000) and his wife, Gloria, are interred here. Rouleau was the owner of the Rouleau Granite Company.

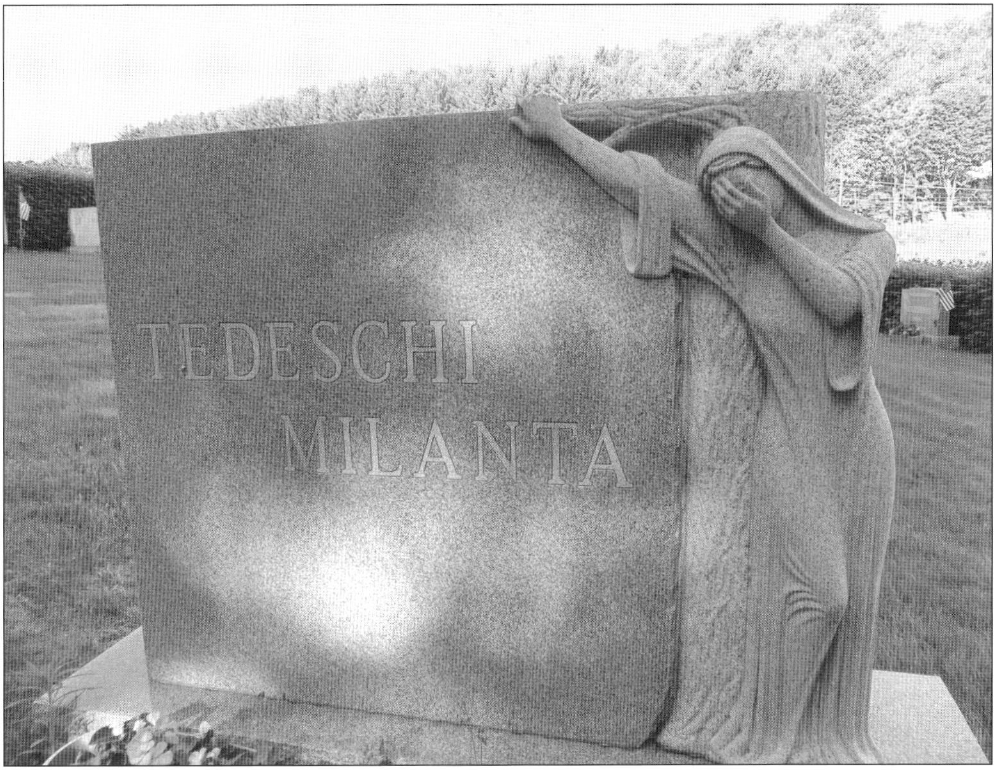

Tedeschi-Milanta Monument (2011). This monument, featuring a weeping Virgin Mary in front of a tree-stump, marks the resting place of Benita Milanta (1908–2011), a native of Carrara, Italy, and the future resting place of her daughter Anna Maria Tedeschi and her husband, Piero, both also natives of Italy.

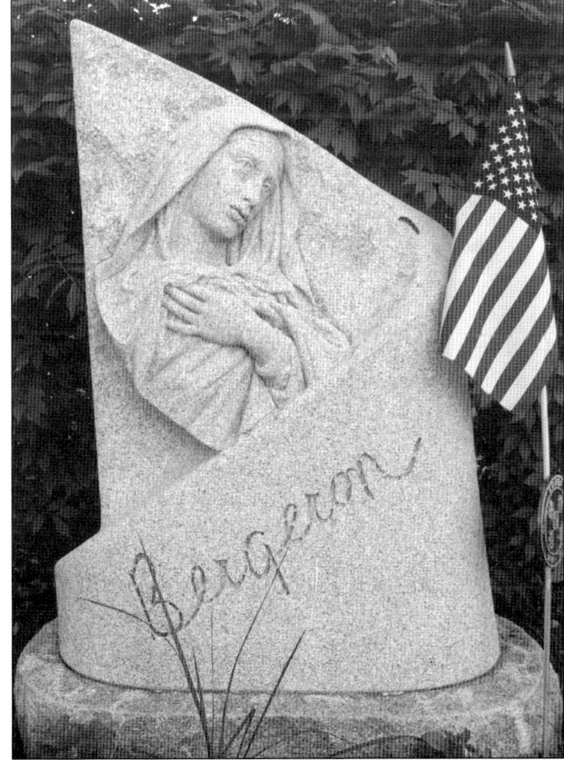

Bergeron Family Monument (1985). Giuliano Cecchinelli sculpted this monument of the Virgin Mary. Buried here are Robert Bergeron (1931–2009), his wife, Catherine (1932–2010), and their son Christopher (1958–1984)—the family of current Hope Cemetery director Jeff Bergeron. Robert was a Korean war veteran, blacksmith, and Barre's mayor from 1984 to 1990.

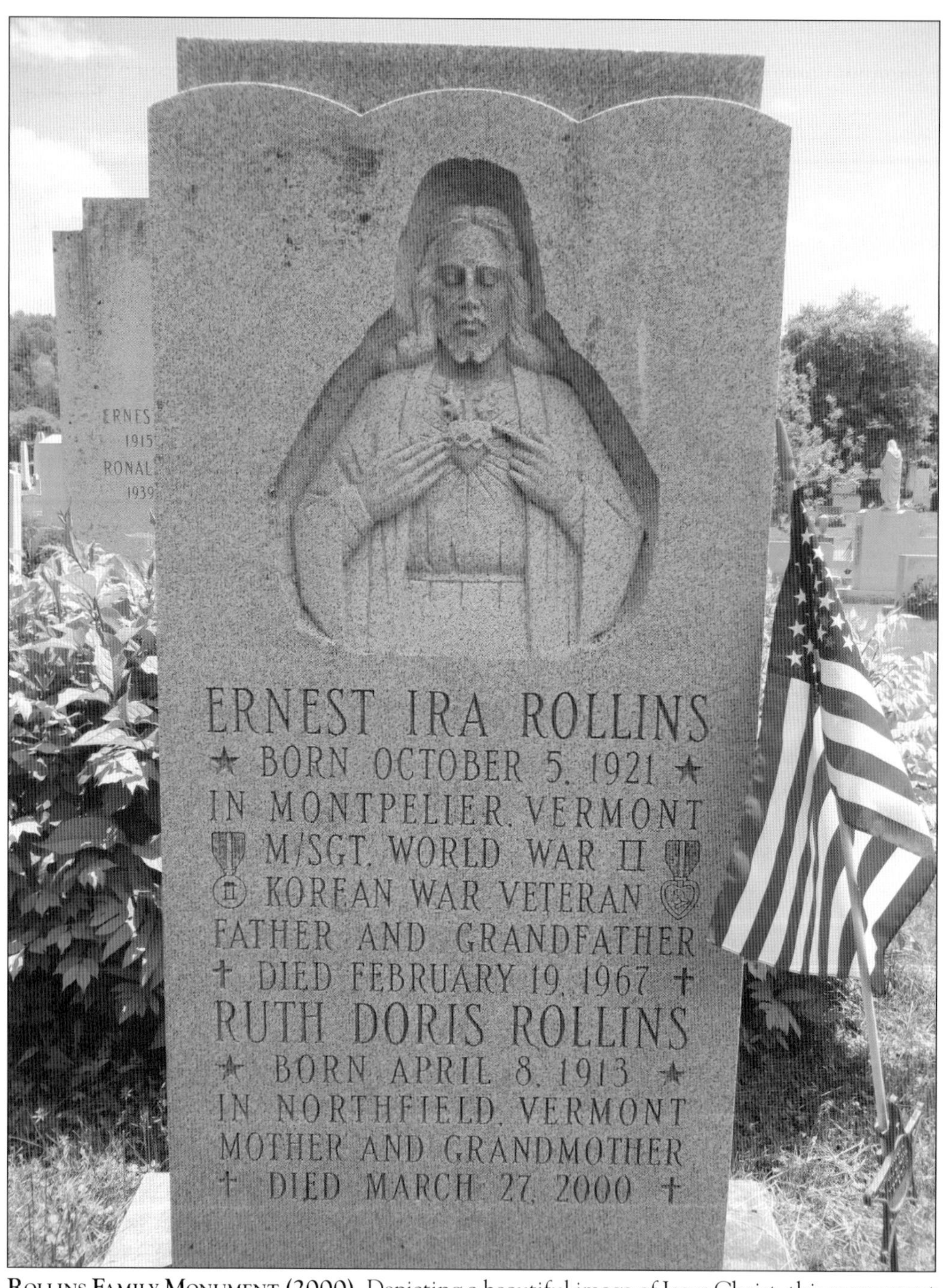

ROLLINS FAMILY MONUMENT (2000). Depicting a beautiful image of Jesus Christ, this monument was erected by the couple's children. Ernest Rollins was a World War II and Korean War veteran; records show that he rose to the rank of first sergeant by the end of World War II and earned a Purple Heart medal in Korea in March 1951, when he was badly wounded during a missile attack while serving in the 11th Airborne Division. An image of the Purple Heart is depicted on the monument, but note that it is superseded by the prominent depiction of the Sacred Heart of Jesus.

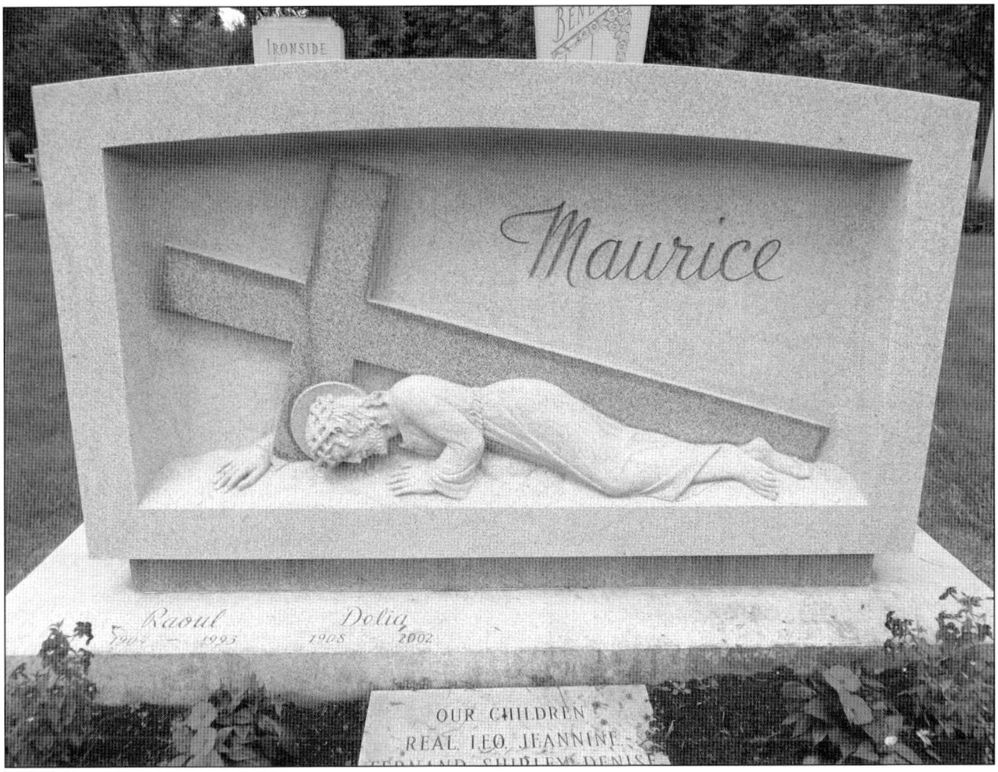

MAURICE FAMILY MONUMENT (1993). This modern monument is indicative of the family's faith and was possibly carved by the patriarch of this family, Raoul Maurice (1904–1993), a French Canadian immigrant from Québec who arrived in this country in 1923–1924 and worked as a stonecutter. The image of Christ with the cross is one of the most powerful to be found in Hope.

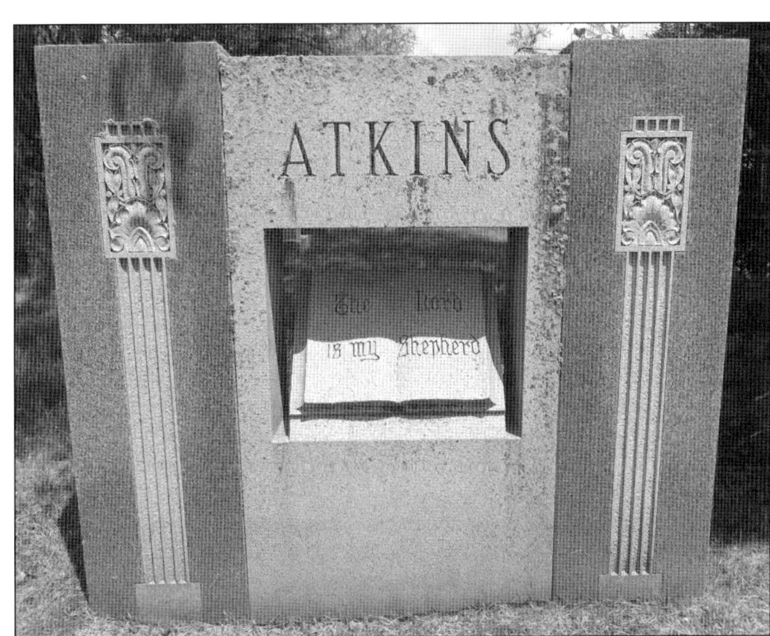

ATKINS FAMILY MONUMENT. The Christian faith of this family is on full display on here, showing the Bible flanked by Corinthian columns. Interred here are Harland Atkins (1887–1957), his wife, Ada (1884–1969), and their child Arden (1912–1993).

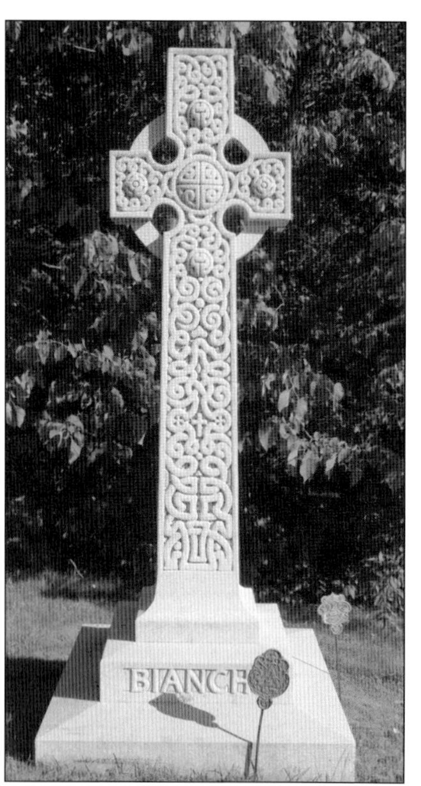

Bianchi Family Monument (1917). This impressive Celtic cross monument offers a departure from others in Hope. It is distinguished by its circular nimbus and its interlace elements with bands that are looped, braided, and knotted, the whole perhaps symbolic of eternity. High crosses like this were first used in Ireland in the eighth century. The patriarch of this family branch was Carlo R.G. Bianchi (1850–1917), an immigrant stonecutter from Italy.

Detail of the Groleau Family Monument. Created by Giuliano Cecchinelli, this simple stone found in the Hillside section features a finely carved dove with an olive branch in its beak. Mentioned in the Bible dozens of times, the dove has many symbolic meanings, being indicative of peace, the Holy Spirit, as well as innocence and beauty.

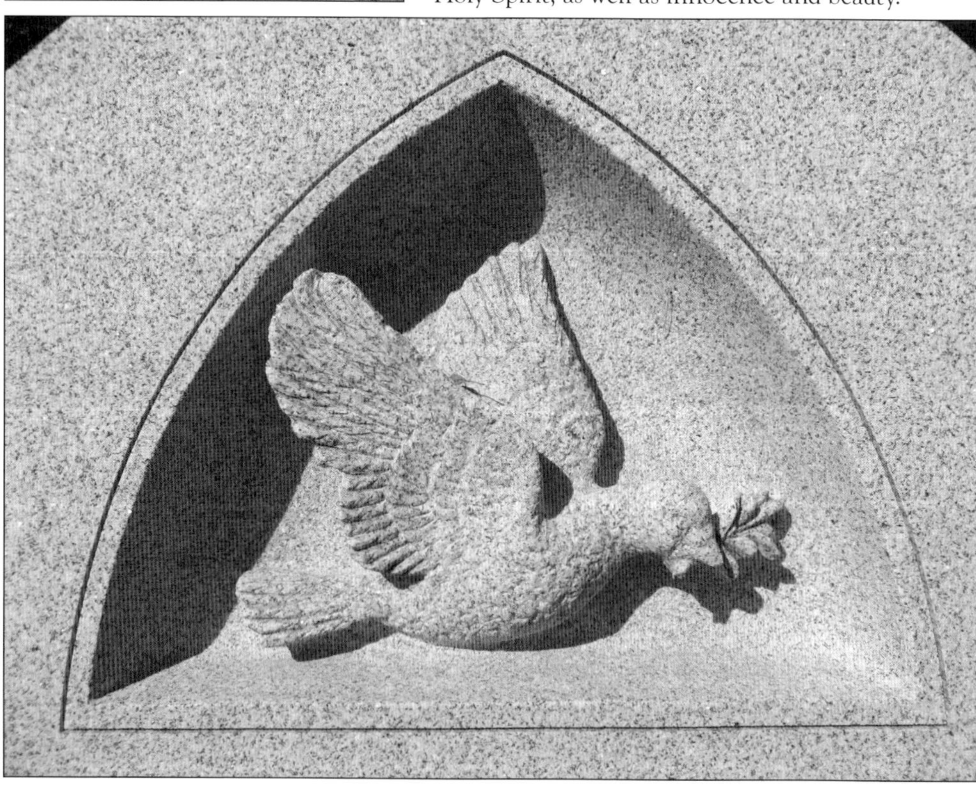

Three

The Nature of Hope

Just as the very essence of Hope Cemetery lies in its garden-style setting, so too are elements of nature found throughout on the granite monuments within. Based on even older European traditions, naturalistic themes have long been a vital element in American mortuary traditions since the founding of New England. While the multitude of plants, including a wide variety of flowers, carved in stone look pretty, many also carry a symbolic meaning—some well known, others more obscure to us today. Examples include the rose, symbolic of love, but, when in full bloom a symbol of death in the prime of life, or, when in a bud form that is drooping or broken, a young life cut short; the lily, a symbol of Christian purity and innocence; the morning glory, a Victorian symbol of unrequited love but also of the Resurrection as they bloom and wither all in a single day; the daisy, a symbol of true love, purity, innocence; laurel leaves in wreath form are a symbol of achievement; ferns are a symbol of sincerity, but, being one of the oldest plants on earth, also of the beginning of life. One example that is important for Barre is the carnation. While it is traditionally a symbol of pure love, the red carnation (as well as the red rose) also became associated with the Socialist movement and many members not only wore them on their lapels as a symbol of support but also had them carved on their monuments. As to other naturalistic monuments, one form perfected by Barre's stonecutters and very popular early in the 20th century was that of shell-rock carving, whereby a block of granite is given a rough-textured finish. Even the backs of these monuments, where just the shell-rock finish is present without decoration, are works of art, all done by hand.

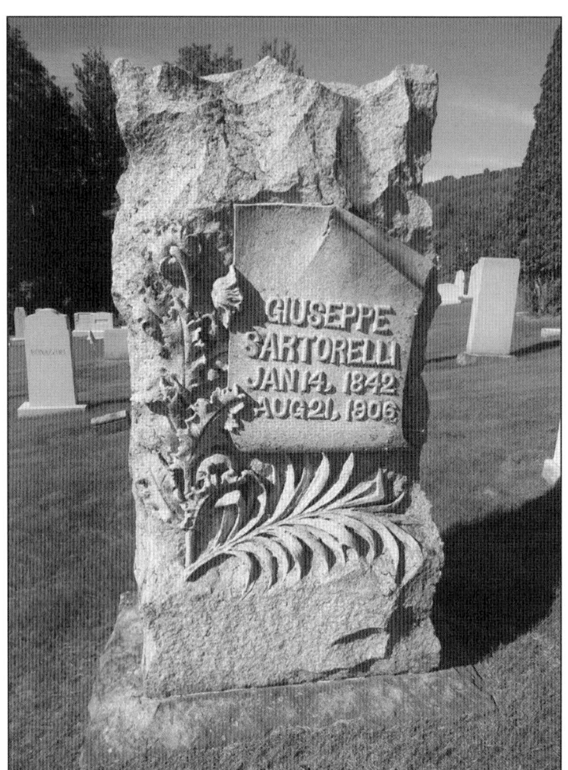

GIUSEPPE SARTORELLI MONUMENT (1906). Sartorelli was a stonecutter who arrived here from Italy in 1890 and lived in Williamstown. His monument features several flowers, with the daisy at left and the lily below. The stone itself is finished in the shell-rock style, which is especially notable at the top of the monument.

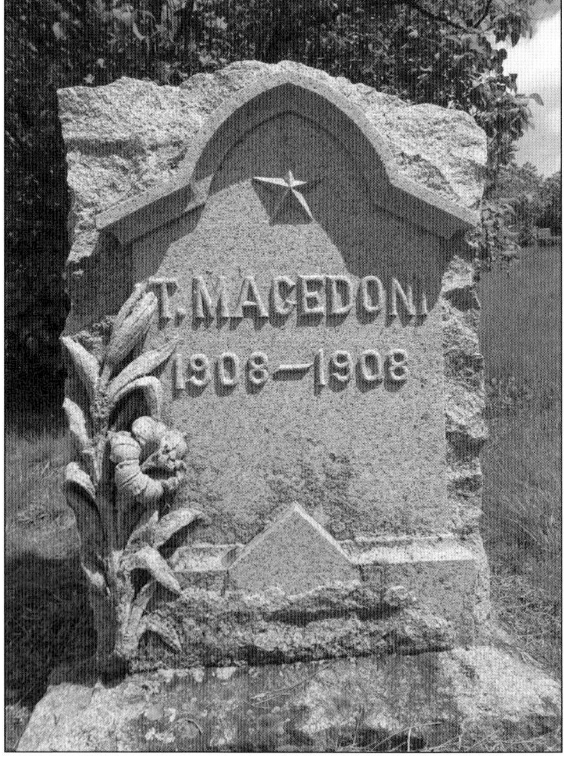

TROVATORE MACEDONI MONUMENT. This incorrectly dated stone marks the grave of an infant, the son of stonecutter Charles and Pierina Macedoni, born on January 9, 1910, and died a month and two days later. Note that the carved lily at left shows one flower drooping and another bud that will never bloom. The monument was likely erected years later, thus accounting for its inaccurate date.

MARCIASI FAMILY MONUMENT (1909). A fine example of shell-rock carving serves as the background for this monument. The stone was almost certainly carved by Onorato Marciasi, a stonecutter from Carrara, Italy, who immigrated here in 1880. His son-in-law Joseph Beltrami, also buried here, was also a stonecutter.

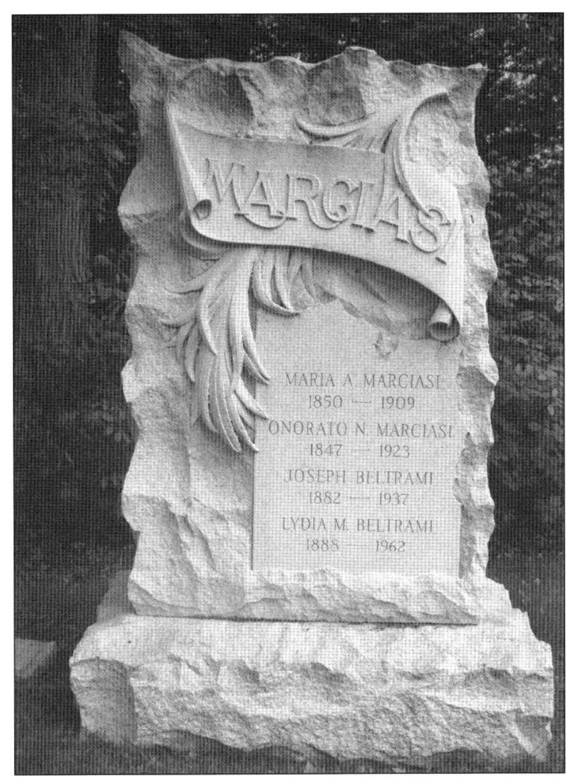

JOHN C. ALLAN MONUMENT (1912). Allan was a stonecutter from Peebles, Scotland, who, in his will, directed that there "be erected a monument of suitable design at my grave . . . of an approximate value of five hundred dollars." His monument is notable for the variegated shell-rock carving at the base and the profusion of lilies and roses, as well as the column with a broken arch, above which is Masonic symbolism.

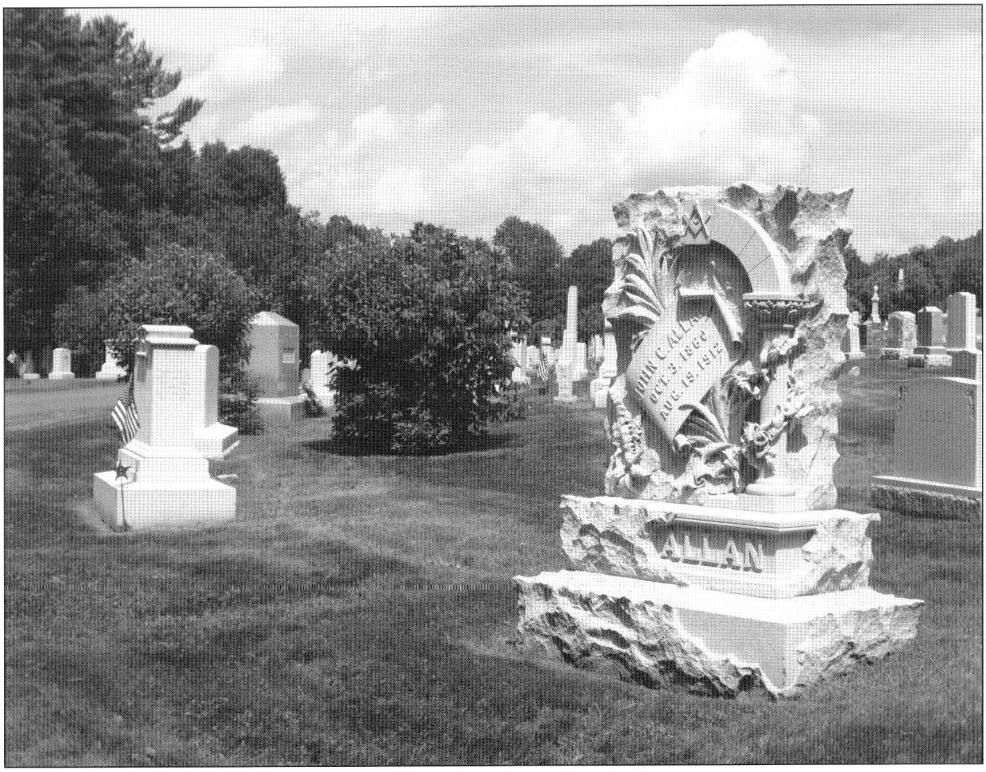

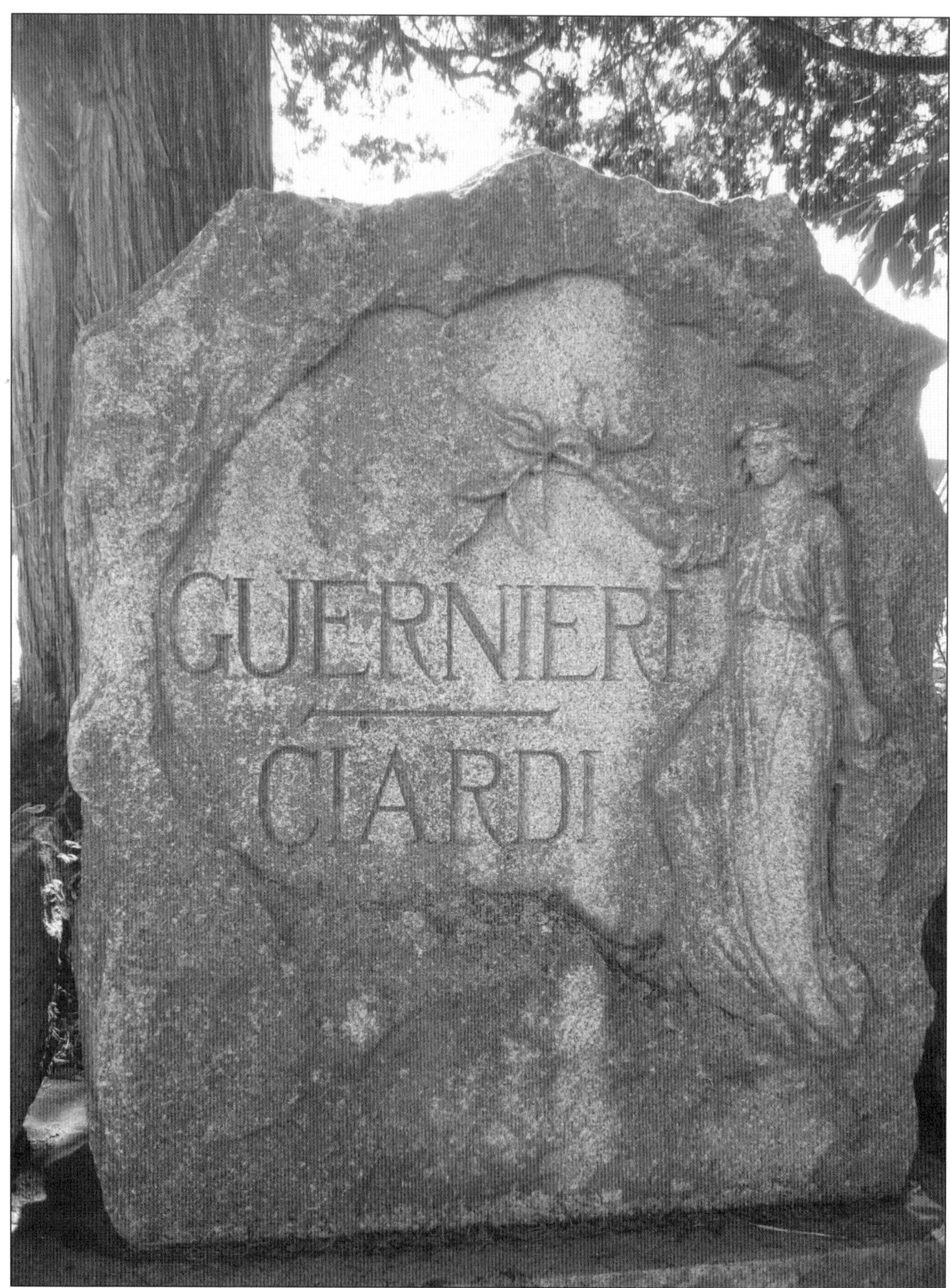

GUERNIERI-CIARDI FAMILY MONUMENT (1930). This monument depicts a young woman, perhaps in the likeness of Brunetta Guernieri, holding a drooping flower. Located under a tree at the back of the Morningside section, it is one of the hidden treasures of Hope Cemetery. The monument was carved by Angelo Ambrosini (1880–1932) in response to the early death of Brunetta Ciardi Guernieri (1896–1930), who arrived in this country from Genoa, Italy, in 1902. Also memorialized here is Riccardi Ciardi (1862–1916), Brunetta's father, who first worked in the granite trade and then became a merchant. Active in the Socialist Party, he died by suicide via arsenic poisoning.

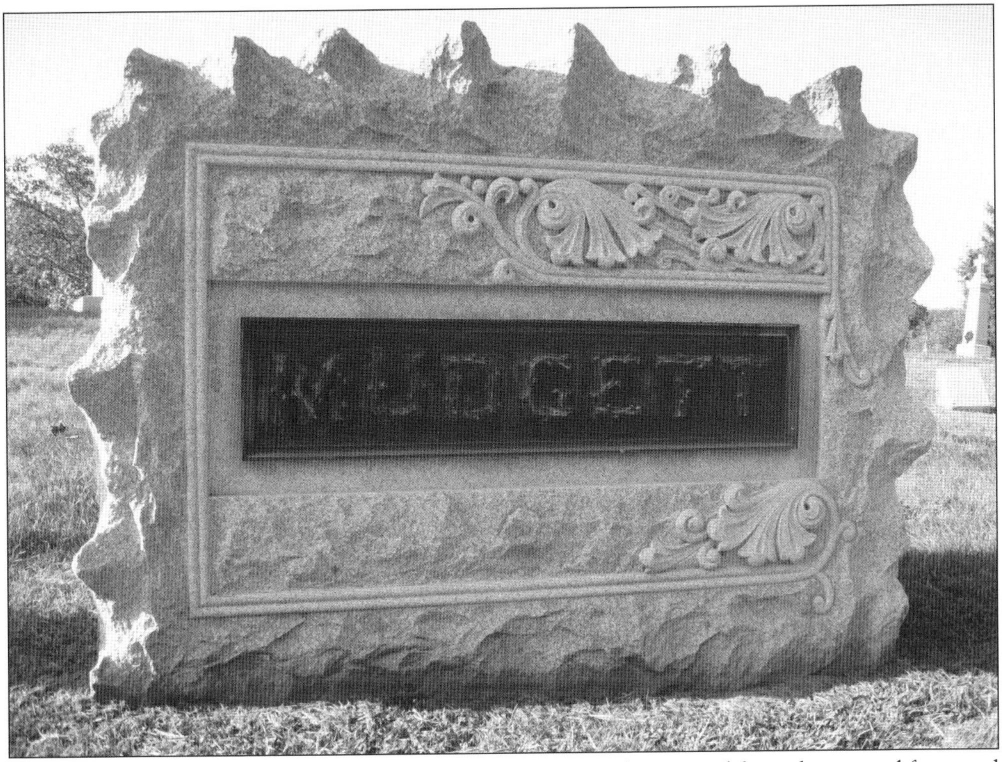

MUDGETT FAMILY MONUMENT AND GROUND MARKER (1909). Unusual for its horizontal form and brass nameplate inset, this monument is another of the overlooked treasures in Hope Cemetery. The points of the shell-rock carving, which surround the stone, are eye-catching, as is the stylized floral border. The inclusion of the brass nameplate shows true artistry, as the letters are done in rustic fashion in the form of tree branches. Even more unusual is the fact that the accompanying ground markers (below) for individual family members were also executed in the same style.

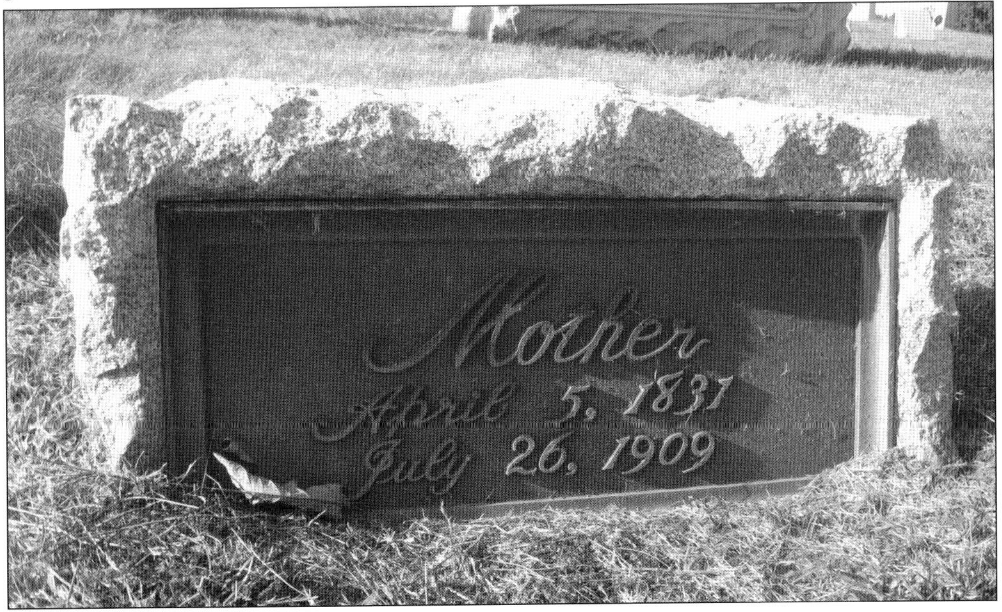

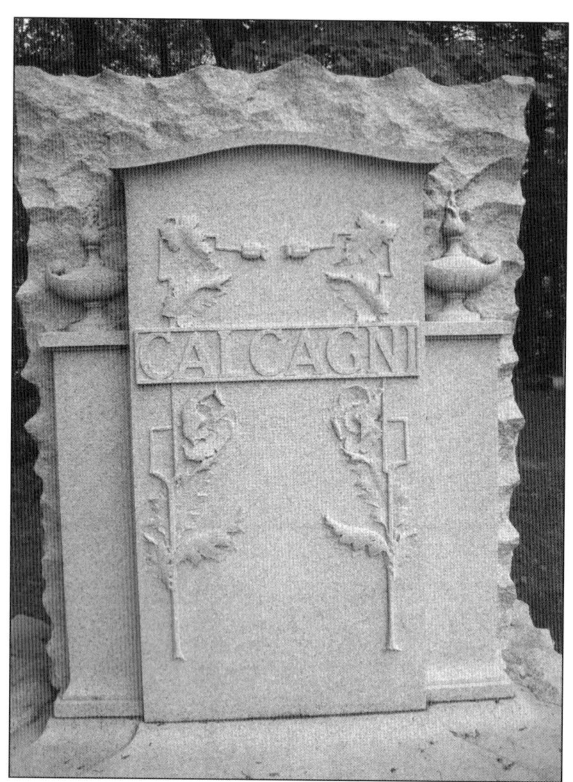

CALCAGNI FAMILY MONUMENT (1918). Multiple symbolism is at play on this monument for Nathalma Calcagni (1849–1918) and her husband, stonecutter Constantino Calcagni (1841–1920). Shell-rock carving serves as the background for the drooping daisies at center, their stalks executed in an oddly squared-off manner, while flanking them are columns topped off with a lamp with an eternal flame, symbolizing the Resurrection and immortality.

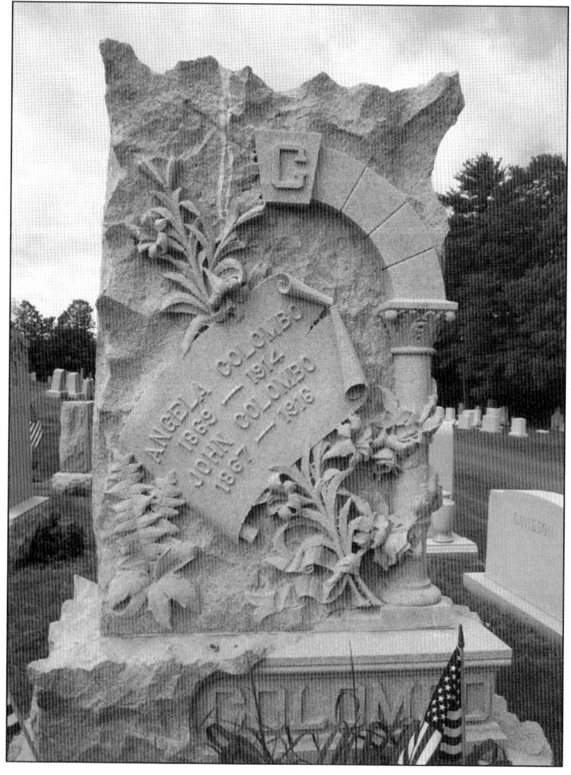

COLOMBO FAMILY MONUMENT (1916). Variegated shell-rock carving and ferns adorn the base of this finely executed monument. It also features a column intertwined with roses, symbolic of the couple's love, and a broken arch above, all against a background with larger-than-life lilies at center. John Colombo, who immigrated from Italy in 1887 and worked as a stonecutter, may have carved this stone.

Broggini Family Monument. Three naturalistic elements make up this monument. They are the shell-rock tablet, with the single lily at center, flanked by a broken tree trunk. The oval inset likely held a portrait of the deceased. Memorialized here are Dario Broggini (1905–1975) and Rose Broggini Stratton (1909–1974), his sister. Dario worked for the Valz Granite Company as a stonecutter and likely made this monument long before he died.

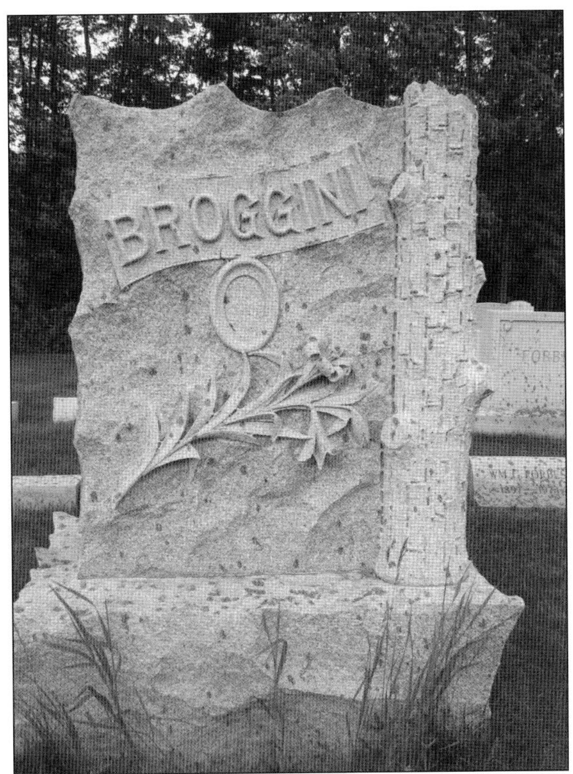

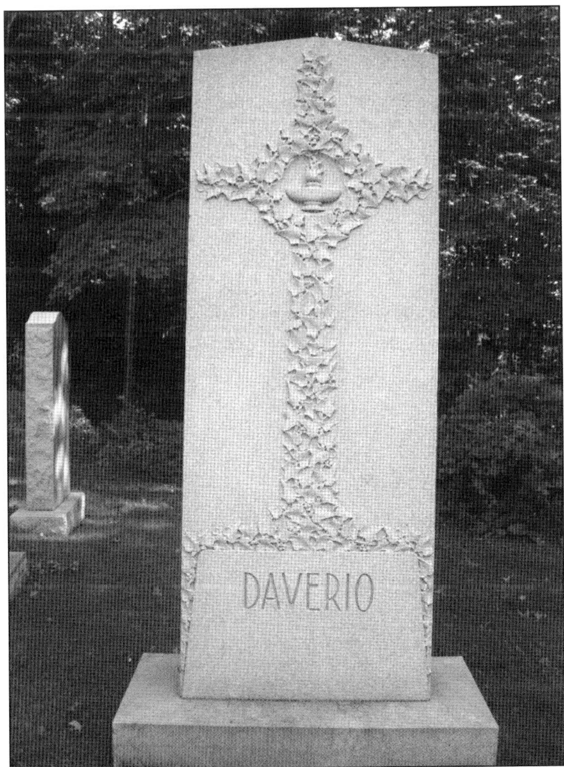

Daverio Family Monument (1939). This monument is notable for its exquisite cross made out of ivy, a plant symbolic of immortality, a theme augmented by the lamp with the eternal flame at center. Maurillio Daverio (1887–1939) was a stonecutter who arrived here from Italy in 1901.

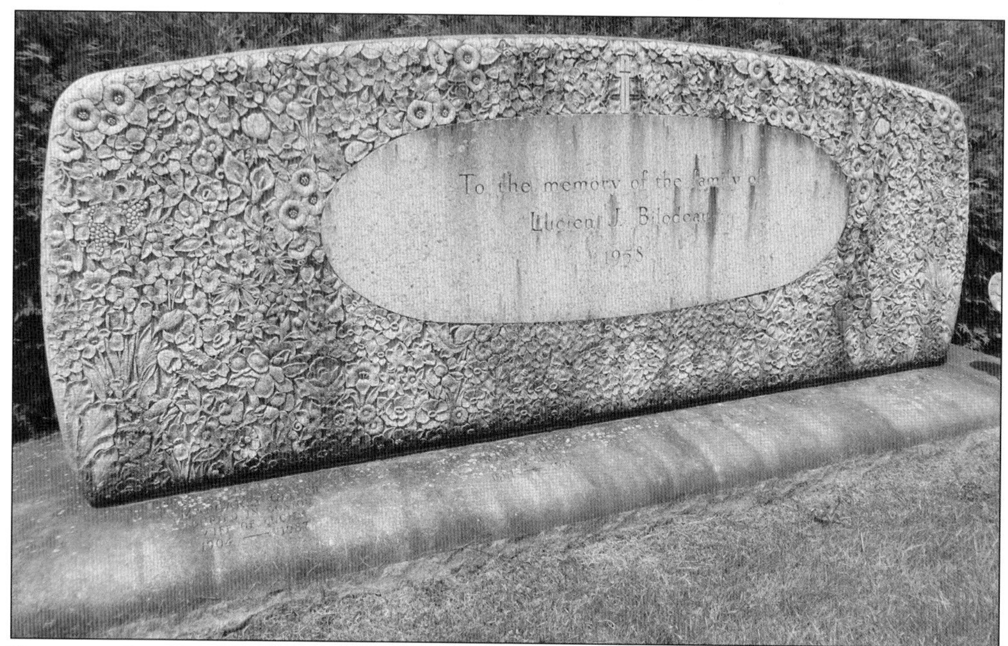

Bilodeau Family Monument and J.O. Bilodeau Advertisement. This family has had a long history in the monument business in Barre, being established by Joseph Bilodeau, a French Canadian immigrant who arrived in 1900 and soon started his company (below). Joseph's son Lucien Bilodeau (1903–1993) served as treasurer and later assumed control of the family business. Its intricate floral design made using the sandblasting technique, this monument was crafted after the tragic death of Lucien and Mary Bilodeau's son Nelson Bilodeau (1929–1956). Being one of the largest monuments in Hope Cemetery, it is indicative of the family's prominence and wealth in the granite trade, as is true with most of Hope's largest or elaborate monuments.

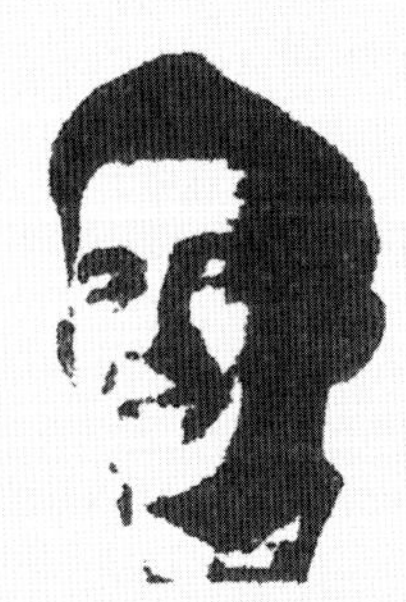

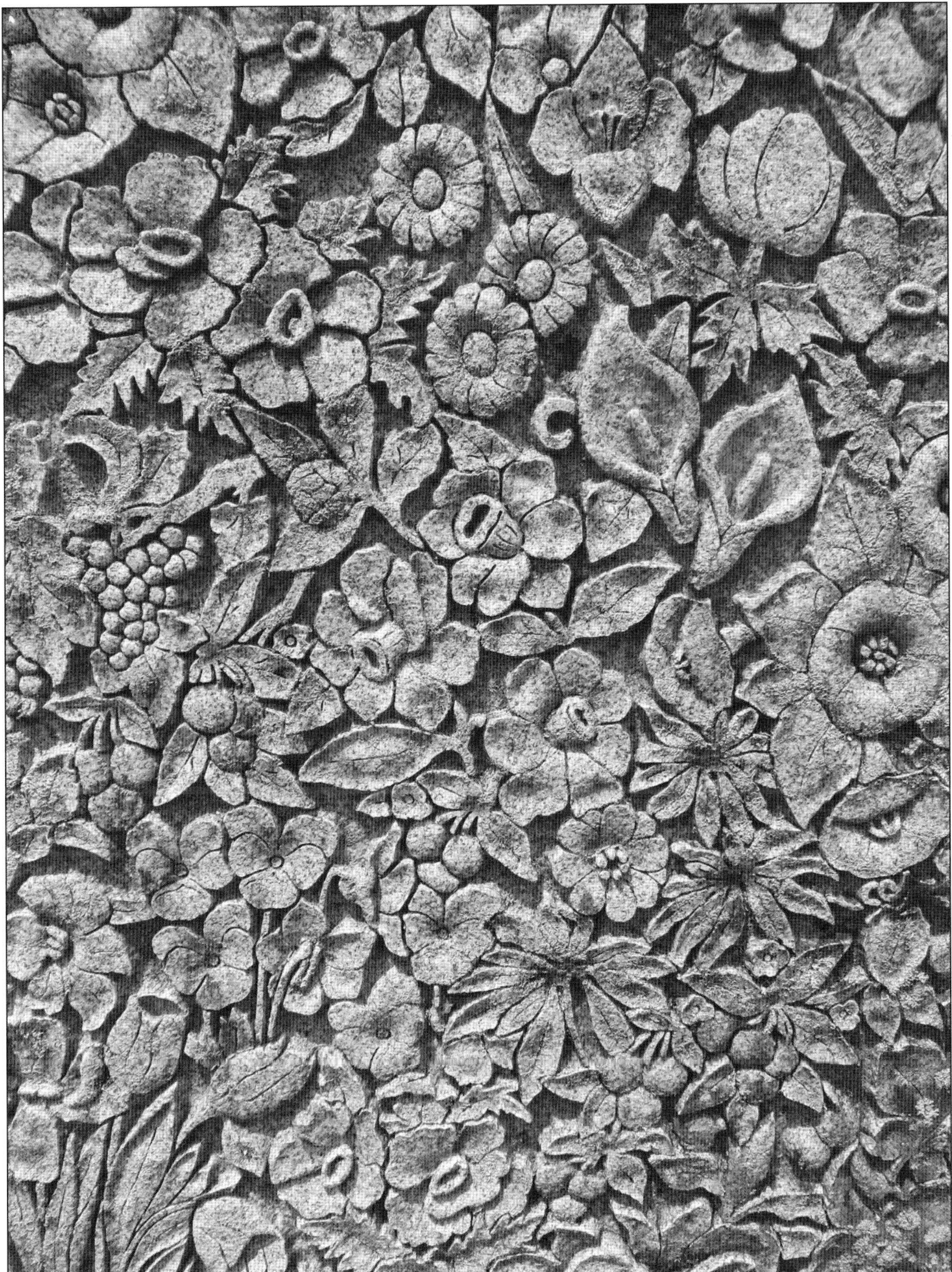

Detail of the Bilodeau Family Monument. The charming design of this monument is readily apparent—the artistic work offering a comforting and joyous form of remembrance to a grieving family. It is covered with hundreds of flowers, including daisies, morning glories, poppies (symbolic of many things, including consolation, remembrance of a fallen veteran, and rest and Resurrection), tulips (symbolic of enduring love), and roses, seen here in detail, as well as grapes (symbolic of the blood of Christ). Not seen here are the several birds hiding near the corners of the stone, including a hummingbird at upper right, symbolic of eternity.

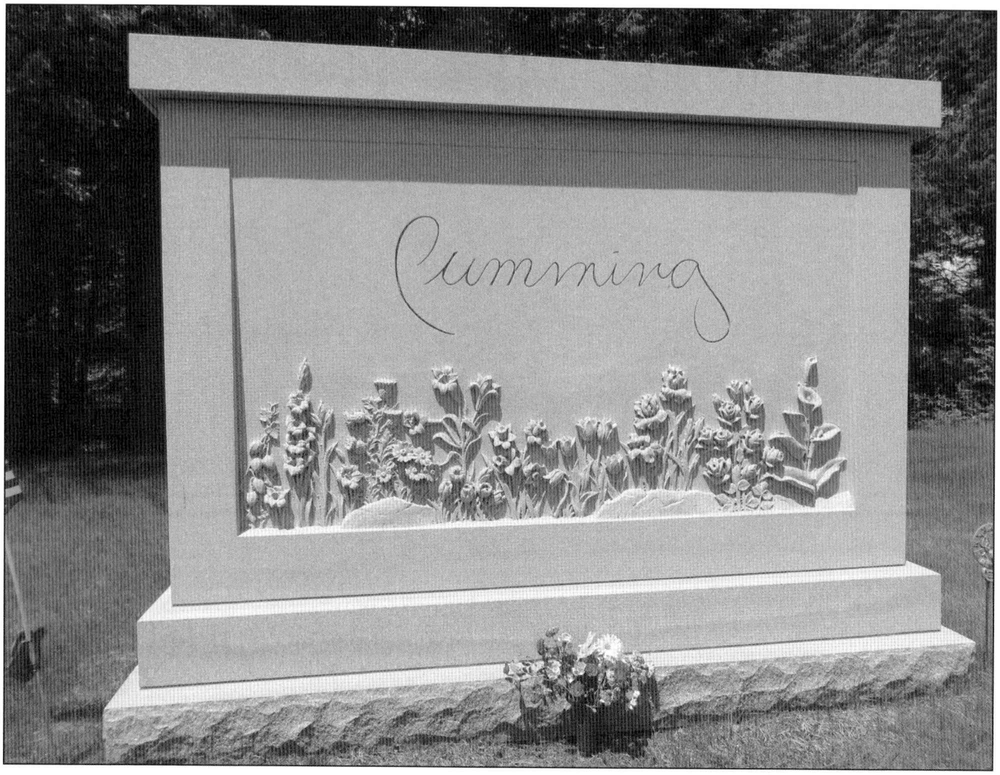

Cumming Family Mausoleum (1977). This structure was made for Francis Cumming (1922–1977), a World War II Army veteran and court reporter for the State of Vermont. It was manufactured by Beck and Beck Company and was designed by Ana Cumming, Francis's wife, and Joe Puricelli of Beck and Beck, with Al Comi doing the drafting work. It is notable for its beautiful floral carvings, cut in bas-relief form.

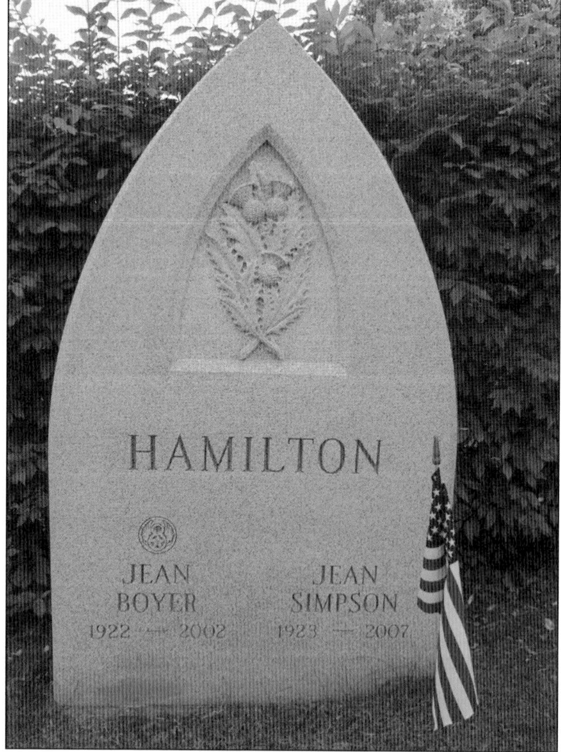

Hamilton Family Monument (2002). Cut in Gothic form, this monument features thistles in a triangular niche. The thistle has long been the national symbol of Scotland, so this may reflect the ethnic heritage of the family. Jean Boyer Hamilton was a veteran of World War II and later a teacher and coach in South Ryegate, Vermont.

Annibale Rovetti Monument (1908). A trained sculptor, the man buried here was born in Cremona, Italy, arrived in the United State in 1892, and was employed as a granite cutter. His monument consists of a beautiful chunk of Barre granite cut in a high shell-rock form, accented with a metallic wreath and floral carvings.

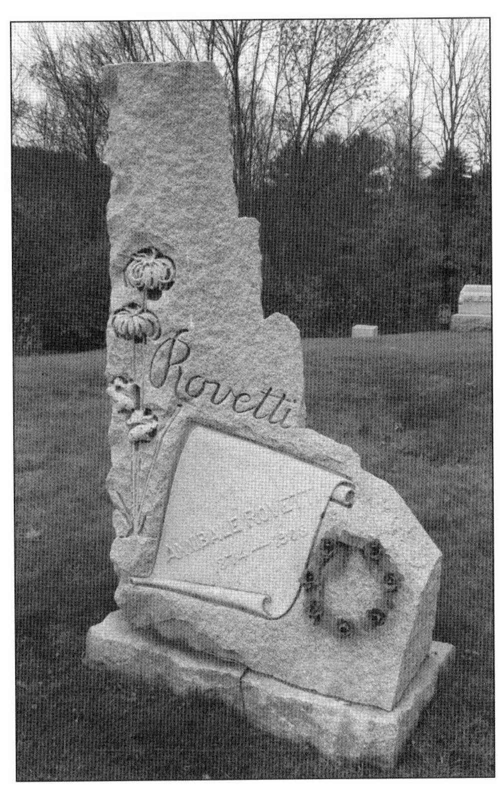

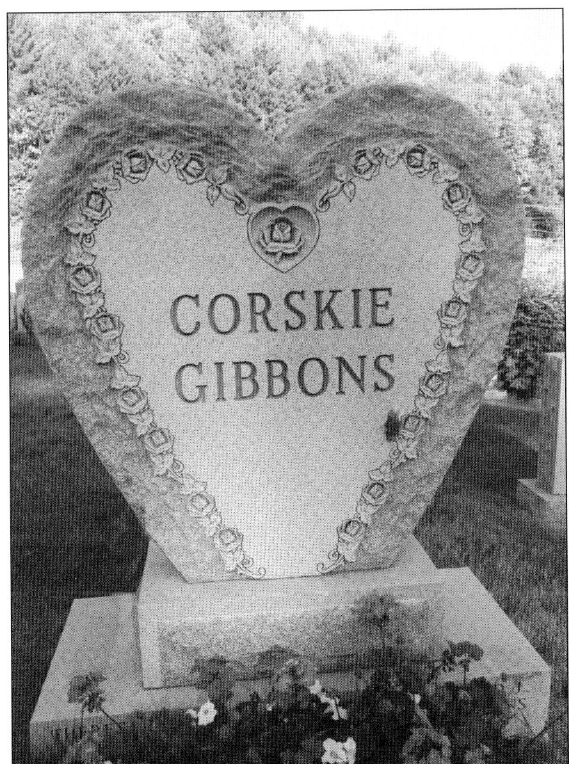

Corskie-Gibbons Family Monument (2007). An abundance of beautiful roses, arranged in a heart-shaped garland form, are the theme for this sculpted modern monument. The heart-shaped design of the stone is enhanced by its shell-rock finish around the edges. The monument was crafted for Theresa Martel Corskie (1925–2007), a native of Winooski, Vermont.

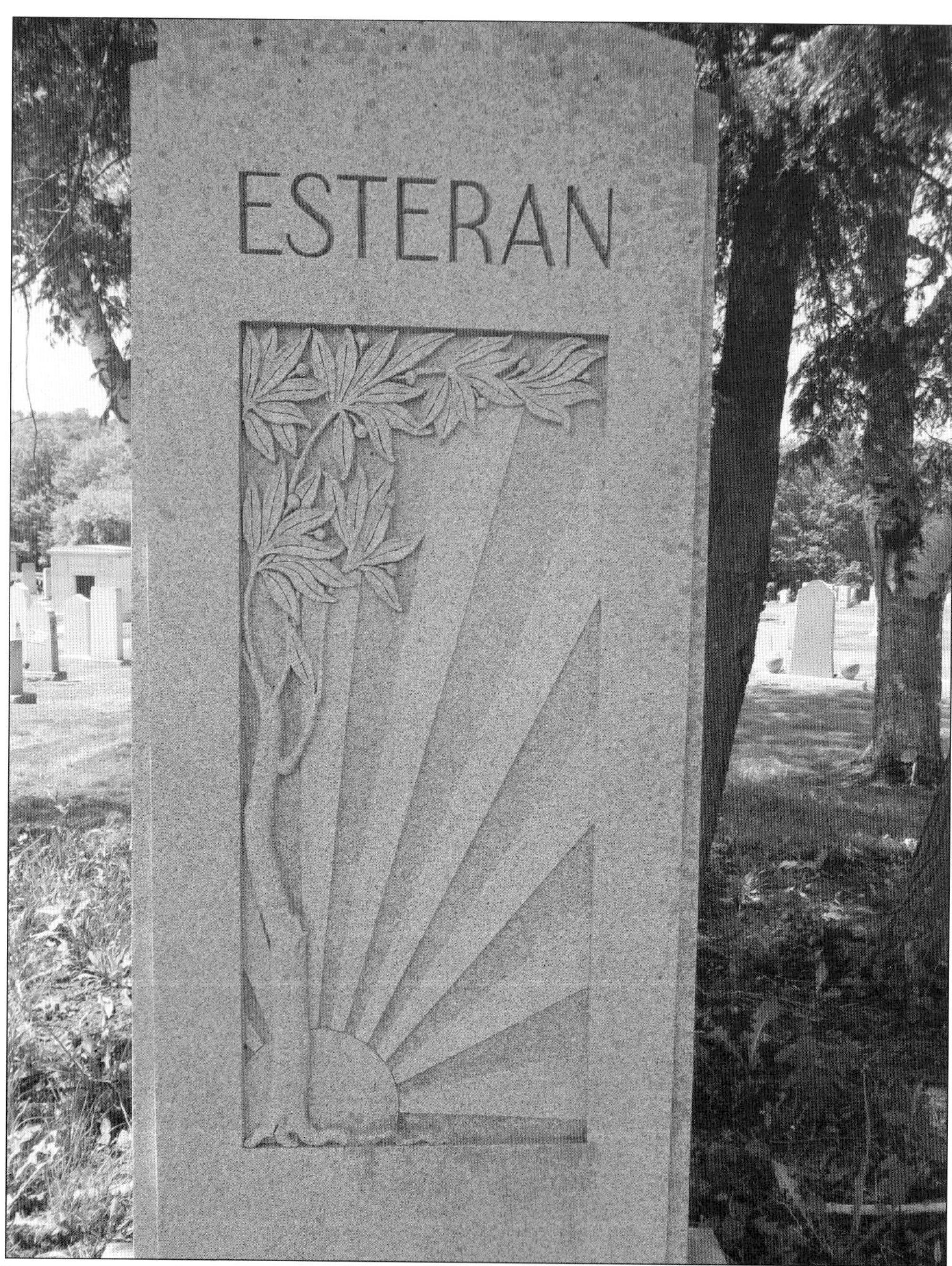

ESTERAN FAMILY MONUMENT (1942). Sculpted in the Art Deco style, this monument cut in bas-relief depicts a sun with rays bursting forth, flanked by an olive tree. The sun has a dual meaning here: its location on the lower portion of the stone is indicative of a setting sun, symbolic of the end of life, while the position of the sun on the horizon, with its glorious shining rays, has religious significance, symbolic of the dawn of the Resurrection. Primitivo Esteran (1883–1942) and Matilde Usle Esteran (1892–1963) were natives of Santander, Spain. He immigrated to the United States in 1907 and was employed as a stonecutter. He may have fashioned this monument, the olive tree, native to the Mediterranean, a reminder of his Spanish homeland.

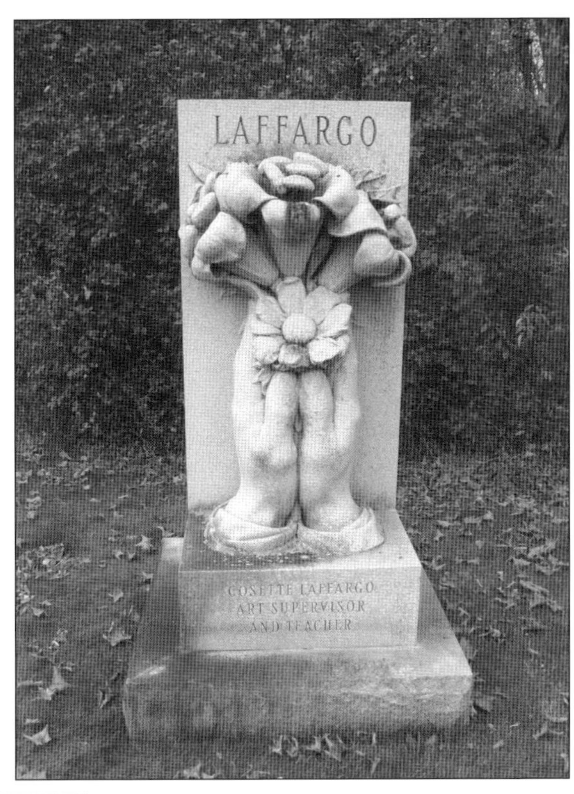

COSETTE LAFFARGO MONUMENT (1969). Laffargo (1908–1969, pictured below) was born in Barre to Virginio and Angela Laffargo. She first worked for the family business, but by 1941, she was working as a teaching assistant at the Mathewson Evening Drawing School in Barre, operated by Italian artisans. From this time forth, Laffargo would work as an art teacher. By 1944, she was an art teacher in the Seymour, Connecticut, public school system and—except for a stint as a teacher at the Hawthorne School in Rock Island, Illinois, from 1946 to 1947—would remain in that school system for the remainder of her career, rising to the level of art supervisor. Her monument was sculpted by Giuliano Cecchinelli and was one of his first commissions. (Below, courtesy of the Aldrich Public Library.)

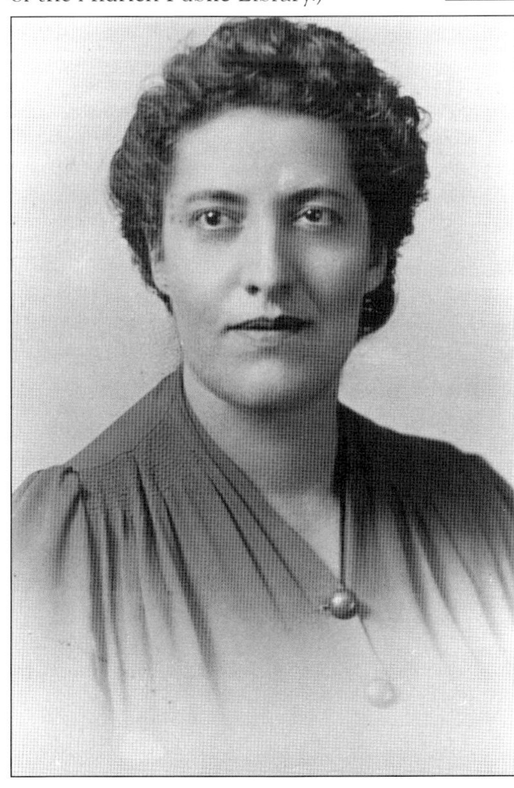

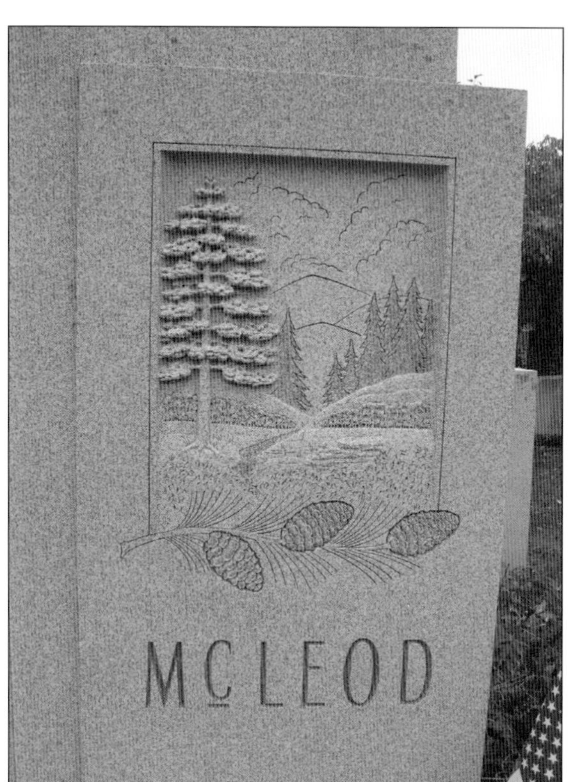

McLeod Family Monument. Modern works like this have an emphasis not on naturalistic elements with a religious meaning but on realistic views of New England nature, such as the pine bough with pine trees and mountains in the background shown here.

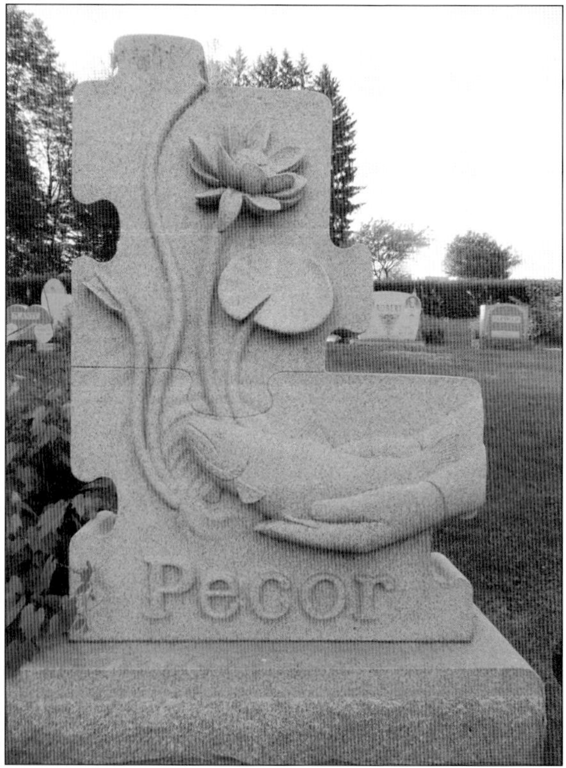

Pecor Family Monument (1997). This sculptured monument has puzzle pieces serving as a backdrop for a scene depicting a lily pad and a fish being released back to nature. Erected in memory of Corey Pecor (1972–1999), an Army and National Guard veteran, the puzzle pieces are perhaps representative of a life yet to be completed, while the natural fishing scene is representative of a hobby shared between father and son.

Four

The Architecture of Hope

Hope Cemetery is most often described as garden-style cemetery in a pastoral setting, and this is certainly true, but it is also another thing: a city for the dead. It started out with one monument, one "house," and year by year, just like any community, it has grown as more monuments have been added. Currently, there are thousands of monuments present, some say as many as 10,000 of them. Like any city, the architecture within Hope is widely varied and, just as with homes on any real city block, some of these granite "houses" have no distinguishing architectural elements visible. However, many of Hope's monuments do feature interesting architectural details that are finely carved. Sometimes, these architectural features are the main theme of a given monument, while others serve as a backdrop to the main theme. The influences for the architecture found within Hope are wide-ranging and reach far back into time and all the way down to the present. Several monuments with an Egyptian influence can be found here, and Greek and Roman classical designs with finely carved Corinthian columns are also common. The architectural elements of Europe's Gothic cathedrals offer a unique perspective. America too has its influences to be found, from monuments that mimic the skyscrapers of the 1930s and 1940s down to the more unusual designs of the modern era. Finally, one cannot forget about the actual houses for the dead, the mausoleums that are found about Hope Cemetery. This form has its origins dating back to 350 BC in the tomb of King Mausolus at Halicarnassus, in modern-day Turkey. Just as with this king, so too are the mausoleums of today final indicators of their owner's wealth and success.

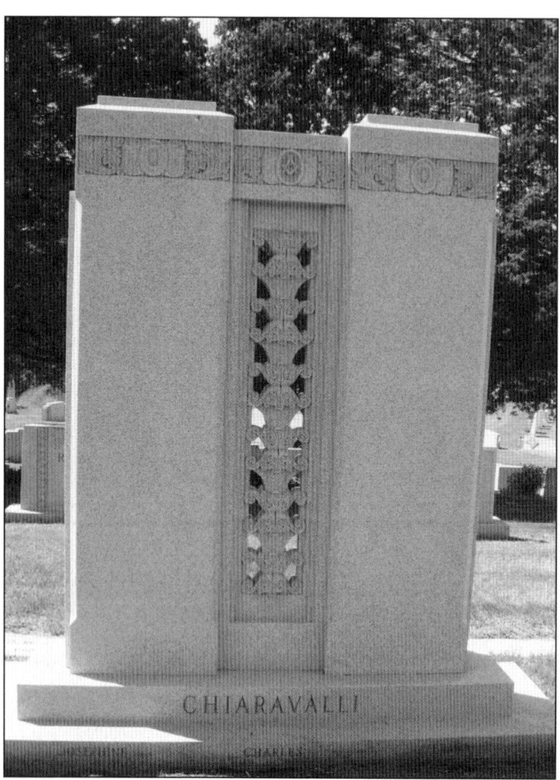

Chiaravalli Family Monument (1946). The twin columns on this monument are separated by an acanthus leaf and scroll panel. At top are bands with a central scroll, flanked by acanthus leaves. The scroll at center features the Masonic emblem indicative of Charles Chiaravalli's (1882–1946) membership. Acanthus leaves are symbolic of immortality and their use in architectural form dates back to the ancient Greeks.

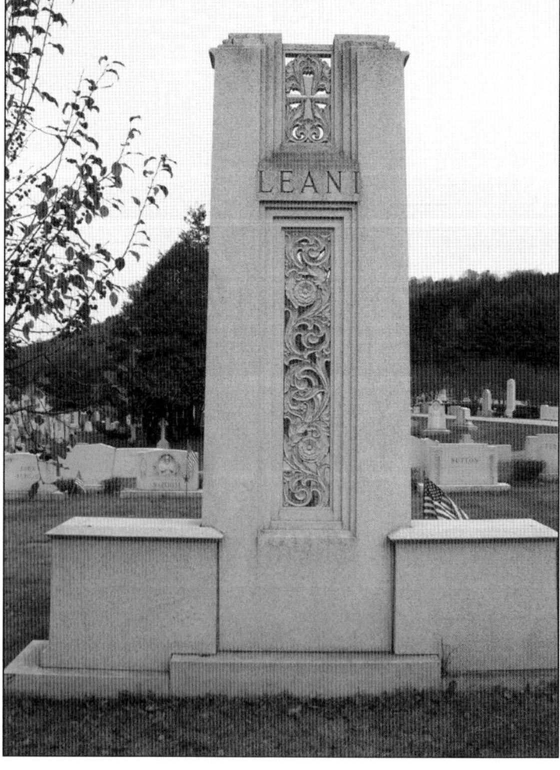

Leani Family Monument (1955). One of the largest monuments in Hope, it was erected by Dr. Aldo Leani (1910–1980) to honor his father, stonecutter Luigi Leani, and mother, Lucia. The column features a center panel with a floral and acanthus-leaf theme, the whole topped off with a cross. The front of the monument has a pedestal with an urn topped by an eternal flame.

Reynolds Family Monument. Located in the Woodside section, this Art Moderne–style monument erected in the 1960s has the look of a skyscraper. Its streamlined form features a panel of roses at center, with the flowers in various stages from the closed bud at top to one past full bloom at center. Buried here are Barre native Clyde Reynolds (1911–1990), a bakery salesman, and his wife, Winona Lita Reynolds (1910–2010).

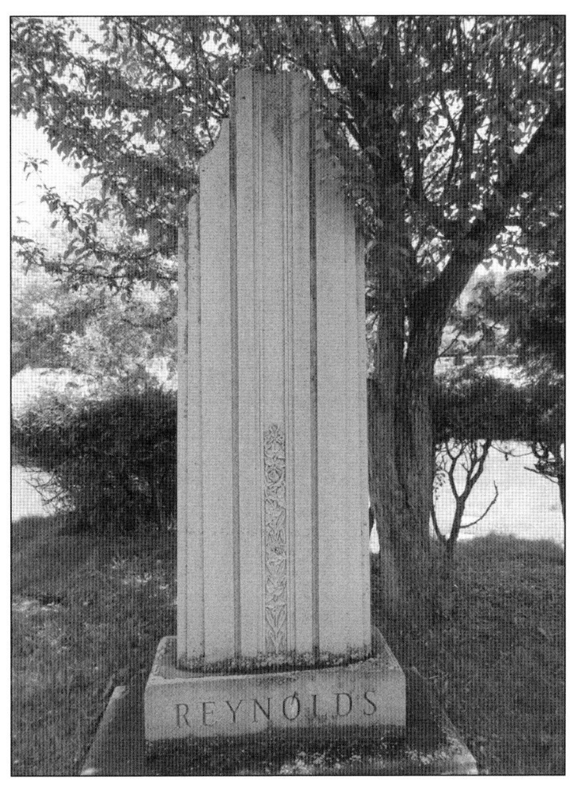

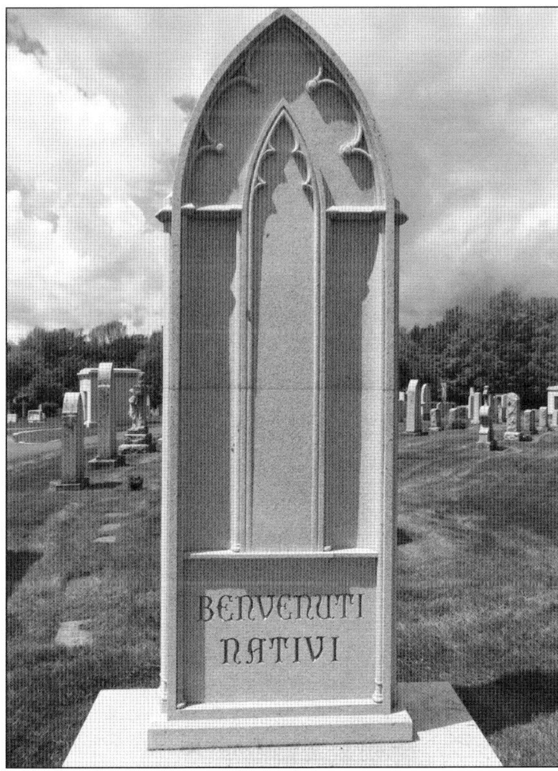

Benvenuti-Nativi Family Monument (1970). The arched windows of Europe's Gothic cathedrals offer the inspiration for this modern monument. Giuseppe "Joseph" Benvenuti (1879–1969), his wife, Anna (1885–1970), and their daughter Sarah Benvenuti Nativi were Italian immigrants, with Joseph arriving in Barre in 1910 and his family following in 1912. He worked in the granite trade.

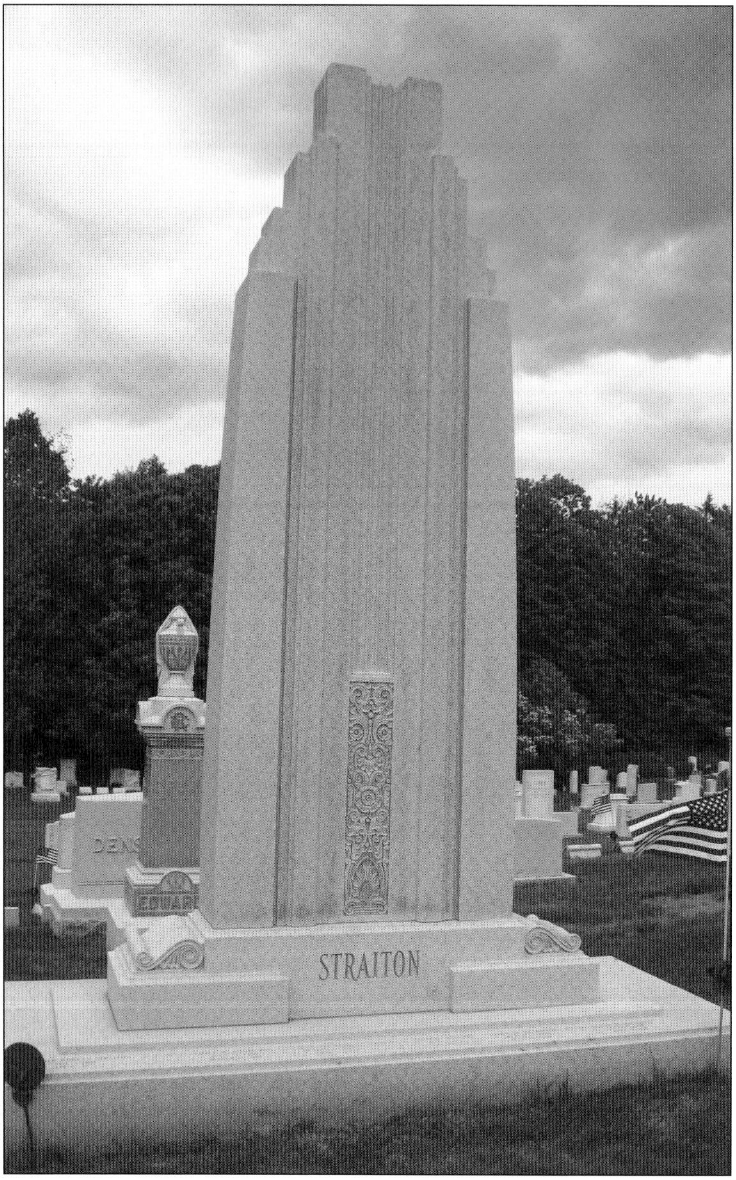

Straiton Family Monument and George Straiton Advertisement. This memorial is one of the most imposing found in Hope Cemetery. The head of this family, George Straiton (1862–1931), was a well-known monument dealer in Barre (below) for many years after his arrival from Scotland in 1882 with his Canadian-born wife, Isabella "Belle" (also called "Lovie") Straiton. This monument was crafted in the Art Deco style of the 1930s, embodied in such buildings as New York City's Empire State Building, and is indicative of the wealth Straiton accumulated during his years in the monument business.

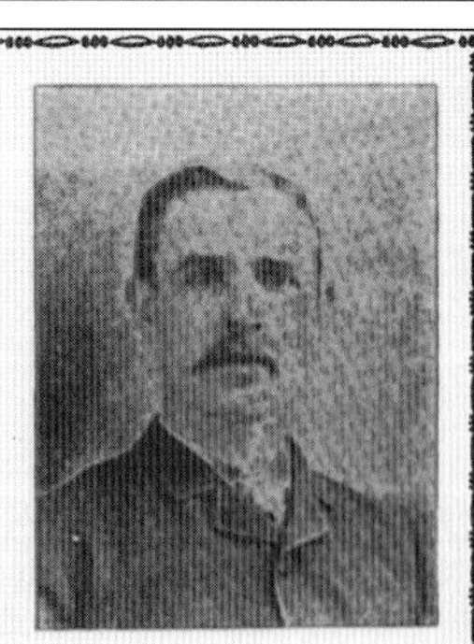

Always Ready for Business!

GEORGE STRAITON,

BARRE, VERMONT

My Specialty is **BARRE GRANITE MONUMENTAL WORK.**

If you are a retail Monument Dealer requiring GOOD WORK, A 1 STOCK AND PROMPT SHIPMENTS send direct to me. You shall have a prompt reply and if the work is entrusted to my care I guarantee satisfaction. Every appliance for the best finishing at bottom prices.

GEORGE STRAITON, BARRE, VERMONT.

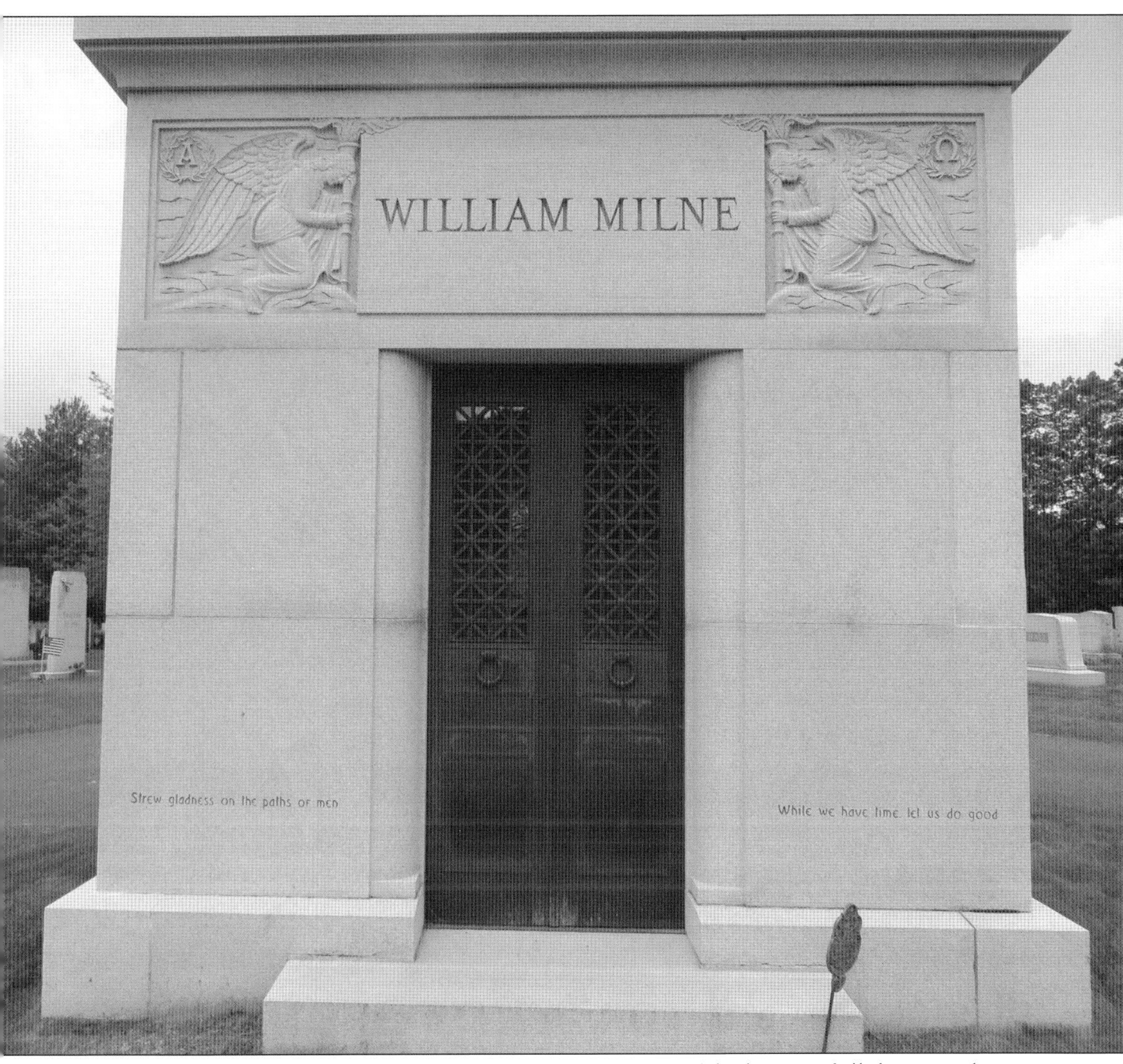

WILLIAM MILNE MAUSOLEUM. Milne's final resting place is one of the largest of all the mausoleums in Hope Cemetery but is also notable for the bas-relief carved panels that flank his name at top, with each of them featuring a winged angel carrying a torch topped off with an eternal flame. This plot was purchased by William (1880–1962) and Ethel Milne in 1937; when their mausoleum was built is uncertain, but it was almost certainly constructed by his own company. Milne was the son of William Alexander Milne and immigrated here from Scotland in 1891.

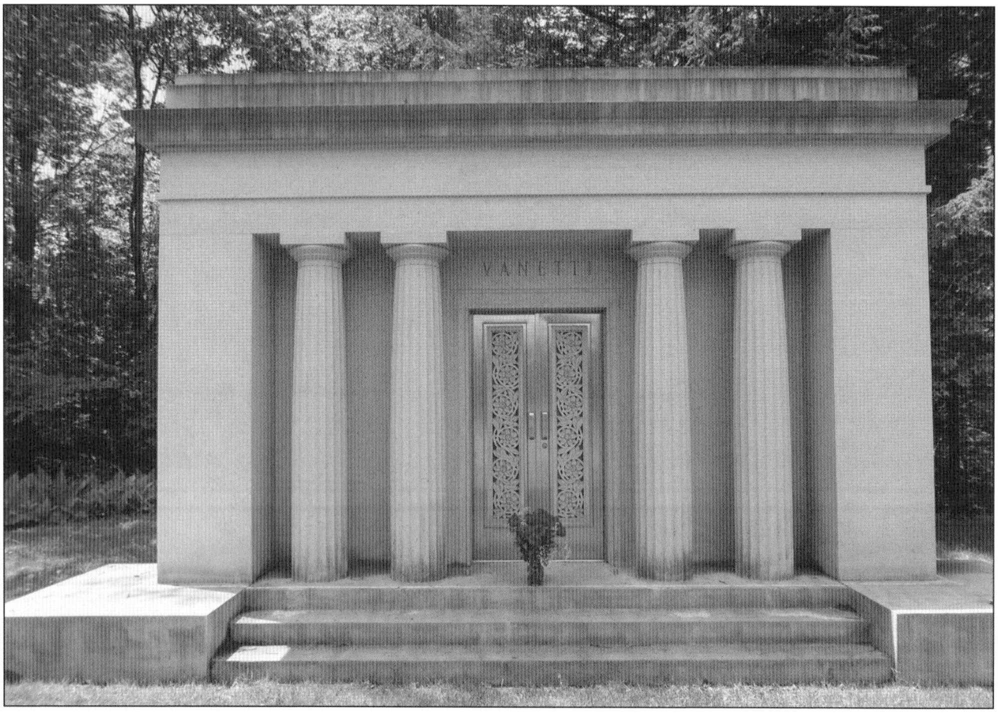

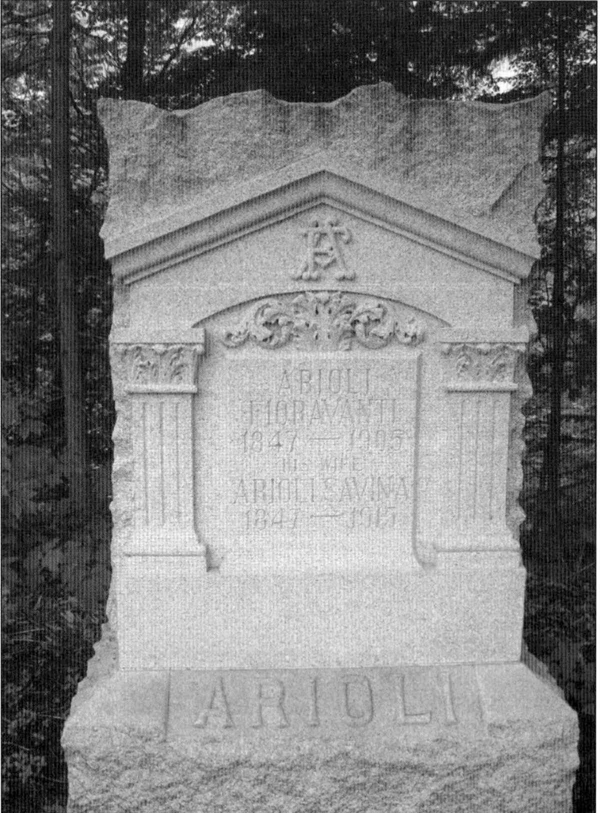

VANETTI FAMILY MAUSOLEUM. This mausoleum is noted for its size and form. The facade features four fluted Doric columns, which help support a roof that weighs 23 tons, and brass doors with exquisitely carved floral granite panels. The Vanetti family was long involved in Barre's granite business, with Aldo Vanetti (1910–1978) and his brother Henry purchasing the Valz Granite Company in the 1940s.

ARIOLI FAMILY MONUMENT (1905). Small Corinthian columns supporting a pediment with the letters "F" and "A" are the highlights of this monument. Fioravanti and Savina Arioli arrived in Vermont from Besano, Italy, in 1898, with Fioravanti employed as a stonecutter, as were his sons John and Joseph. Fioravanti died from pulmonary tuberculosis.

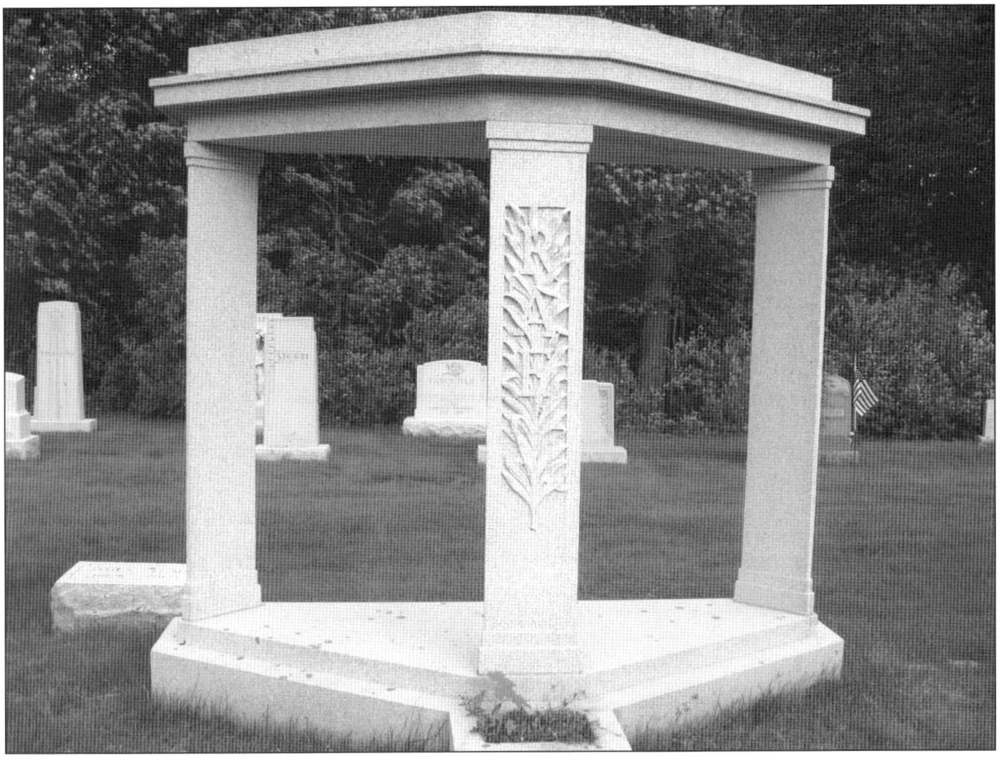

Rae Family Monument (1920). This unique work, fashioned in the form of a shrine or temple, is distinguished by its simplicity. It was likely crafted by the man buried here, James Rae (1858–1920), an immigrant from Scotland who arrived here in 1893 and worked as a stonecutter before succumbing to pulmonary tuberculosis.

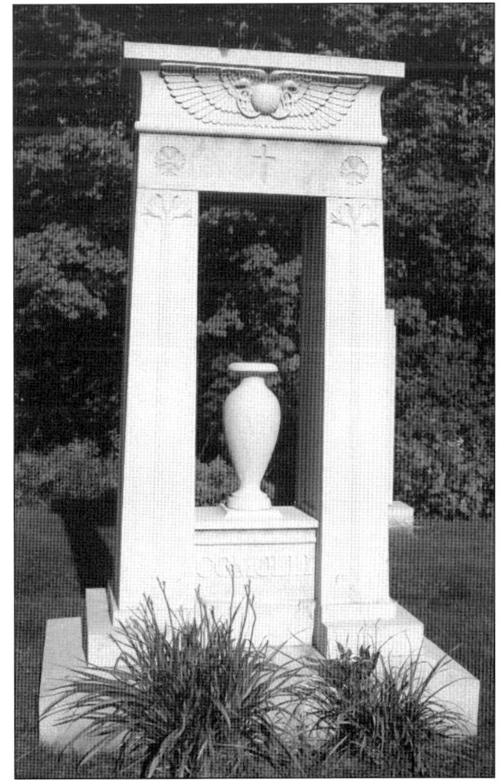

Comolli Family Monument (1917). Cut in the form of an Egyptian temple, this monument features two columns, each adorned with a long-stemmed flower, flanking a funerary urn. Most distinguishing is the double-headed eagle carved at top, which is a Masonic symbol. Angelo "John" Comolli immigrated to Barre in 1886 from Como, Italy, and was a proprietor of one of the city's most successful granite companies.

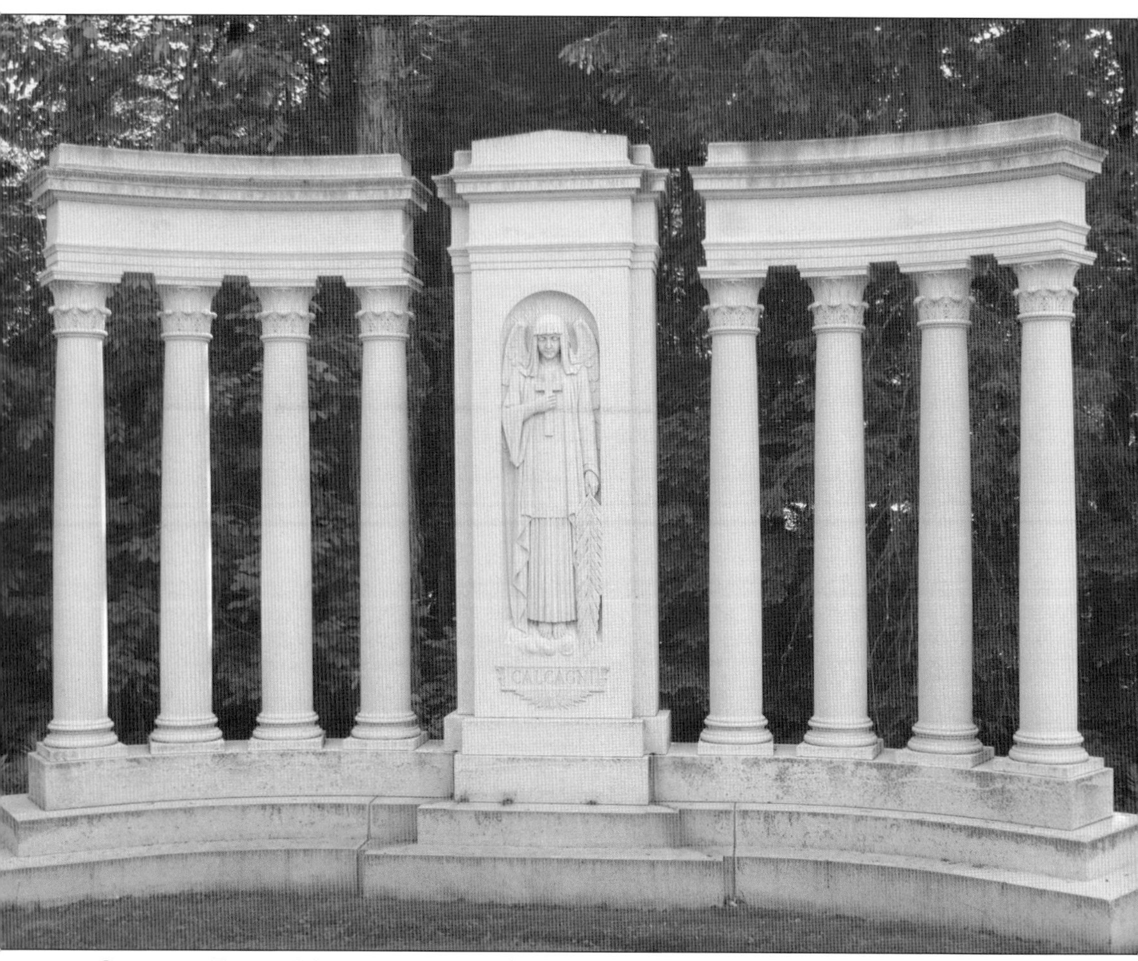

Calcagni Family Monument. Corinthian columns are the dominant element in this large classically styled monument. They flank a large angelic figure holding a cross and carved in bas-relief. Among those interred here are Joseph Calcagni (1874–1926) and his wife, Teresa (1879–1957). Joseph arrived here from Italy in 1892 and began to work for Samuel Novelli, later establishing a partnership with him under the name Novelli and Calcagni. The company grew into one of the most successful granite companies in all of Barre. The Calcagni family continues in the granite trade to this day in the form of the Granite Corporation of Barre, established by grandson Joseph B. Calcagni.

Monti-Casellini Family Monument (1955). This monument, consisting of three columns of the Tuscan order, is beautiful in its simplicity and perhaps representative of the ruins of a Greek temple. Buried here are Felix Monti (1883–1955) and his wife Caroline (1889–1983), as well as their daughter Elva and son in law Salvatore Casellini. Felix was a carver in the granite trade who immigrated here from Viggiano, Italy.

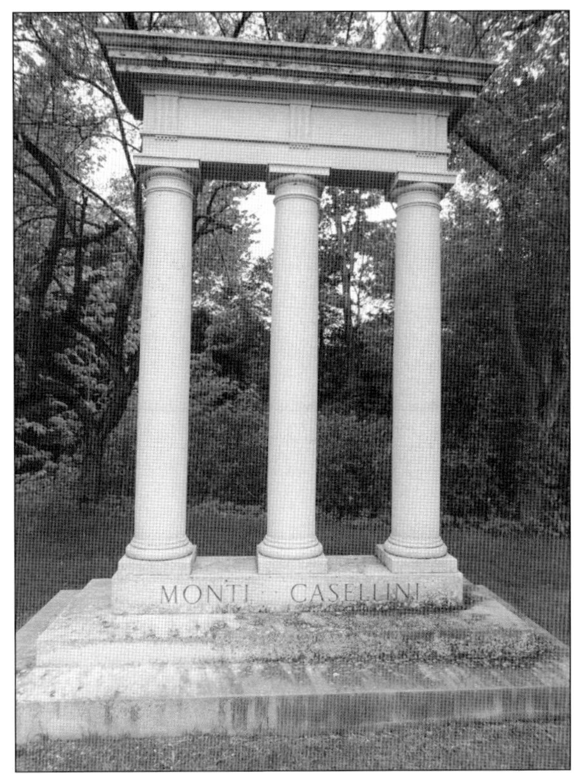

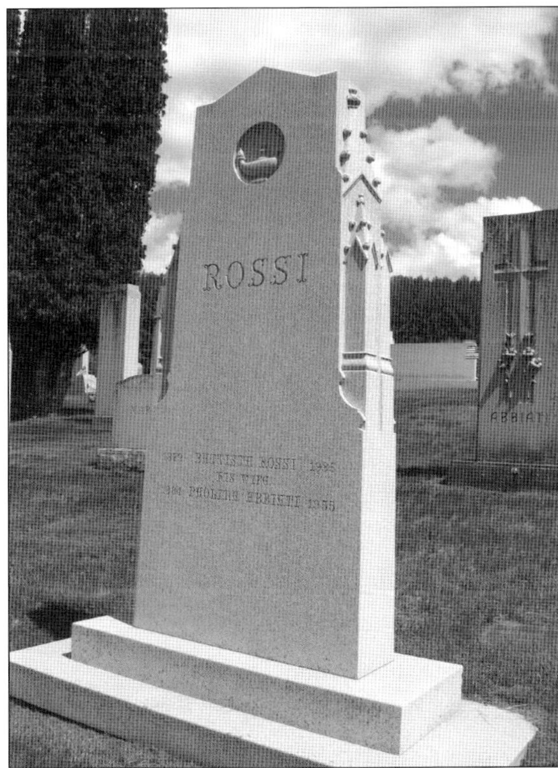

Rossi Family Monument (1935). Viewed from the front, this monument at first appears rather simplistic. However, when the monument is examined from a different angle, its architectural elements are clearly visible. Found on the side are tiered towers carved in Gothic form. Battista Rossi (1879–1935) was a stonecutter from Baveno, Italy, who arrived here in 1899.

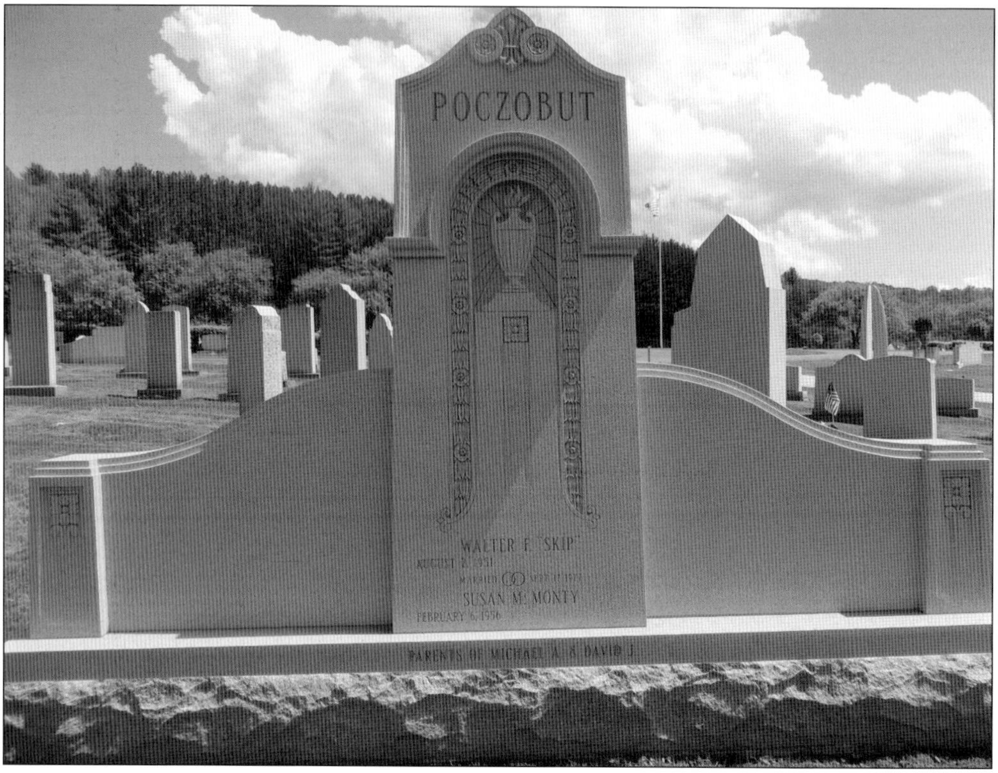

Poczobut Family Monument. No one is yet buried at the site of this monument, a practice common in Hope Cemetery, as those who want to be buried here often pick their resting places decades in advance. The work features a central column and floral designs circling an urn with an eternal flame. The sidewalls have been left blank but offer space for additional memorial carvings.

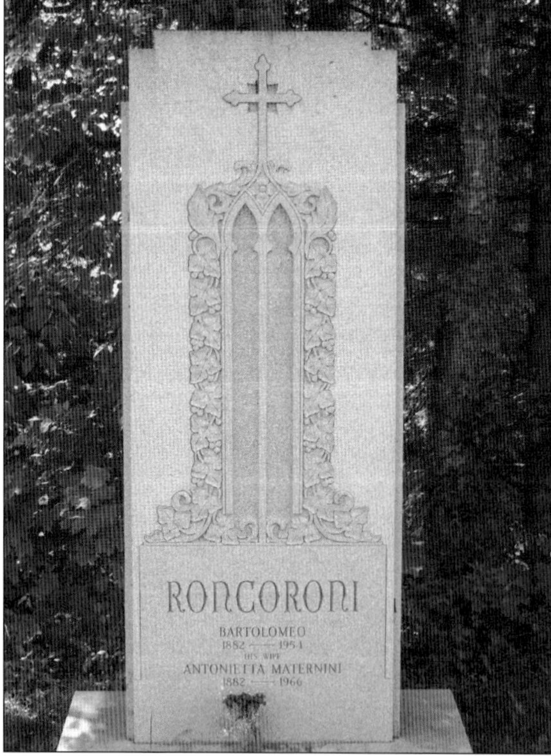

Roncoroni Family Monument (1954). A Gothic cathedral window from their Italian homeland may have served as the inspiration for this monument. Bartolomeo Roncoroni arrived in the United States in 1913—with his wife, Antoinietta, arriving a year later—and served as a stonecutter for many years.

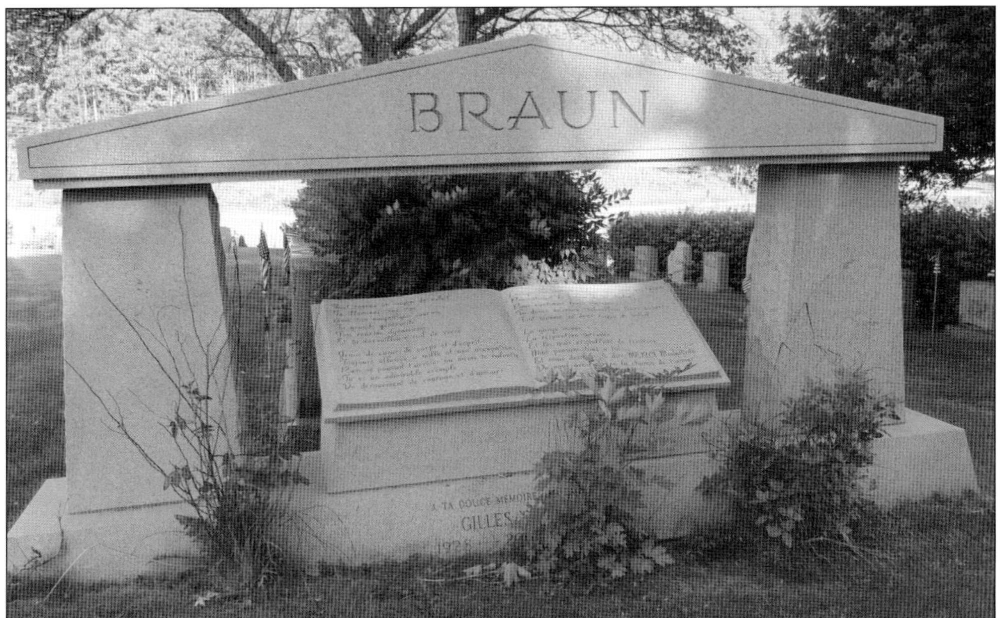

BRAUN FAMILY MONUMENT (1994). This modern monument features a large pediment supported by two large granite blocks. Housed within this shrine is a book of verse, composed by Gilles Braun (1928–2007) in honor of his wife, Madeleine Bergeron Braun (1931–1994). Both were immigrants from Québec—Gilles from Sherbrooke and Madeleine from Coaticook. Quite appropriately, the verse in this book of stone (below) is written in French, its last three lines on the second page reading, in translation, "And we want to say: Thank you Madeleine / For giving us the chance to love / And be loved by you."

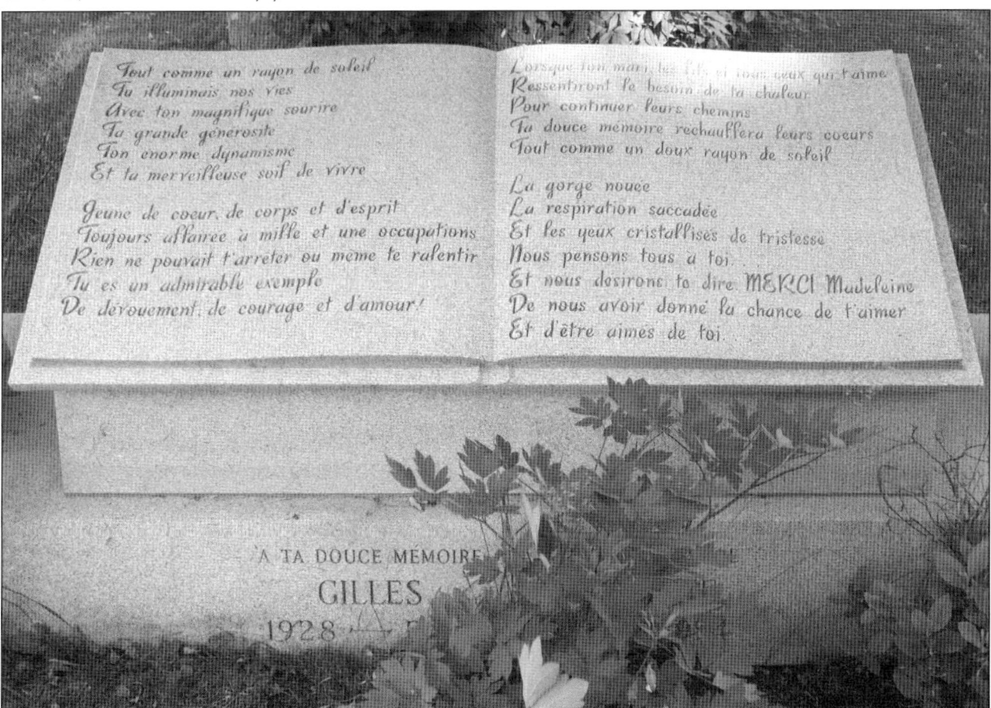

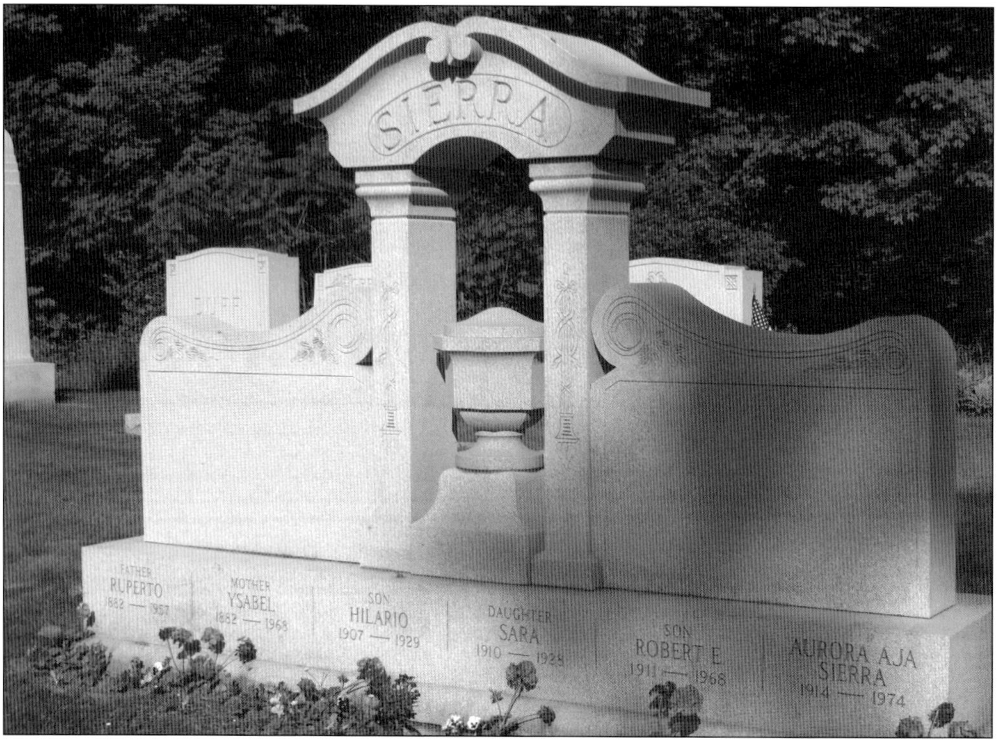

SIERRA FAMILY MONUMENT (1929). The arched pediment design for this family's monument is unique, as are the two inverted torches, with intertwined snakes and an eternal flame, symbolic of death, carved on the columns. These torches represent the lives of the Sierra children, which were cut short at a young age, with Sara dying from tuberculosis in 1928 and her brother Hillario dying 11 months later due to a quarry accident.

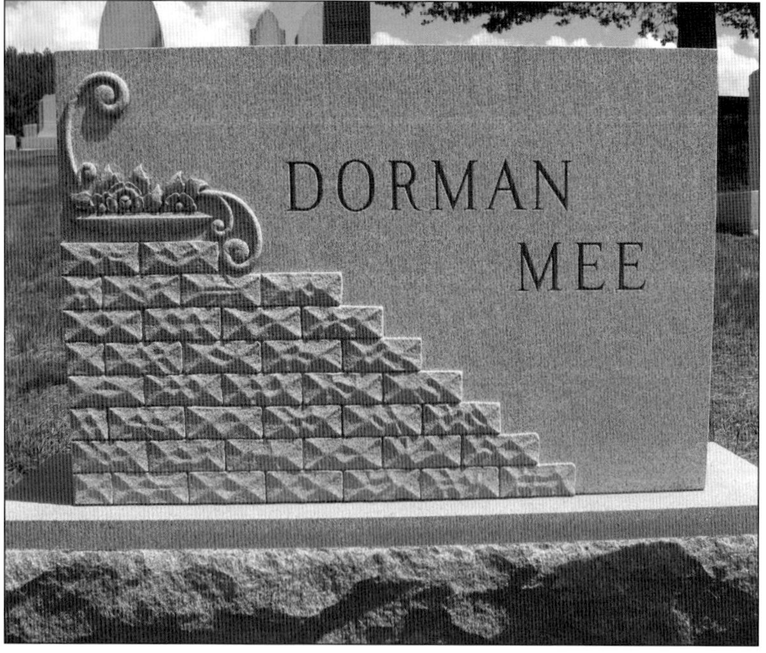

DOORMAN-MEE FAMILY MONUMENT (1988). Buried here are Fred (1902–1988) and Hazel Doorman (1902–1990), as well as Edward (1900–1971) and Helen Mee (1903–1988), the two women being sisters. Their monument is simple yet elegant, featuring a textured granite brick wall and stairway, with a floral basket at top.

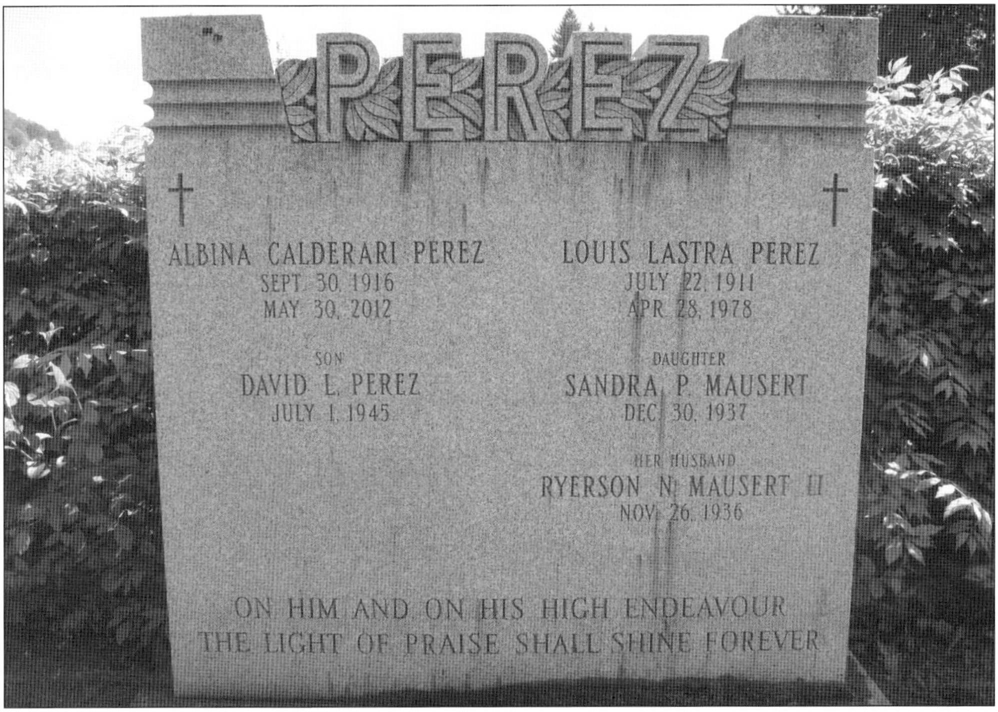

Perez Family Monument (1978). Though this monument has an easily identifiable religious message, it is visually striking for the family name carved at top, interspersed with olive tree leaves, an indicator of their Spanish heritage, in the style of an old-fashioned movie theater marquee from the 1930s.

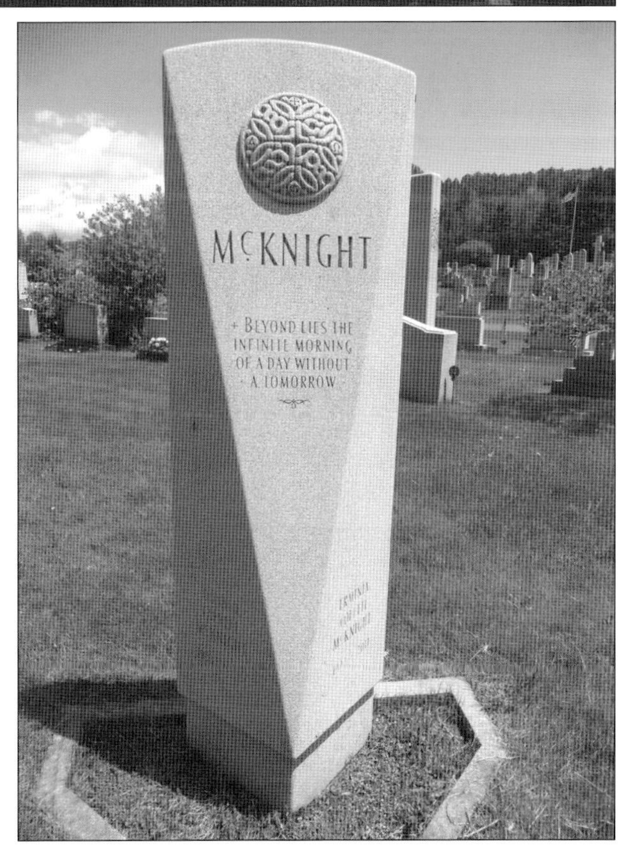

McKnight Family Monument. This modern monument is notable for its overall form and shape, its front offering a tapered effect whose lines are pleasing to the eye. Not surprisingly, this creation marks the burial plot for an architect, Donald Farrell McKnight, and his wife, Erminia Coletti McKnight (1907–2011). McKnight, who owns McKnight Associates Architects in Barre, likely designed this stone.

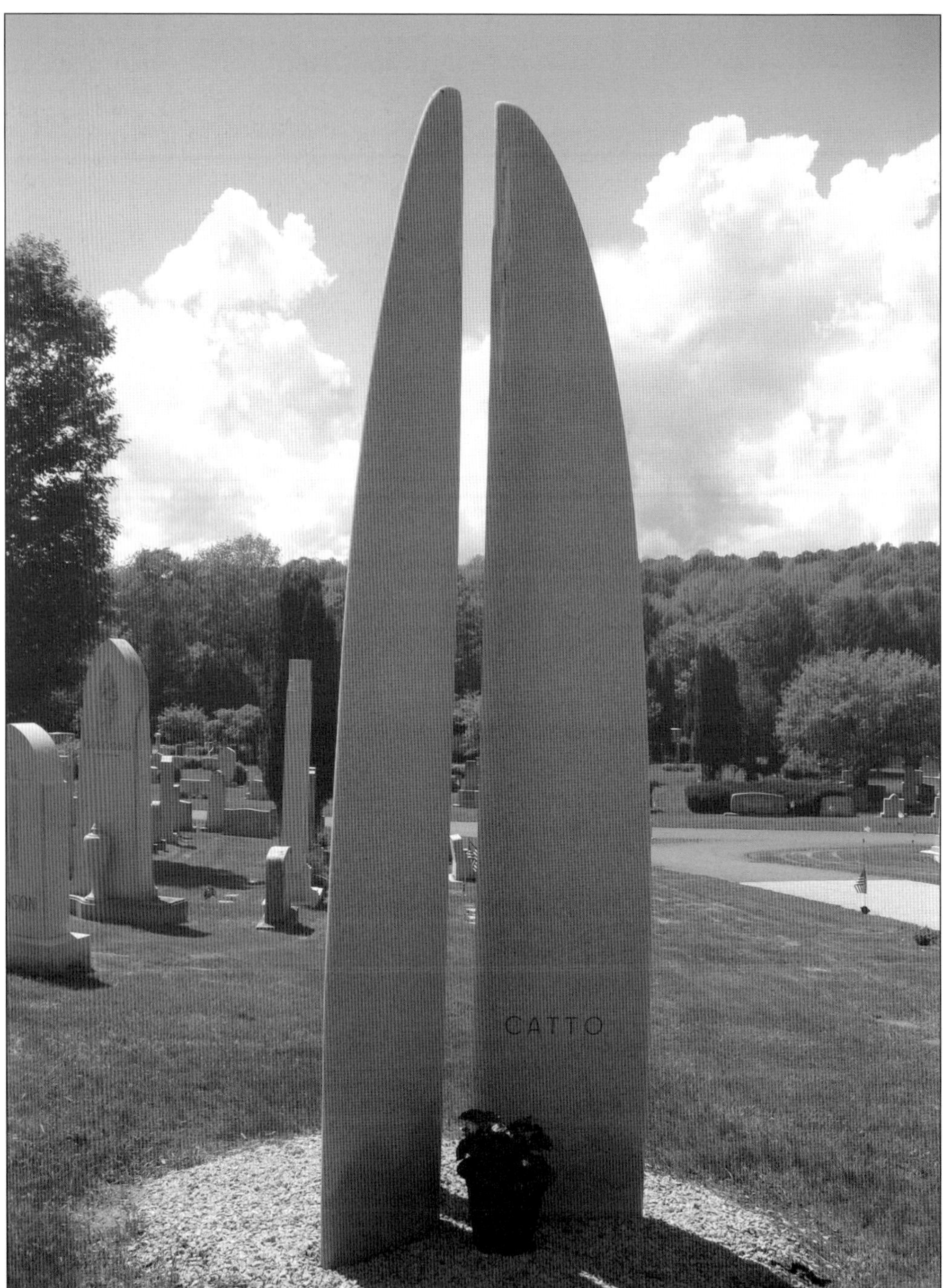

Catto Family Monument (1961). Noted for its three uniquely curved components that soar skyward, this striking monument marks the graves for Vincent Catto (1893–1960), a well-known merchant in Barre, and his wife, Rena Mammolo Catto (1897–1959). It was designed by Rena's nephew, architect Paul Mammolo, a Barre native who practiced his trade in East Hanover, New Jersey, and is also interred in Hope Cemetery. Once surrounded by tall shrubs and partially obscured, it is now one of the most visible monuments in all of Hope.

Five

Hope in the Modern Era

For many visitors to Hope Cemetery today, the most intriguing and delightful monuments are those that are created in the form of sculptured or shaped objects. Because of the skill of Barre's modern-day monument artists, the sky seems to be the limit when it comes to the works they produce, and it is only here, in this open-air museum, that they can be seen in abundance. What is also interesting about Hope Cemetery is the fact that many of the modern monuments here do not mark anyone's final resting place—at least not yet. Plots here are coveted, and individuals and families will often purchase them and have a personal monument created and erected sometimes years or even decades in advance—and in some cases, no burials may ever take place. While there are many unusual monuments here, to maintain the decorum and beauty of the cemetery, regulations are in place that govern the size and content of monuments, and all monument designs must be approved by the Barre Cemetery Commission. The commission also has the right to reject any monument design if it is deemed to be unsuitable for any reason. One of the most integral rules that has been put in place to maintain the look of Hope, as well as support the local business, is that requiring monuments to be made "of only first grade, clear Barre granite." While these regulations have evolved over the years, the results speak for themselves, as Hope has continued to maintain its unique character and beauty and looks to do so far into the future.

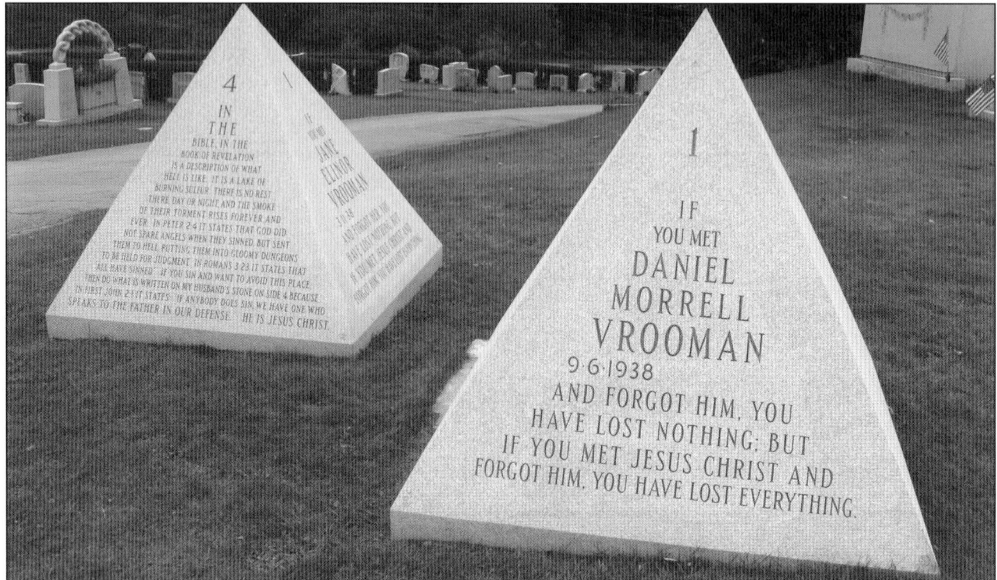

Vrooman Family Monuments. Located near the entrance to the cemetery, this set of pyramids, the side of each of which is lettered with religious messages, is eye-catching and helps to set the modern tone for Hope Cemetery. The owners of this plot live out of state and may never be buried here, but the messages they wish to convey will certainly inspire and delight visitors far into the future.

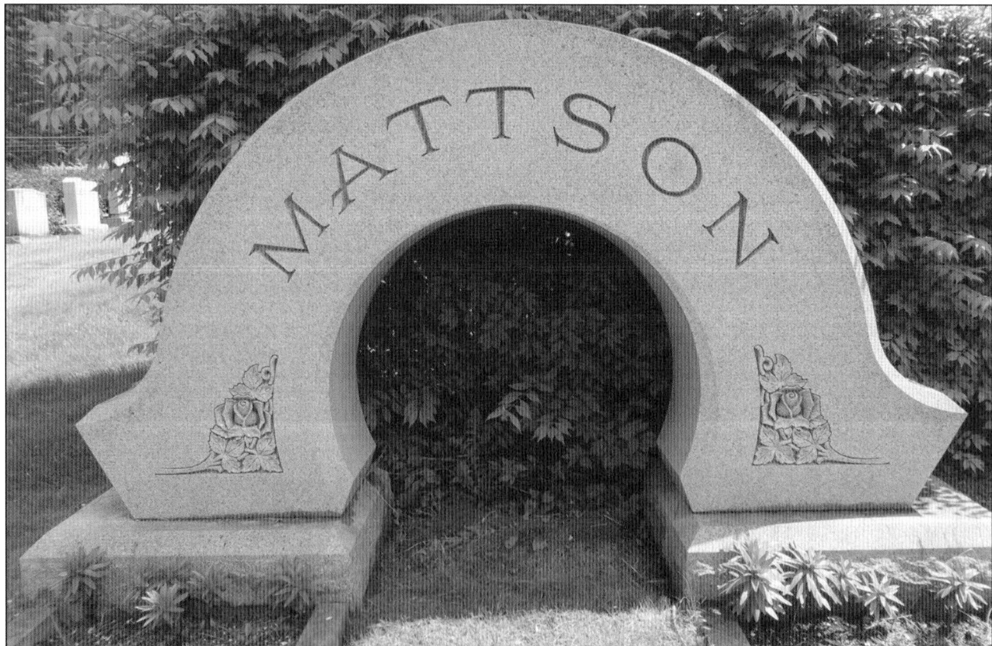

Mattson Family Monument. Family connections are the theme here, as the graves of two brothers, Allan (1950–2014) and Kenneth (1945–1995), are connected by this circular arch design. Allan had a long involvement with the granite business, both as a banker and a vocational instructor for students learning the trade, as well as working for the family business, Chioldi Granite Company (now Northern Mausoleum Services).

Bettini Family Monument (1960). One of the cemetery's most visited monuments, this easy chair marks the final resting place of Guerrino (1892–1960) and Jennie Bettini. While it may represent a place of relaxation for Guerrino, the empty chair is also a symbol of his loss. Interestingly, it is not the first stone chair carved in Barre; Novelli and Corti created a smaller version in 1901 for a client.

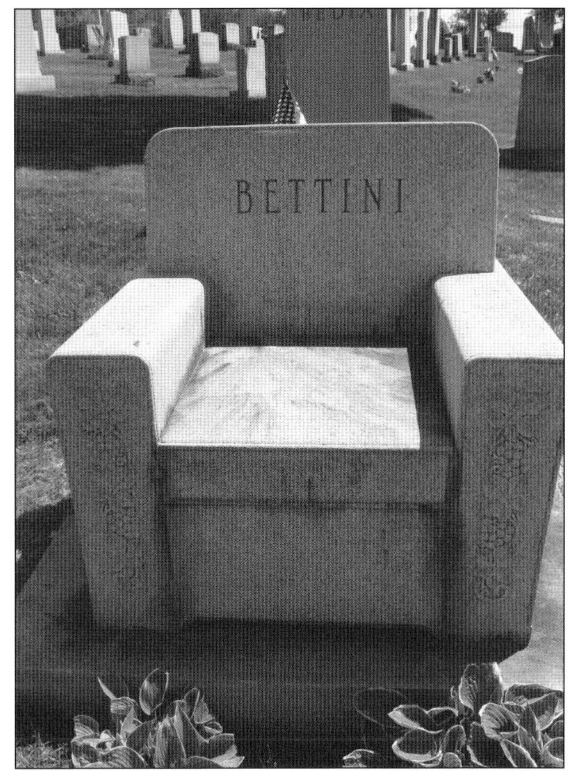

Douse Family Monument (2016). This finely crafted granite bench provides a place of reflection and remembrance for the friends and family of Kimberly Douse (1977–2016), beloved wife, married to Jason Douse in 2003; mother of two; and second-grade teacher at Barre City Elementary School.

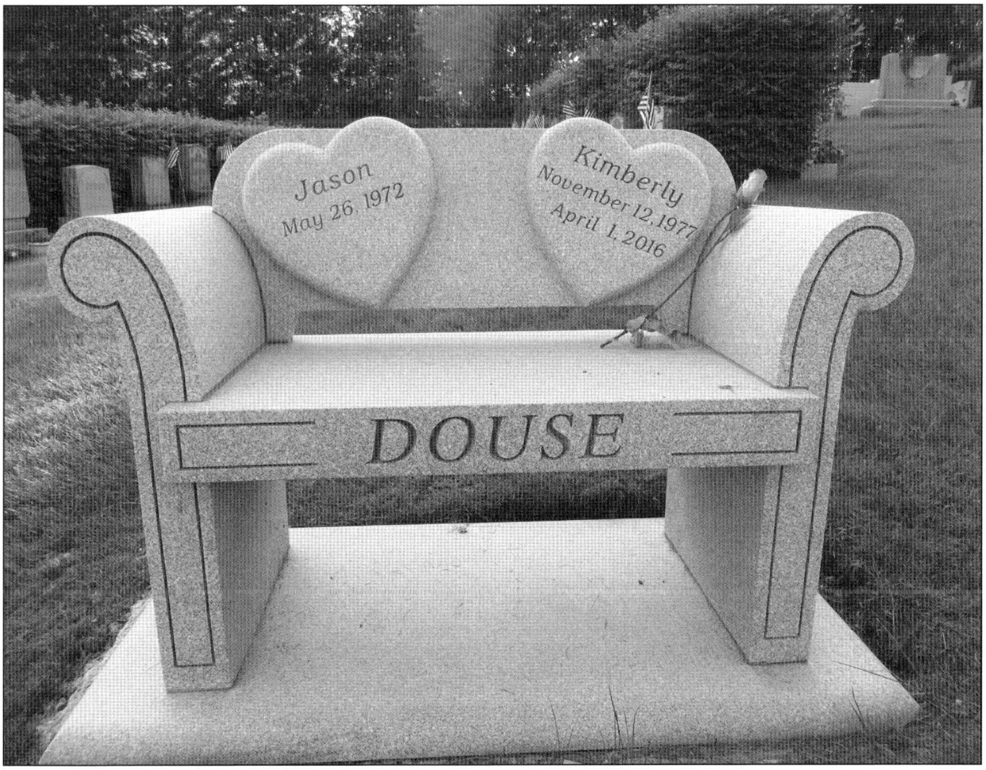

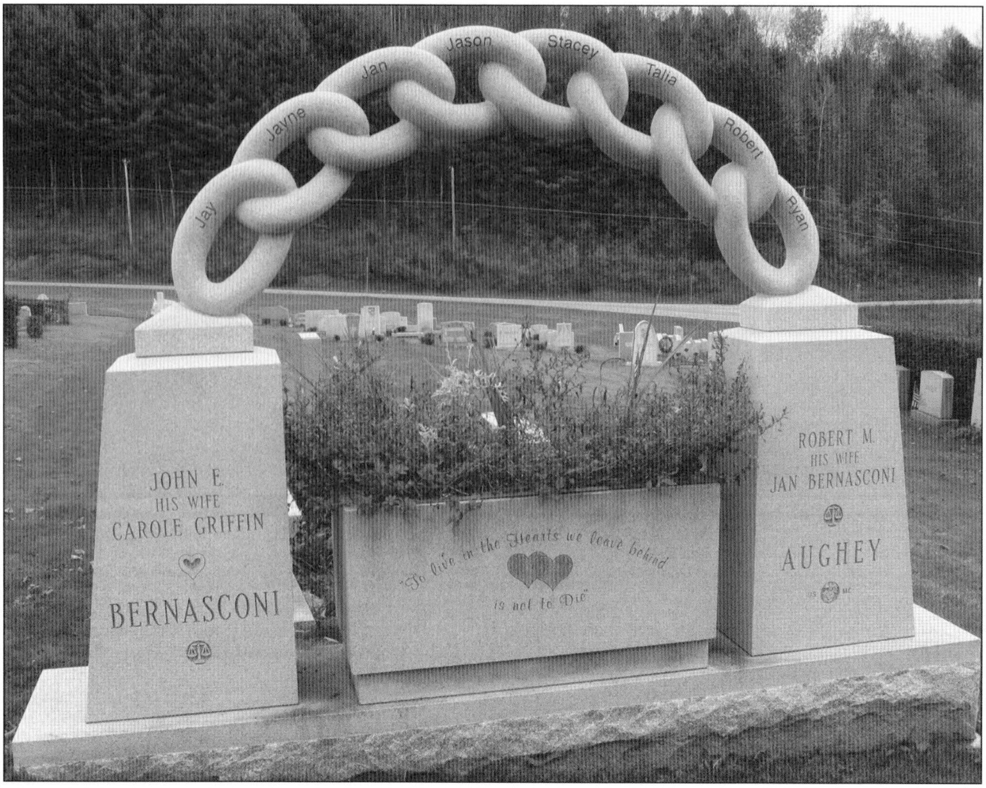

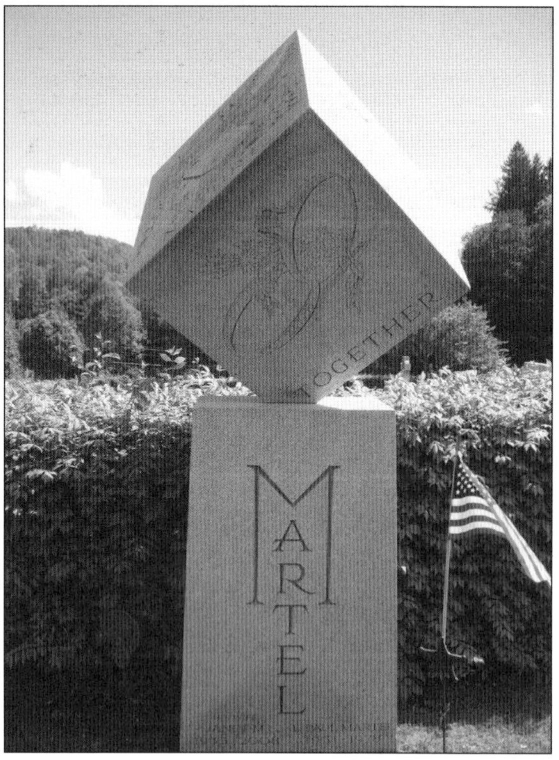

Bernasconi-Aughey Family Monument. Memorialized here are Jan Bernasconi Aughey (1962–2012) and her parents, John and Carole Bernasconi. She followed in her father's footsteps as a lawyer and was well known for her family-law practice. Jan was the inspiration for this monument, whose individual links list her husband, sons, brother, and nieces. Jan "fervently believed" that "to live in the hearts we leave behind is not to die."

Martel Family Monument (1979). The facets of this family's life and values they "cherished" are depicted on this precisely balanced cube monument produced by Buttura and Sons. Paul Martel (1931–1978) was an insurance salesman and executive. One side lists his family members in the "Tree of Life," while others depict images representing "Nature," "Faithfulness," "Love," "Together," and "Salesman."

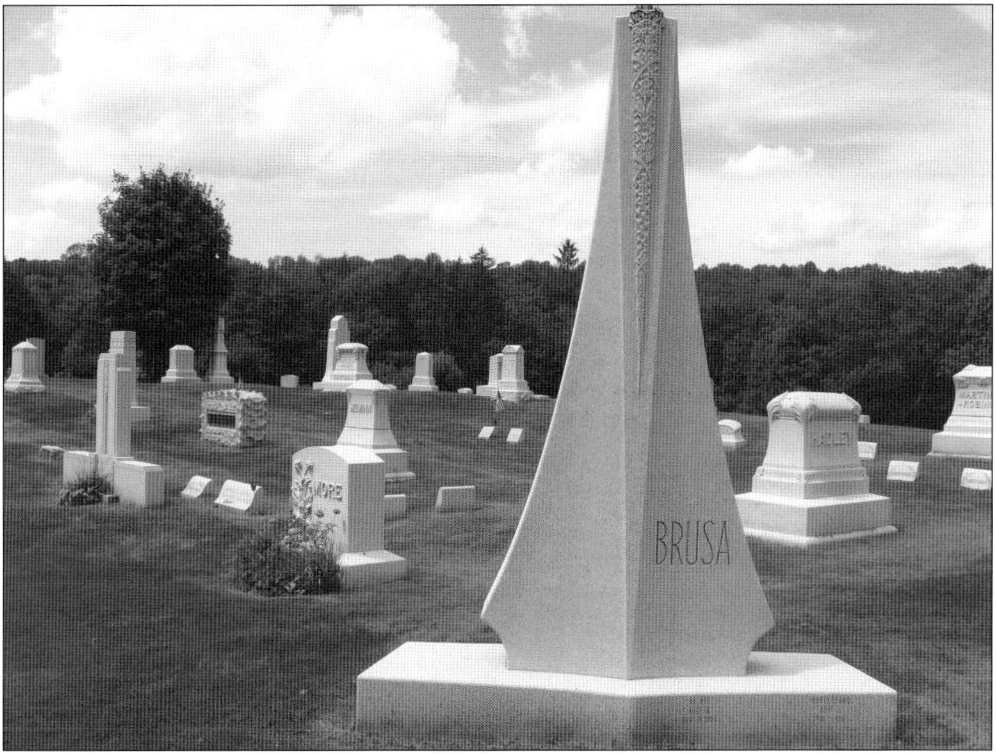

Brusa Family Monument (1992). The impressive nature of this aerodynamic monument is indicative of the lifelong work of Ateo Battista Brusa (1906–1992). Ateo, the son of John Brusa, would succeed his father in the family granite business, Brusa Brothers, by the 1950s and gained further prominence in the industry as director of the American Monument Association.

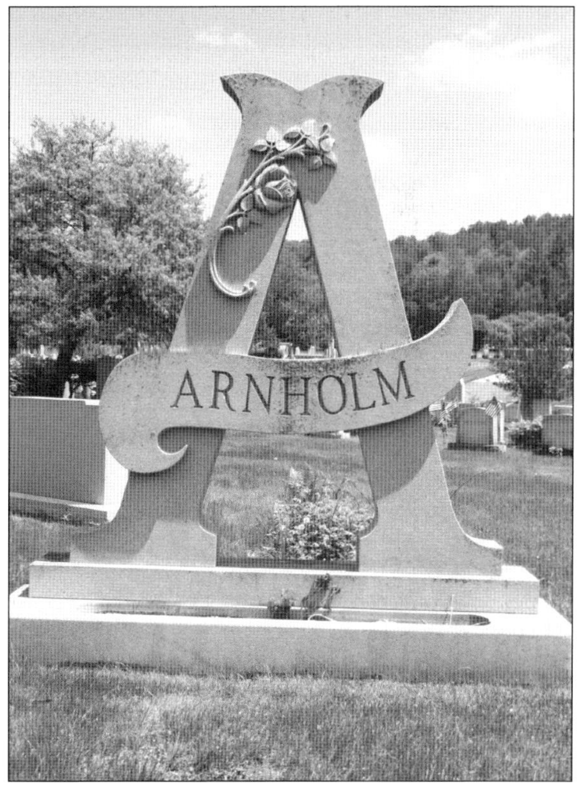

Arnholm Family Monument (1997). An artful monument, this is the largest letter found in Hope. Charles Arnholm Jr. (1917–1997) was the son of a Danish immigrant who worked in the automotive business and owned his own garage. He married Rachel Nichols (Arnholm) in June 1940, and together, the couple would raise nine foster children.

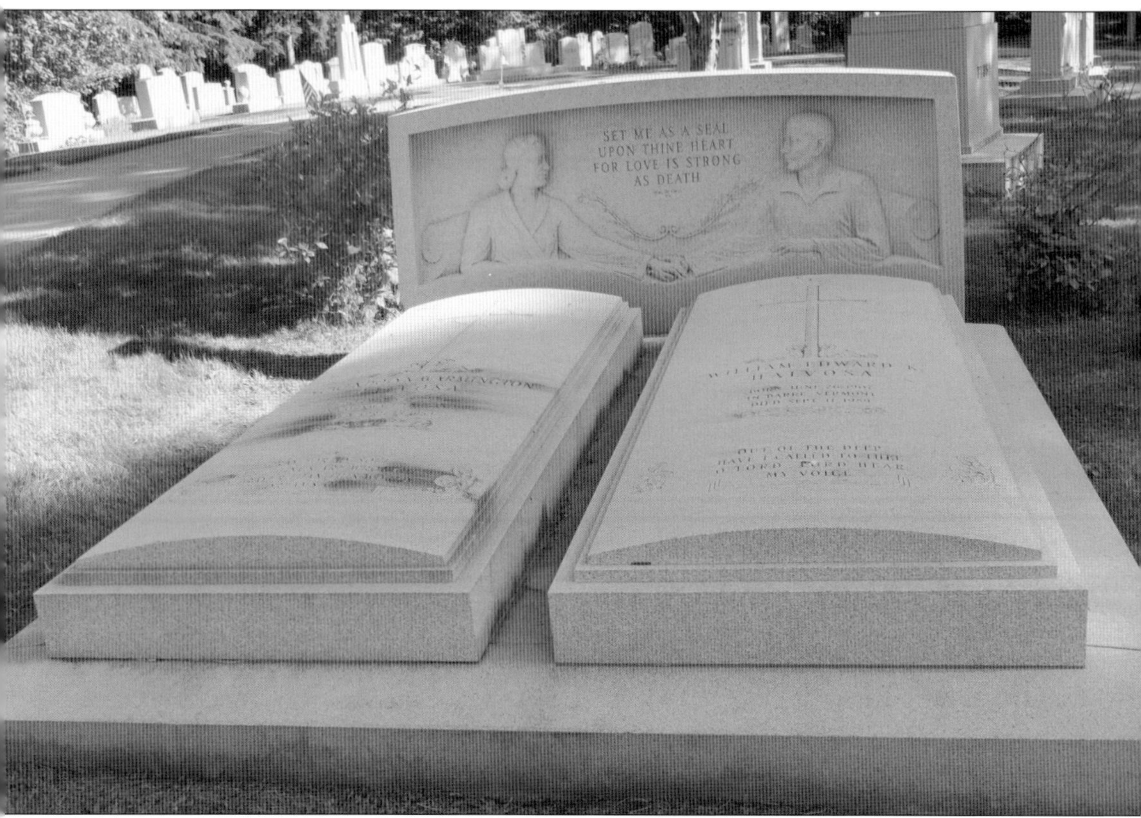

HALVOSA FAMILY MONUMENT (1953). Few monuments take the phrase "laid to rest" to such literal and artistic heights as this one does. It was designed and created at Rock of Ages Corporation, carved by Bruno Sarzanini for Doris Gwendolyn Warmington Halvosa (1904–1953), a native of Cornwall, England, who died of cancer, and her husband, William Edward K. Halvosa (1907–1989), who helped design the monument. This unique display of a couple's eternal love has made it a tourist favorite. Both loved poetry and "were in the habit of writing poems to one another." Halvosa was an accountant at the Rock of Ages Corporation. Works of this type, which cover the entire grave, are known as ledger-style monuments, with their long tradition of use in English cemeteries being a factor in Halvosa choosing this style.

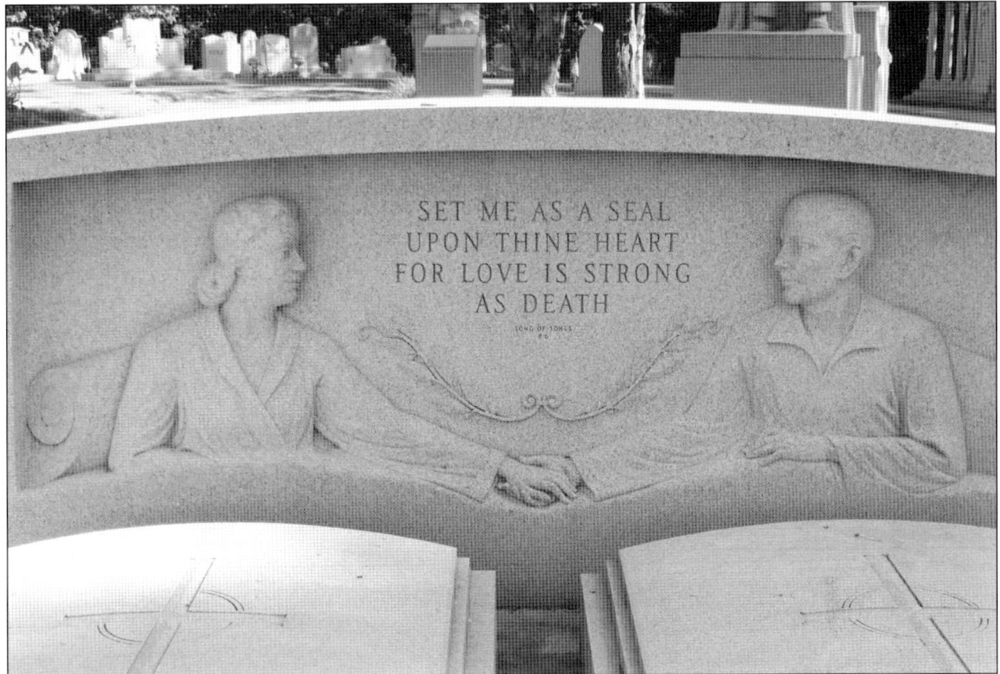

Detail of the Halvosa Family Monument. This view shows the "headboard" of the Halvosa's ledger-style monument, with the couple, dressed in their pajamas, carved in bas-relief style in nearly lifelike size. Symbolic of the couple's divine romantic love for one another is the verse carved in stone from the Song of Solomon in the Old Testament.

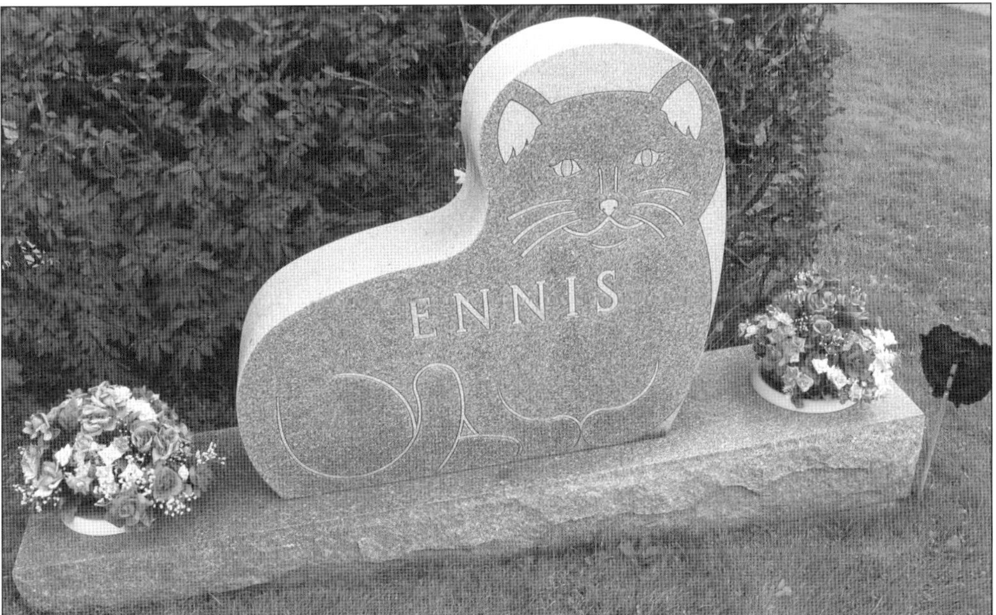

Robert S. Ennis Monument (1996). This is the only monument in Hope Cemetery fashioned in the form of an animal. Ennis (1918–1996), a native of Barre who was a veteran of World War II, worked in the construction trade. Though uncertain, the choice of this monument may indicate that Ennis was a cat lover, perhaps having a beloved feline as a companion.

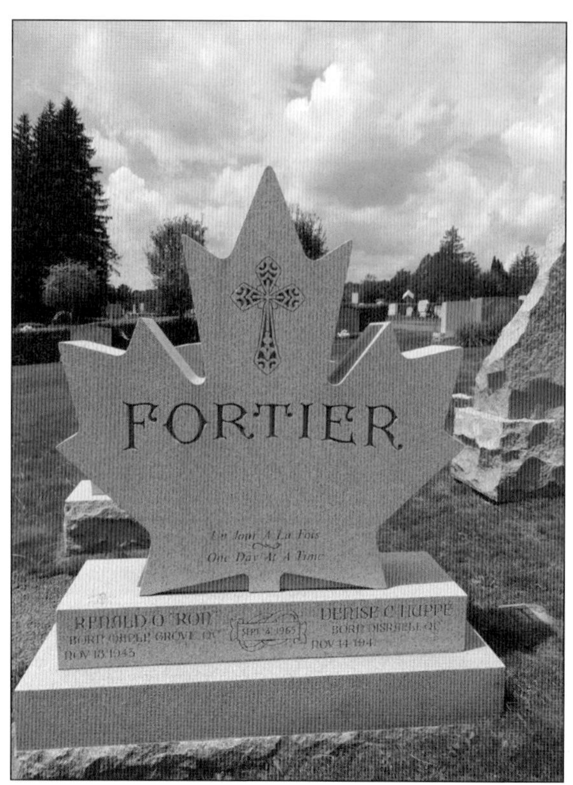

Fortier Family Monument. It seemed inevitable that a monument in the form of a maple leaf would one day be erected here; not only is Vermont a leading producer of maple syrup, but Hope Cemetery is located on Maple Avenue. However, this monument has another intended meaning, for the Fortiers are natives of Québec. Renald O. "Ron" Fortier, a native of Maple Grove, was a longtime granite artisan who crafted this monument.

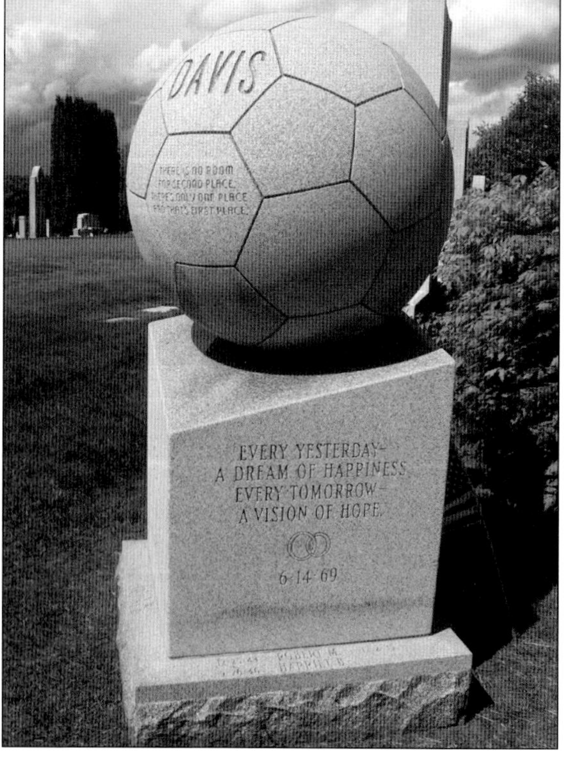

Davis Family Monument. Erected after the death of Brian M. Davis (1945–1985), a native of Pennsylvania, this monument honors his passion not only for the game of soccer—with the wording on the giant soccer ball reading, "There is no room for second place. There's only one place and that's first place"—but also for his wife, Harriet, as this side view shows the couple's marriage date.

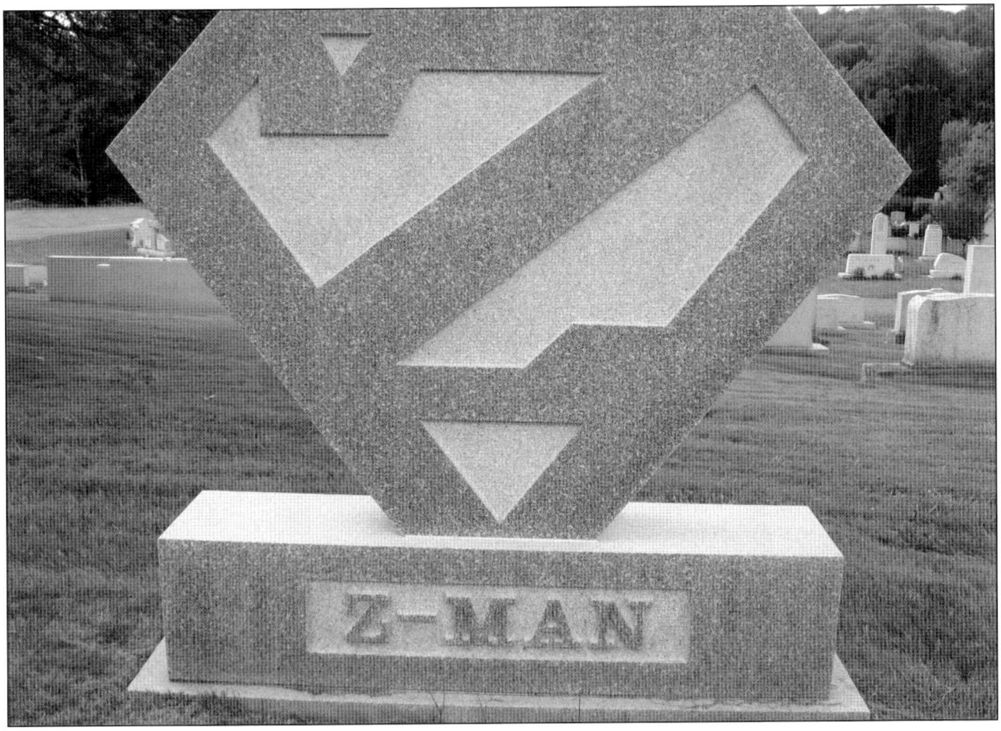

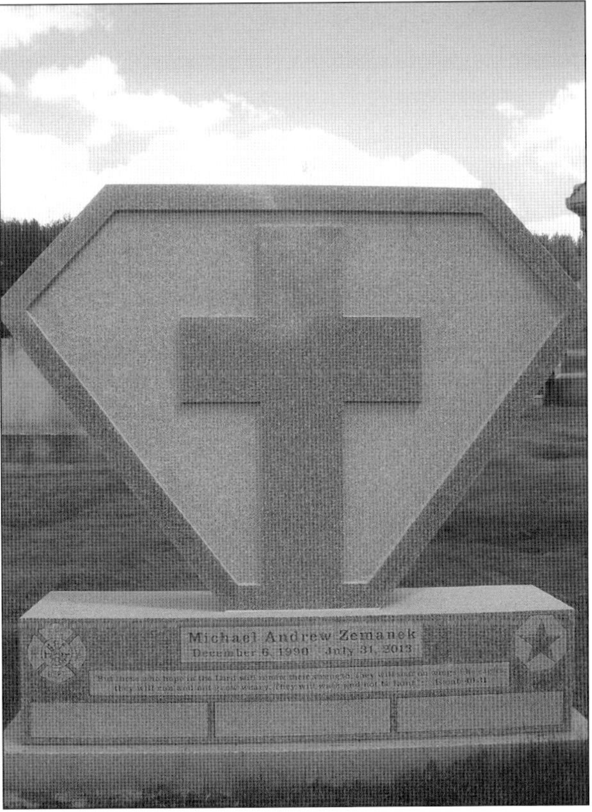

Michael A. Zemanek Monument (2014). In the shape of the Superman logo, this is the only superhero-themed monument in Hope Cemetery. Called a "squared away hard charger" to whom "police work, community service, and swimming were very important," Zemanek (1990–2013) was a real-life superhero, graduating with honors from Norwich University and later from the Vermont Police Academy. He served as a deputy sheriff in Orange County; in the police force of several local communities, including Barre; and as a volunteer firefighter. One side of the monument (above) is modern in nature, giving Zemanek's nickname, while the other (right) is morc traditional with its Christian and service-related images.

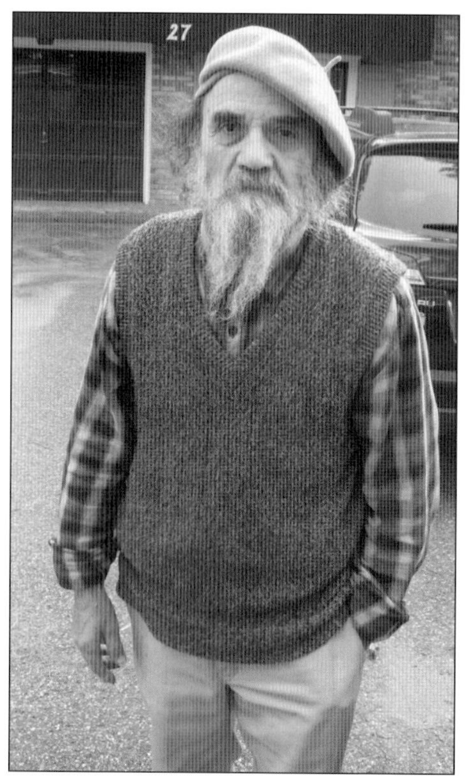

Giuliano Cecchinelli Sr. and Cecchinelli Workshop. The last of the old-time granite artists, Giuliano Cecchinelli has sculpted a number of the modern monuments at Hope Cemetery, as well as many other works of art, including the model for the Italian American Stonecutter Monument located in Barre. He is steeped in the stonecutters trade, having been born in Carrera, Italy, and attending the art institute there to learn his trade before following his father Alberto to America in 1961. He was first employed at the marble works in Proctor, Vermont, but later moved to Barre. The many works he has created since that time are reflected in one of his workshop's rooms (below), filled with the plaster models for his granite works of art. Like the stonecutters of old, he states of Hope Cemetery, "This is my showroom."

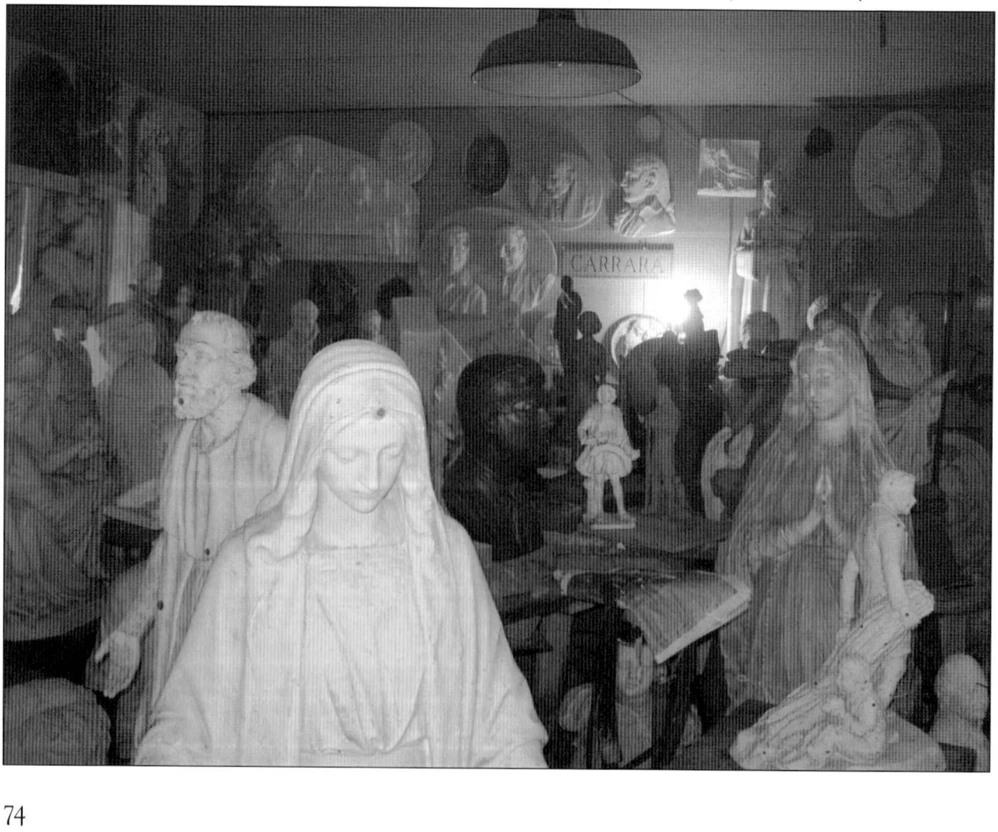

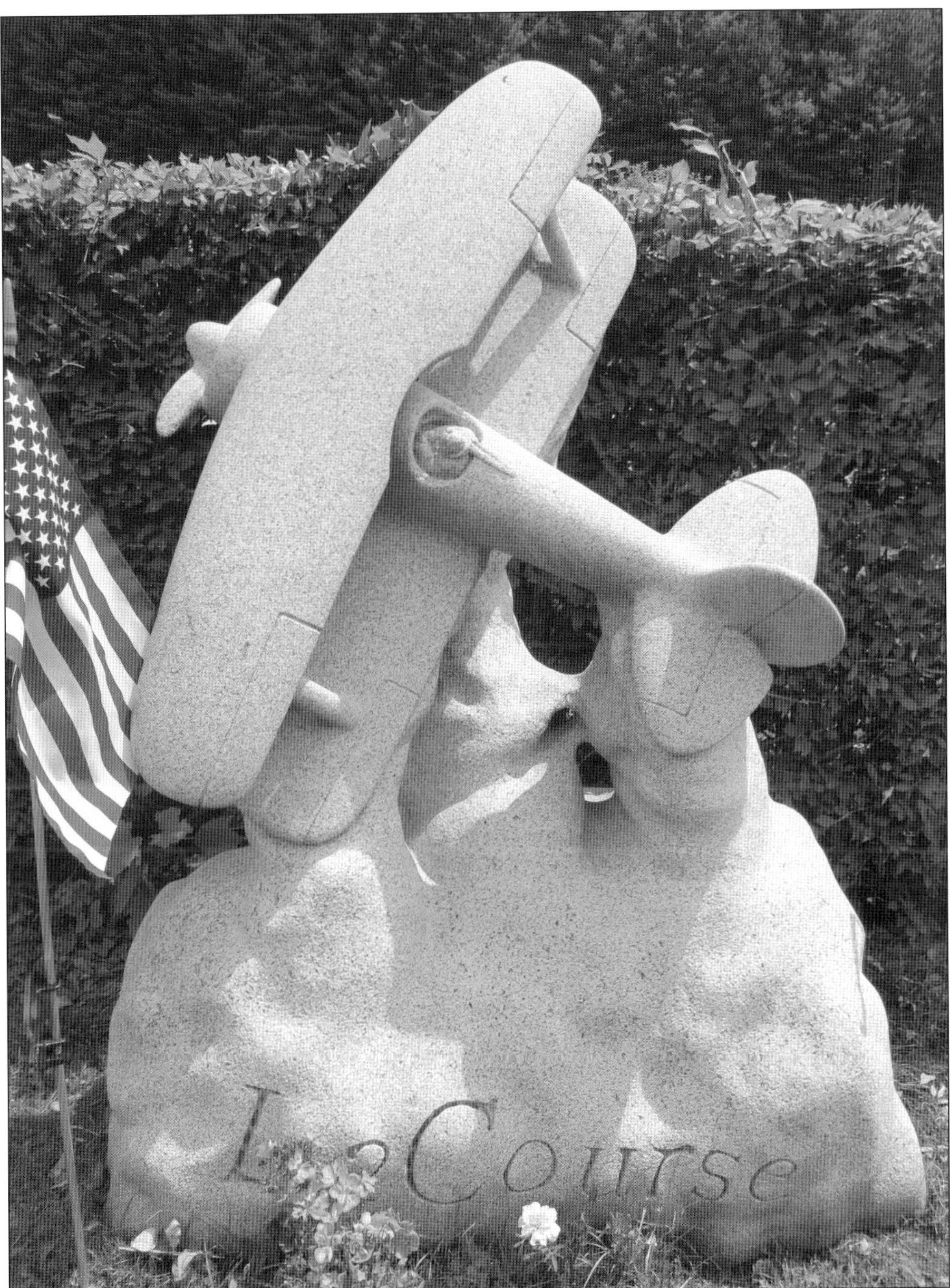

LaCourse Family Monument (1988). Monument-making soared to new heights with the addition of this memorial to Hope Cemetery. Crafted by Giuliano Cecchinell Sr., it honors the service of Roland LaCourse (1918–1988), who served as pilot in the Civil Air Patrol in his younger days, as did his wife, Caroline Mae Dodge LaCourse (1937–2007), who was employed by the Rock of Ages Corporation when the couple married in May 1957.

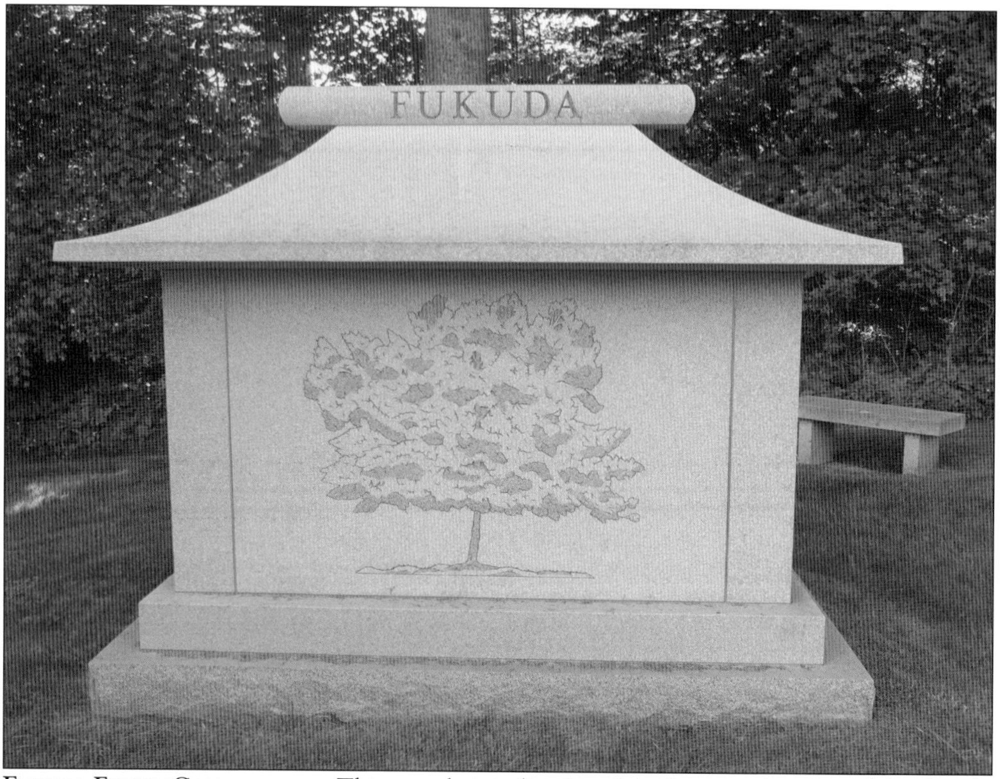

Fukuda Family Columbarium. This pagoda is indicative of the Japanese heritage of this family. Dr. David Fukuda (1921–2006) was born in California to Japanese parents and moved with them back to Japan in 1934; he later gained a medical degree. David moved with his wife, Dr. Michiko Fukuda, from Japan to Vermont in 1951 and, after further training, would become central Vermont's first full-time anesthesiologist.

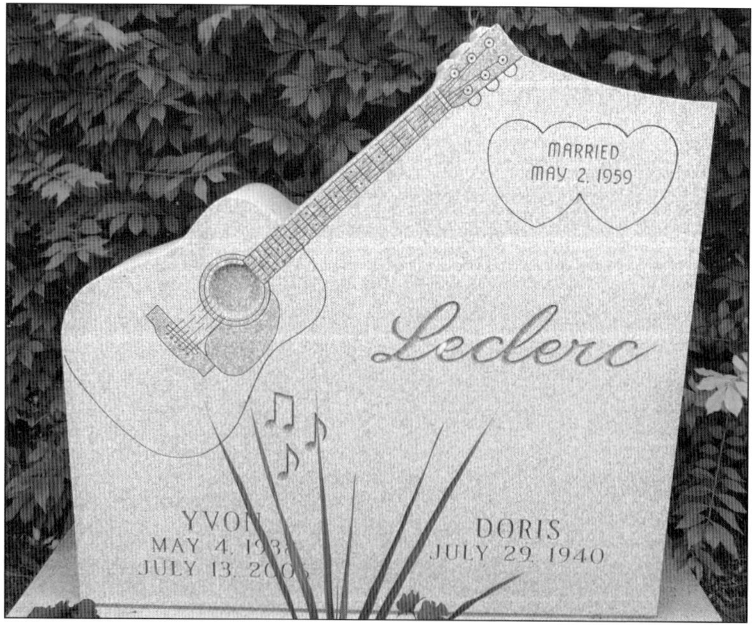

Leclerc Family Monument (2006). Musical interests are reflected throughout Hope Cemetery, with this example designed by Jeff Martel of Granite Industries of Vermont. Yvon Leclerc (1938–2006) was employed in the granite trade in Barre for over 30 years, but was also known for his devotion to playing the guitar.

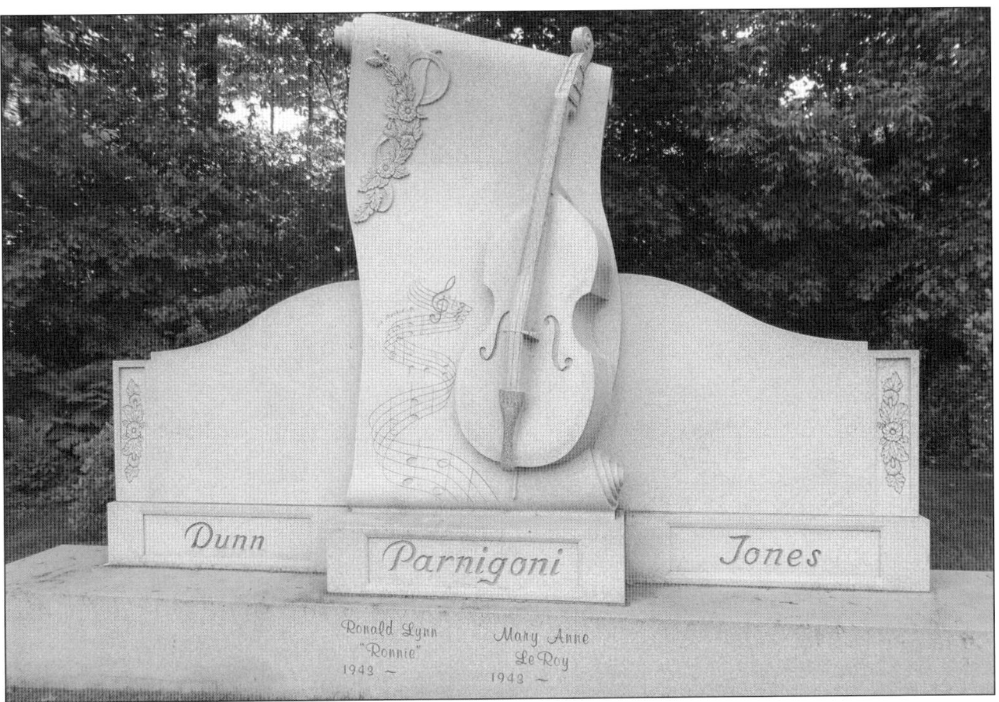

Parnigoni Family Monument. A beautiful cello is the centerpiece in this attractive monument, which marks the future burial site of a well-known Barre couple who have been active in the Rotary Club. Ronnie Parnigoni is president of Parnigoni Brothers Granite, a company active in the granite business in Barre for over 100 years. Note that the musical score on this monument is for the gospel song "He Touched Me."

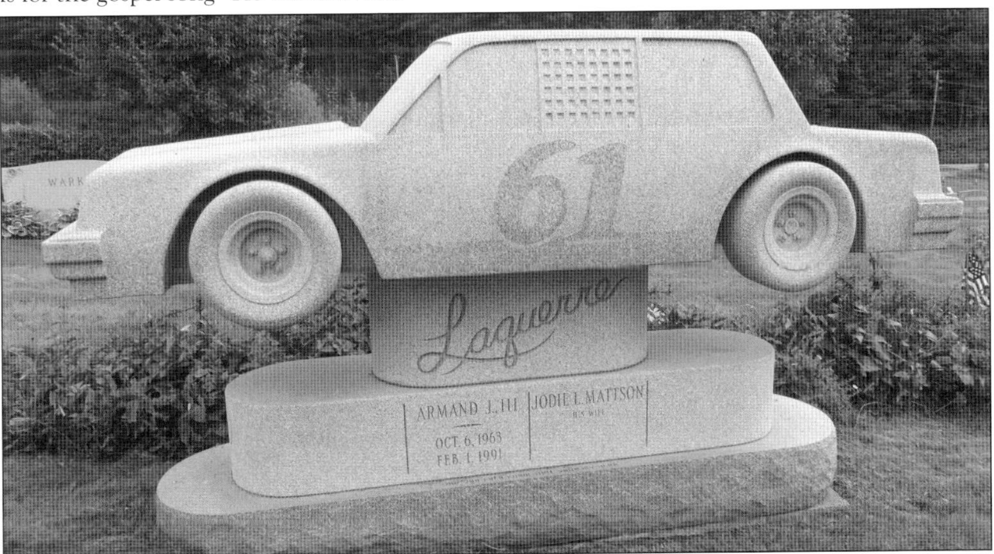

Armand J. Laquerre III Monument (1991). This impressive race car is one of the most famous monuments in Hope Cemetery, celebrating the racing profession of Armand "Joey" Laquerre (1963–1991), who died in a snowmobiling accident. His family was the first family of racing in Vermont, and Joey carried on that tradition, winning the Thunder Road track championship in 1990 in the car depicted here.

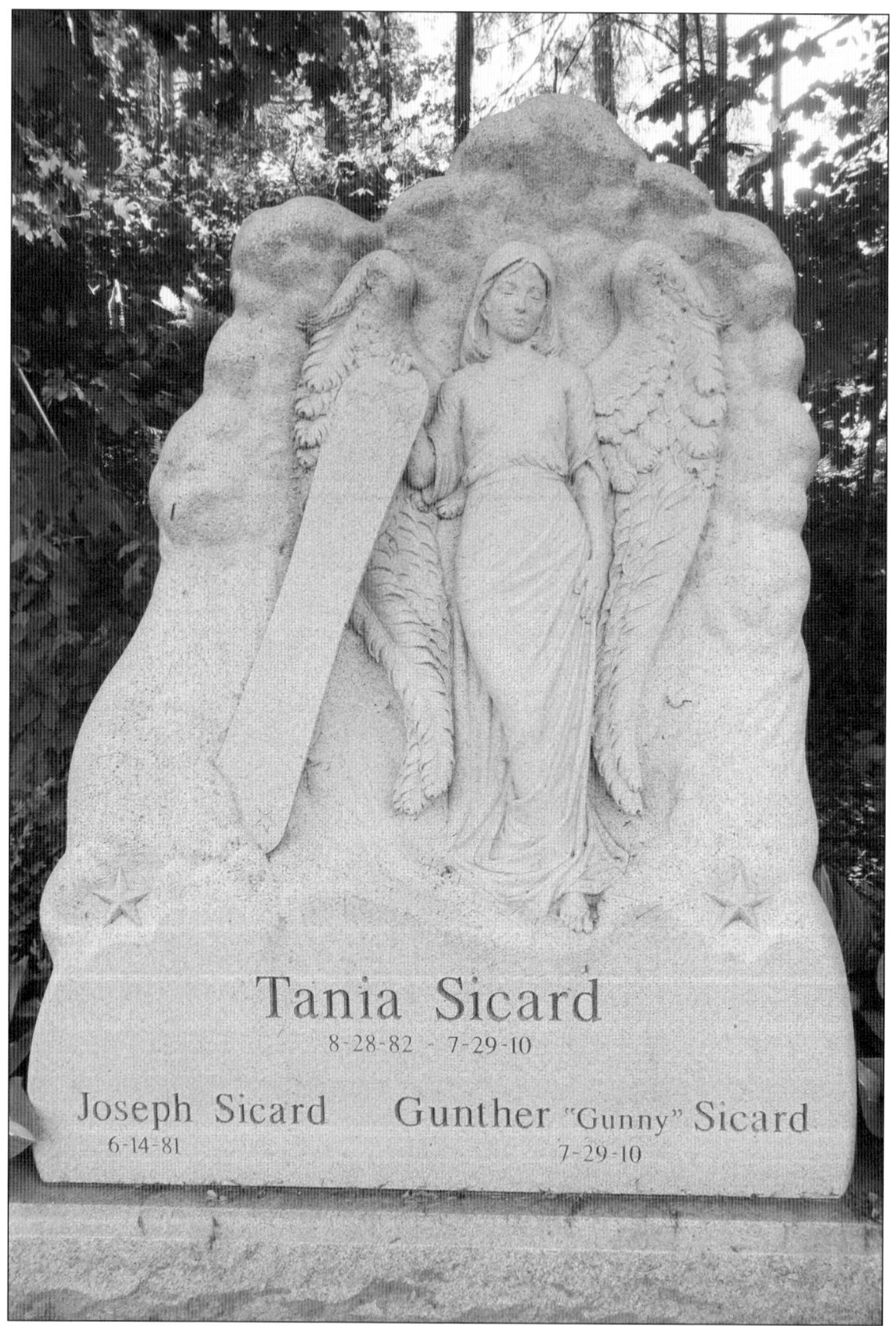

Sicard Family Monument (2011). This beautifully carved angel is a heavenly likeness of Tania Sicard, a young wife and mother who is buried with her son "Gunny" Sicard. She was a native of Maine and moved to Vermont with her parents. After graduating from college in 2005, she worked as an EMT and paramedic in Massachusetts, moving to Barre after her marriage to Joseph Sicard in 2009. Tania was an avid outdoorswoman, as evidenced by this work of art, where she is depicted holding a snowboard, a unique modern addition to an otherwise classic monument form.

Six

The Faces of Hope

The reasons for visiting a place like Hope Cemetery are many and varied. No matter what the reason, thoughts and questions cannot help but come to mind while passing its monuments. What were the lives of those buried here like? How did they die? And, most importantly, what did they look like? In most cemeteries, the answer to the last question must be left to the imagination. In Hope Cemetery, however, it can be answered, for the faces of those buried here are often found as a feature on the very monuments that mark their final resting places. Beginning with the monument for Elia Corti in 1903, down to the present, the inhabitants of Hope can be seen everywhere. Early images were sculpted by hand in bust or relief form, a tradition that continues to this day in the work of artists like Giuliano Cecchinelli. Another method of putting images on granite that was popular early on, and has remained so, are actual studio portraits of the deceased, taken while still living, which were burnt in porcelain, usually in an oval or round form, and glued to the front of a monument. Laser technology in the modern era has only increased the options for portraits in stone. No matter how or when they were made, through these portraits, one can see such details as their hairstyles and mode and manner of dress, and facial expressions, thereby helping to bring them closer to one's understanding more than any written description could ever achieve. Indeed, if it is true that a single picture is worth a thousand words, then the portraits in stone found here offer words enough for a book all their own.

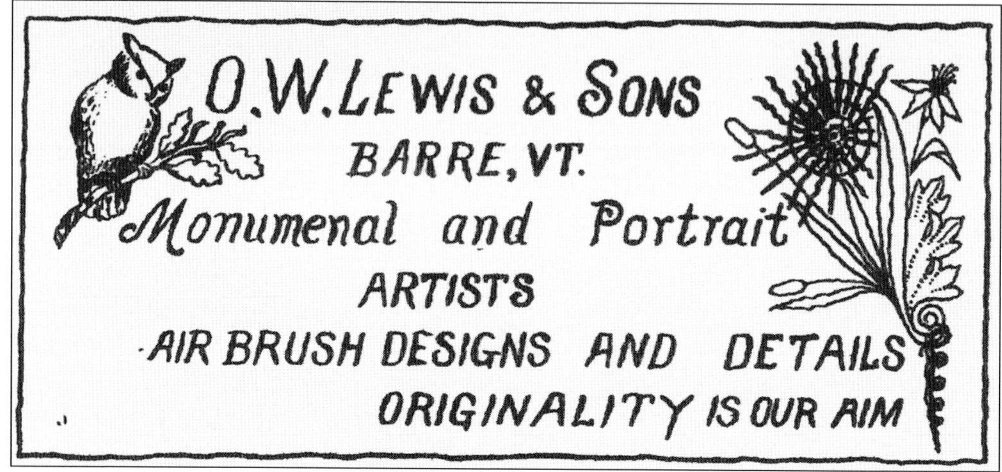

O.W. Lewis and Sons Advertisement (1904). Almost from the very beginning when Hope Cemetery was established, monumental portraits were offered by artists in many different forms. This charming advertisement from the trade magazine the *Reporter* in January 1904 highlights just one shop in Barre that specialized in portraiture. Note the misspelling of the word *monumental* here.

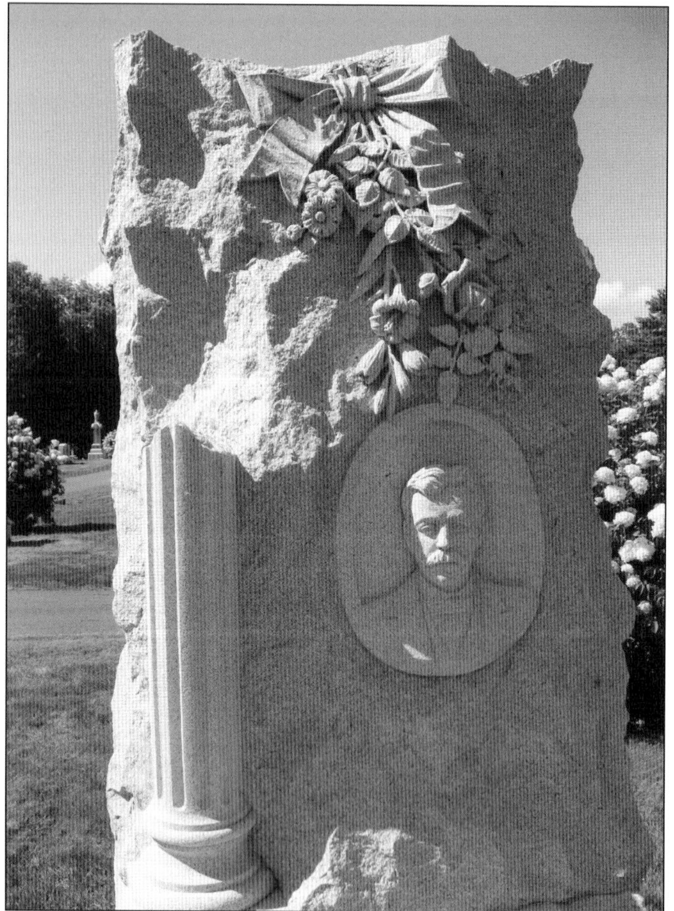

G. Colombo Monument (1905). This portrait, done in cameo-relief form on a shell-rock finish backdrop, pictures Italian immigrant stonecutter George Colombo (1861–1905) as he would have looked in the prime of life. The broken column is a symbol of a life cut short. Colombo arrived in the United States in 1884 and had a career as a granite artist lasting some 20 years.

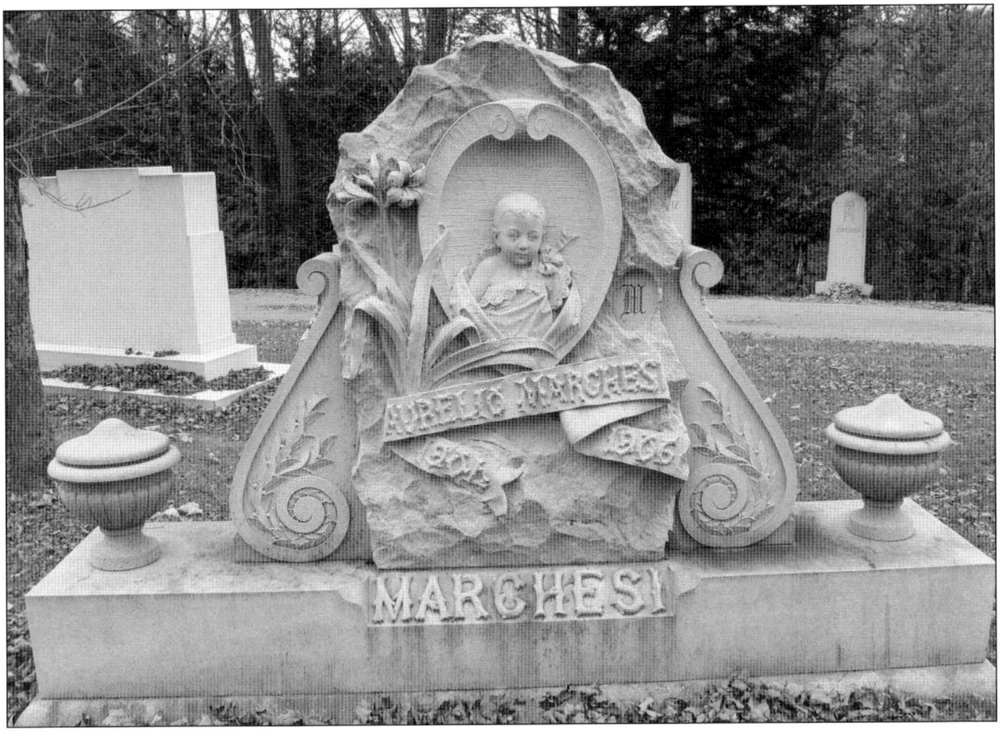

Aurelio Marchesi Monument (1906). A portrait of a young boy, the son of Italian immigrants Charles and Antonia Marchesi, is the focus of this beautifully sculpted monument. Aurelio died in February 1906 from the effects of marasmus, a childhood disease that results in the body wasting away. Because Charles Marchesi was a stonecutter, it is possible that he created this monument for his son. The haunting portrait of the deceased child (right) was done in cameo-relief form. Note that the lettering on the monument was done in rustic fashion. The base and urns of this monument were later additions, while the original part was crafted not out of Barre granite, but from a reddish granite that came from Westerly, Rhode Island.

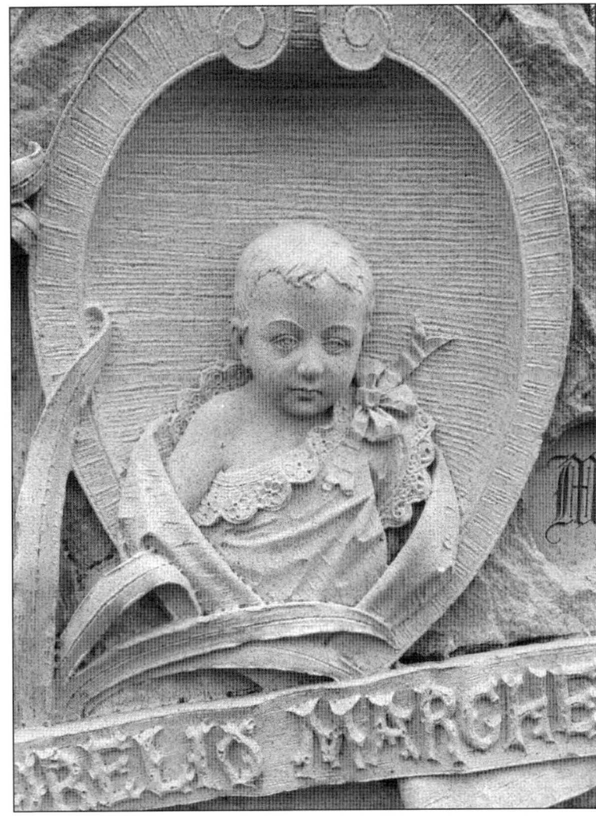

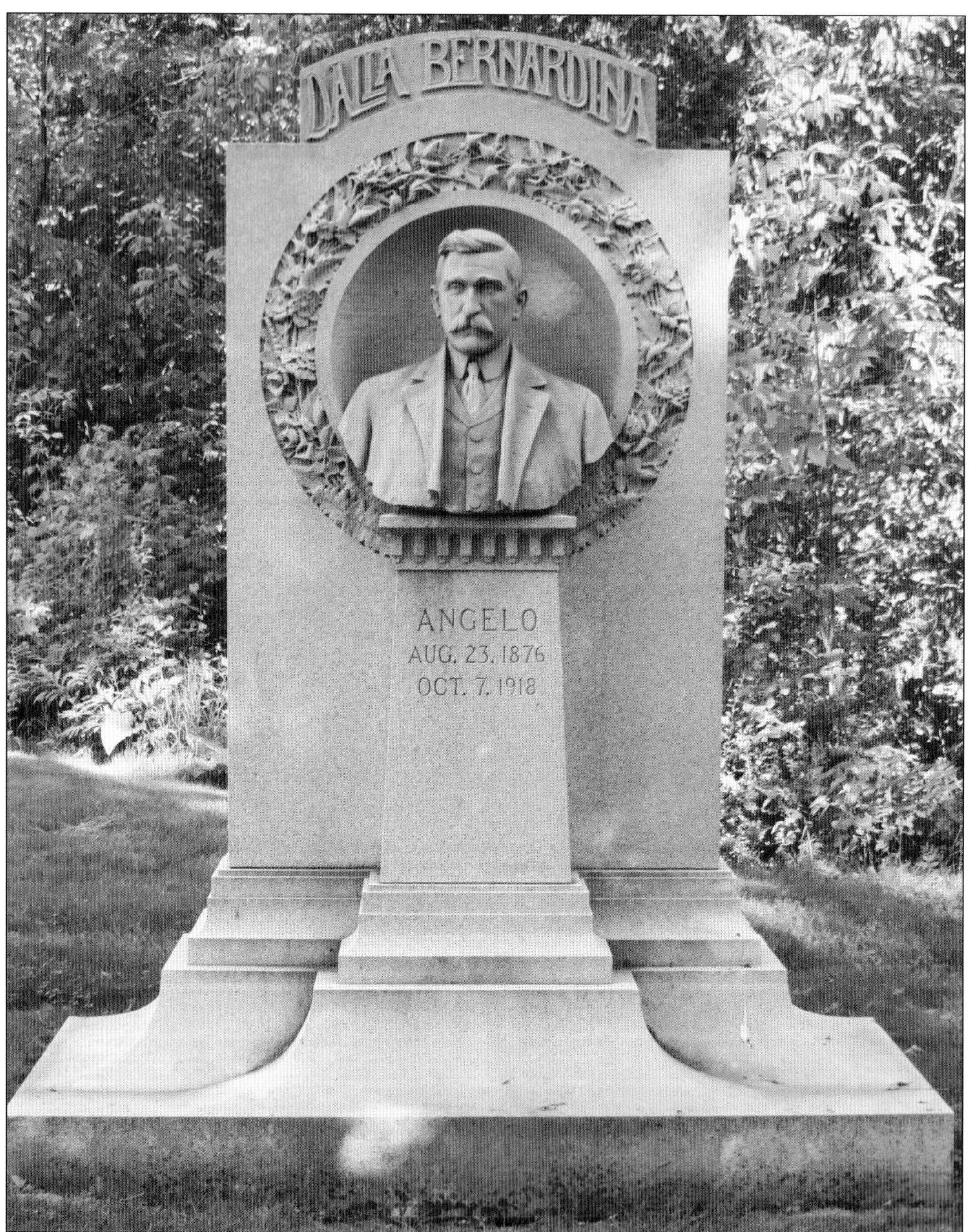

Angelo Dalla Bernardina Monument (1918). This monument offers a striking portrait in stone of an Italian immigrant whose full name was Michael Angelo Dalla Bernardina. He arrived in this country from San Ambrogio, Italy, in 1897. Dalla Bernardina worked in Barre as a granite cutter but died in October 1918 after a seven-day illness; he was one of hundreds to die in Barre during the Spanish flu pandemic. The reddish coloring of the bust of Dalla Bernardina is interesting; its appearance, corroborated by local oral history, shows that it was fashioned not out of Barre granite as is now required of all monuments, but of either quartzite or red granite, which came from Westerly, Rhode Island, crafted by a friend of the deceased, probably Joseph Pelligrini, a stonecutter in the Westerly granite industry.

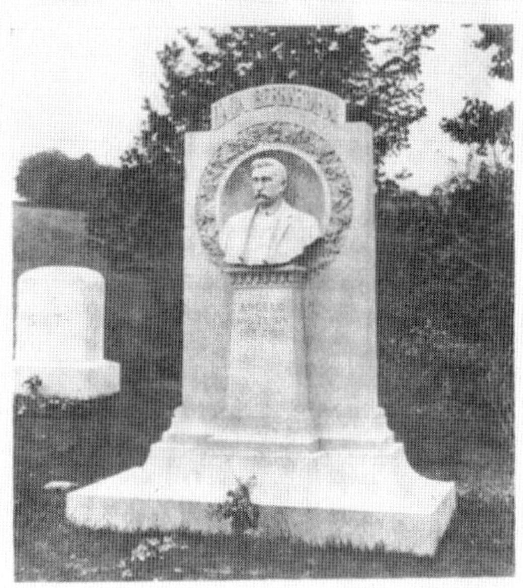

A Hammered Memorial In Tablet Form

THE Dalla Bernardina memorial is a most effective example of the tablet form which is becoming so popular. The velvety smoothness of the hammered surface lends an air of stateliness. The carved sunken wreath relieves it of severity and forms a most fitting frame for the bust.

There is a fine example of carving in this memorial, effectively worked out and well placed. Individuality characterizes the whole monument. It speaks well for the kind of work we turn out. We can give you work of the same high quality.

SOUTH BARRE GRANITE CO. - Barre, Vermont

SOUTH BARRE GRANITE COMPANY ADVERTISEMENT (1920). The high quality of the monument for Angelo Dalla Bernardina (opposite page) was evident from the beginning and, though not produced in Barre, was offered up as an example of what Barre's stonecutters were capable of if given the chance. This advertisement appears in the October 1920 issue of trade magazine *Granite, Marble, and Bronze*.

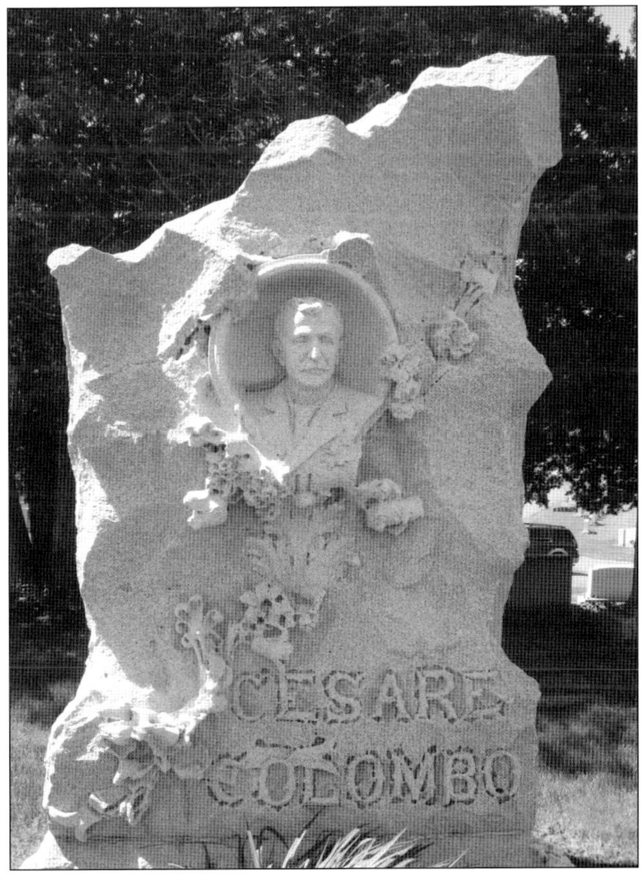

CESARE COLOMBO MONUMENT (1908). Colombo (1857–1908) was a stonecutter from Como, Italy, who arrived in the United States at New York aboard the liner *La Normandie* in 1890 and became a naturalized citizen in 1899. This impressive shell-rock form was cut by Giuseppe Induni (see page 115) and is signed by him on the right side of the monument—a rare example of a signed work in Hope Cemetery.

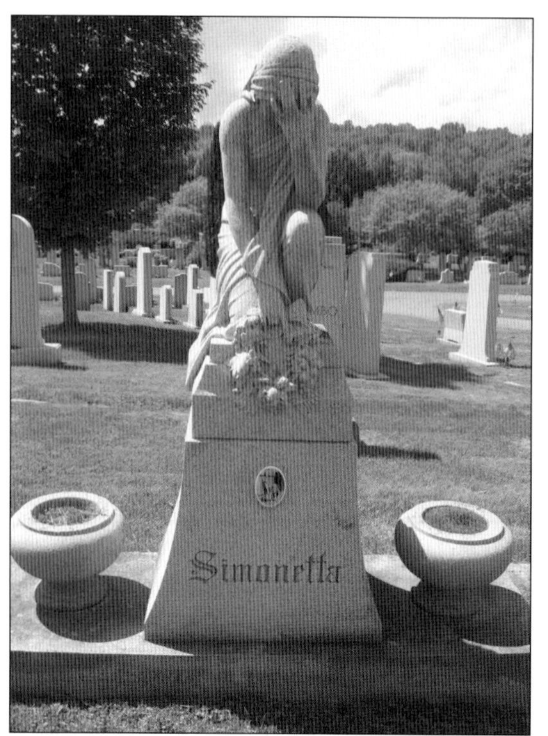

Cecilia Simonetta Monument (1963). A statue of a weeping woman is what first catches one's eye here from a distance, drawing attention to the monument of Cecilia Simonetta (1890–1962); upon closer inspection, her porcelain portrait is of more interest. It depicts her as a young woman in a demure pose featuring her high-heel shoes; the photograph was taken after her arrival here from Italy in 1913, likely in the late 1920s or early 1930s. Her husband, Paul Simonetta, worked in the granite trade, but after he died, Cecilia supported herself by operating a dress shop throughout the 1950s.

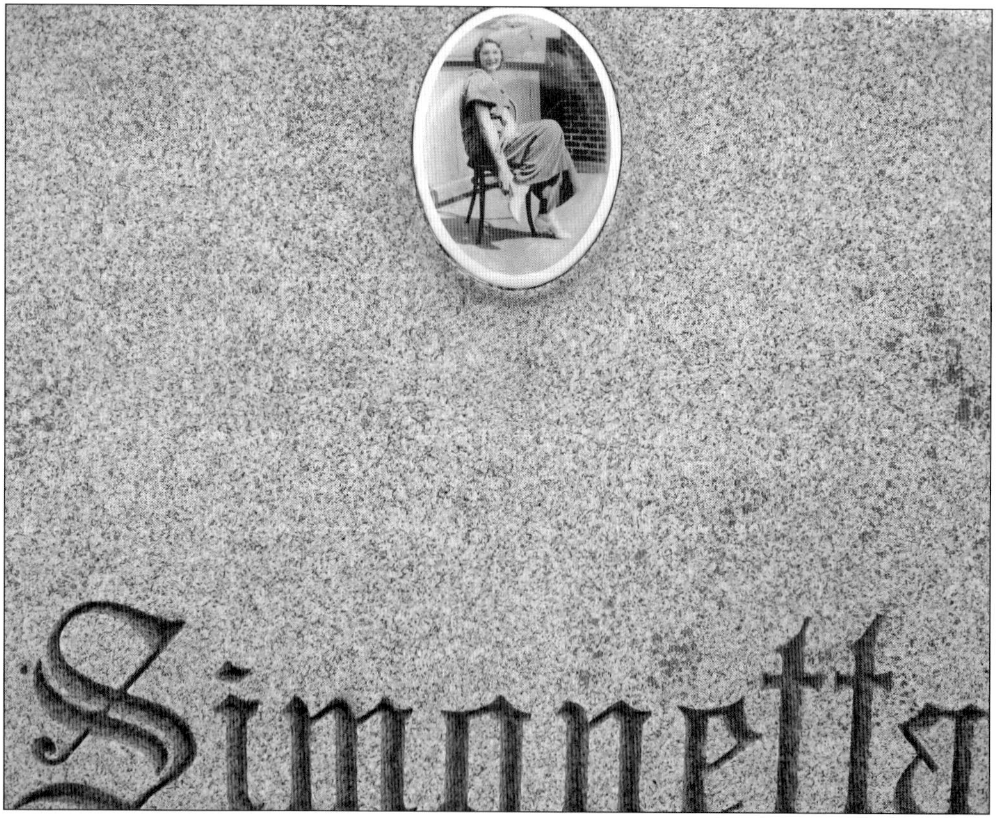

Simonetta

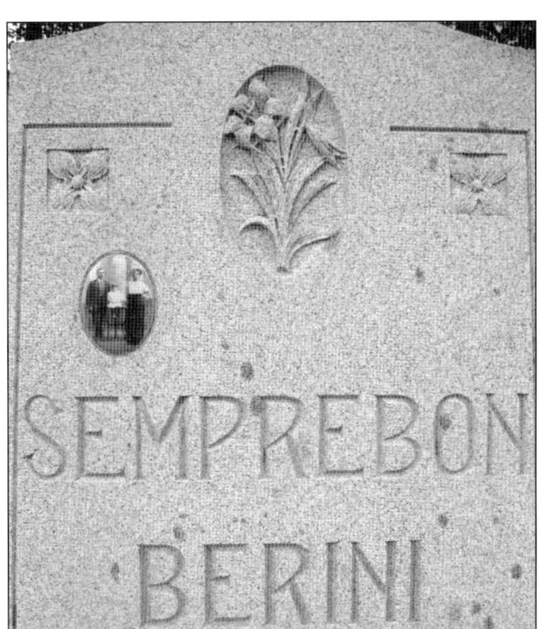

SEMPREBON-BERINI FAMILY MONUMENT (1932). A rare family portrait is the highlight of this simple monument. It features Giuseppe "Joseph" Berini (1891–1932), his wife, Regina Cecchini (1890–1956), and their young son Gino Berini (born 1924) at the age of about three years old. Regina was twice widowed; she married her first husband, Joseph Semprebon, in 1910, but he died during the flu epidemic in 1918; she remarried in 1923.

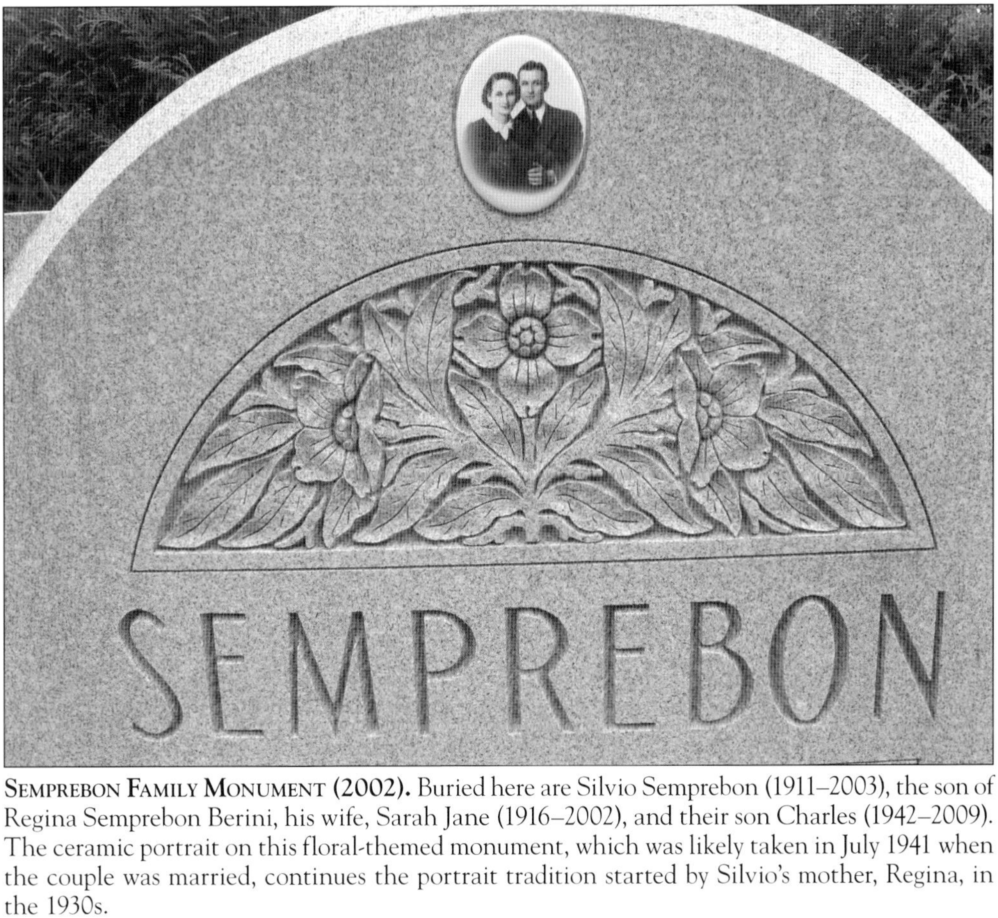

SEMPREBON FAMILY MONUMENT (2002). Buried here are Silvio Semprebon (1911–2003), the son of Regina Semprebon Berini, his wife, Sarah Jane (1916–2002), and their son Charles (1942–2009). The ceramic portrait on this floral-themed monument, which was likely taken in July 1941 when the couple was married, continues the portrait tradition started by Silvio's mother, Regina, in the 1930s.

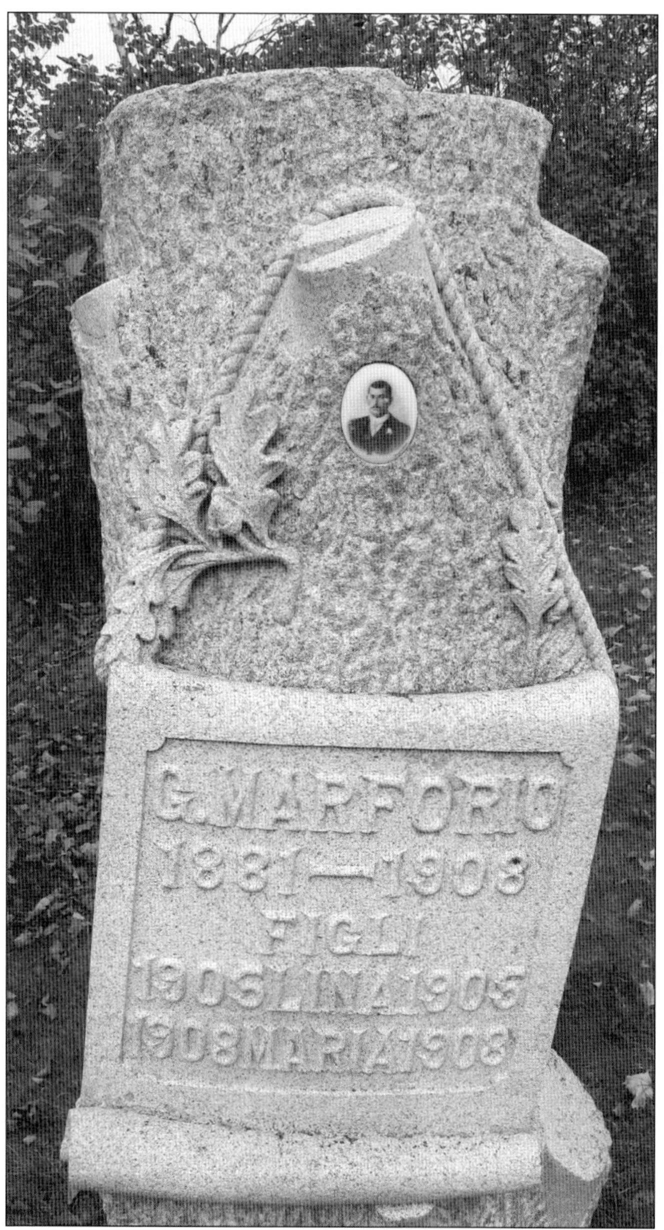

Marforio Family Monument (1908). This tree-stump style monument is symbolic of not one but three lives cut short at an early age. Gaudenzio Marforio was an Italian stonecutter, born in Baveno, who arrived at New York in 1903 and, within a short time, married a woman named Francesca. They moved to Barre, where he worked for Marr and Gordon. His two children (*figli* in Italian, as noted on the monument) died in infancy; "Lina" (short for Angelina) died at the age of three months from infant cholera, and Maria survived less than a year. Note the porcelain portrait of Gaudenzio, who died the same year as his second child. Portraits of this kind were called "dedos," named after Joseph A. Dedouch from Chicago, whose company patented this porcelain portrait technology in 1893 and became the leading provider nationwide of monumental portraiture. Such portraits, previously invented in Europe, were extremely popular both in Italy and amongst Italian immigrant families in America, especially in Barre.

Eugenio A. Carusi Monument (1915). Rising out of a shell-rock base, this life-sized bust marks the final resting place of an accomplished artisan. Carusi (1871–1915) arrived here from Italy in 1894 and soon established his own business. At the time of his death, he was at the height of his carving career; records show he had some $4,000 worth of outstanding income due from commissioned works.

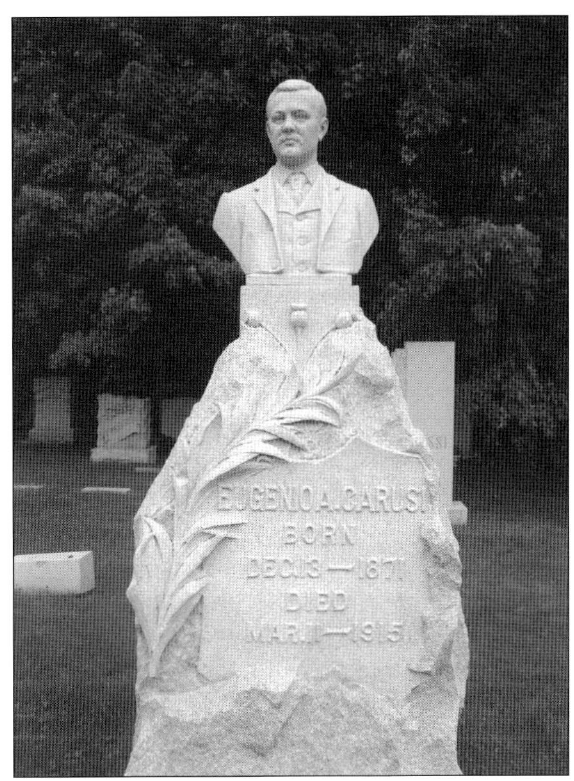

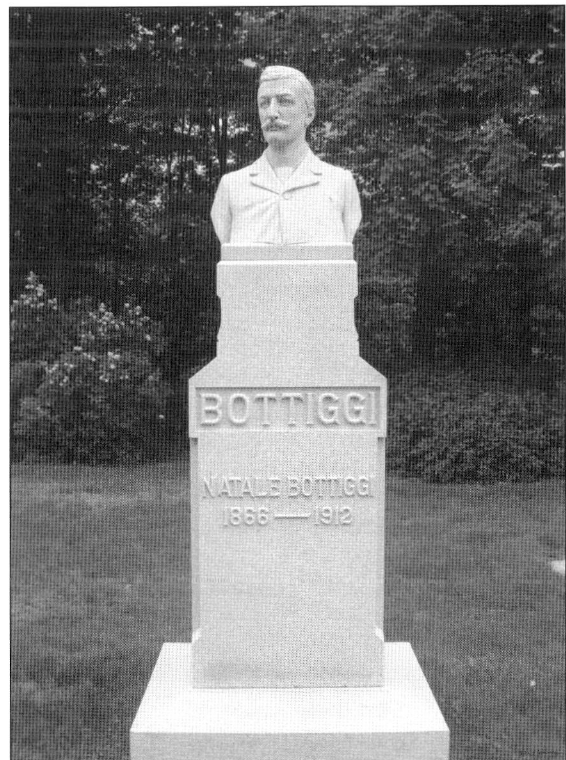

Natale Bottiggi Monument (1912). This stonecutter arrived here from Brens-Useria, Italy, in the 1890s and became a naturalized citizen in 1900. He was employed as a stonecutter by the Scottish firm of Innes and Cruickshank in Barre and would later die from the effects of inhaling granite dust. Whether this bust was carved by Bottiggi himself is unknown.

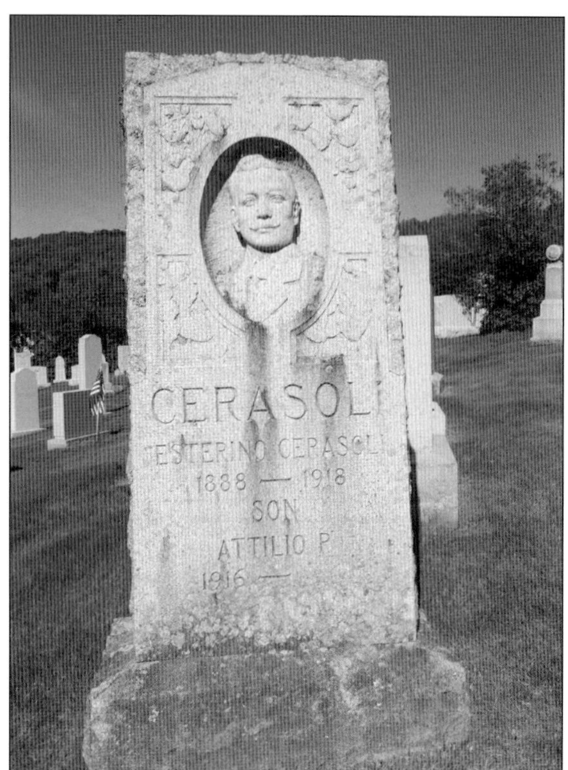

Esterino Cerasoli Monument (1918). Cerasoli (1888–1918) arrived in America in 1905 and by 1908 was in Barre. He was married in New York in 1913, and he and his wife, Beatrice, returned to Barre, where a son, Attilio, was born. Sadly, Esterino was an early victim of the Spanish flu pandemic in Barre. His son died in Ohio in 2002 and, though listed on this monument, is not buried here.

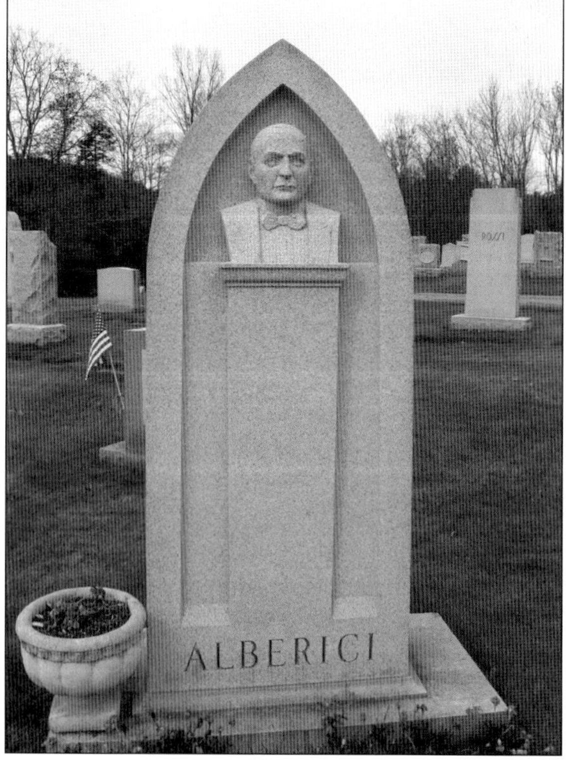

Alberici Family Monument (1932). This Gothic-style monument features a rather austere bust of the family patriarch in America, Salamone Alberici (1881–1932). He emigrated from Tocco da Casauria, Italy, via the port of Naples in 1906 and became a naturalized citizen in 1912. Alberici owned a house on Seminary Street in Barre and died from a sudden heart attack said to have been brought on, in part, by exhaustion.

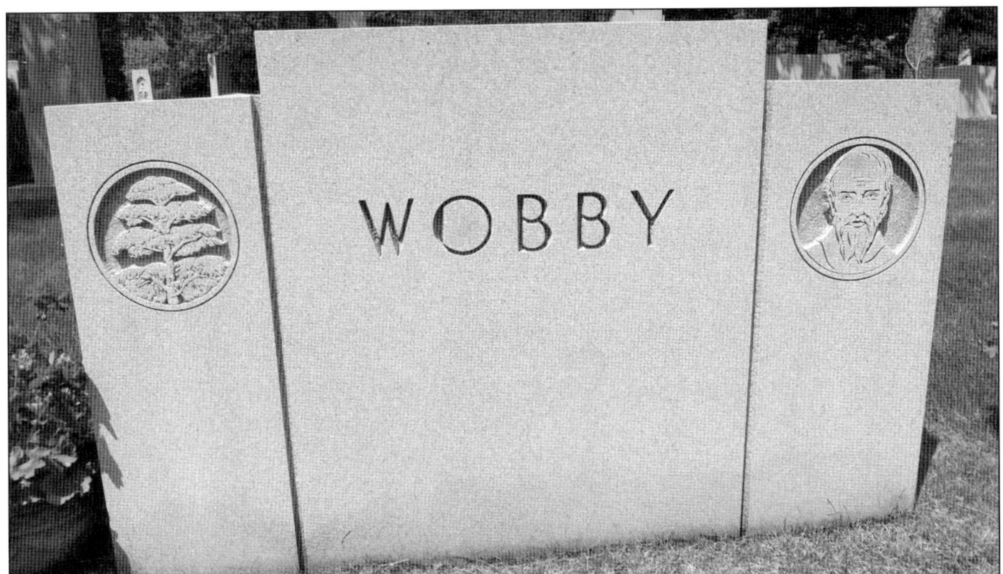

Michael J. Wobby Family Monument. Memorialized here are Michael John Wobby (1897–1967) and his wife, Leona Wobby (1909–1997). The monument features two images: one of Michael Wobby, and the other a cedar tree native to his homeland. Wobby, born in the Mount Lebanon Mutasarrifate, an independent region of Syria, married Leona Handy of Newport, Vermont, in 1928. For many years, they operated Wobby's Market in Barre, a beloved town institution.

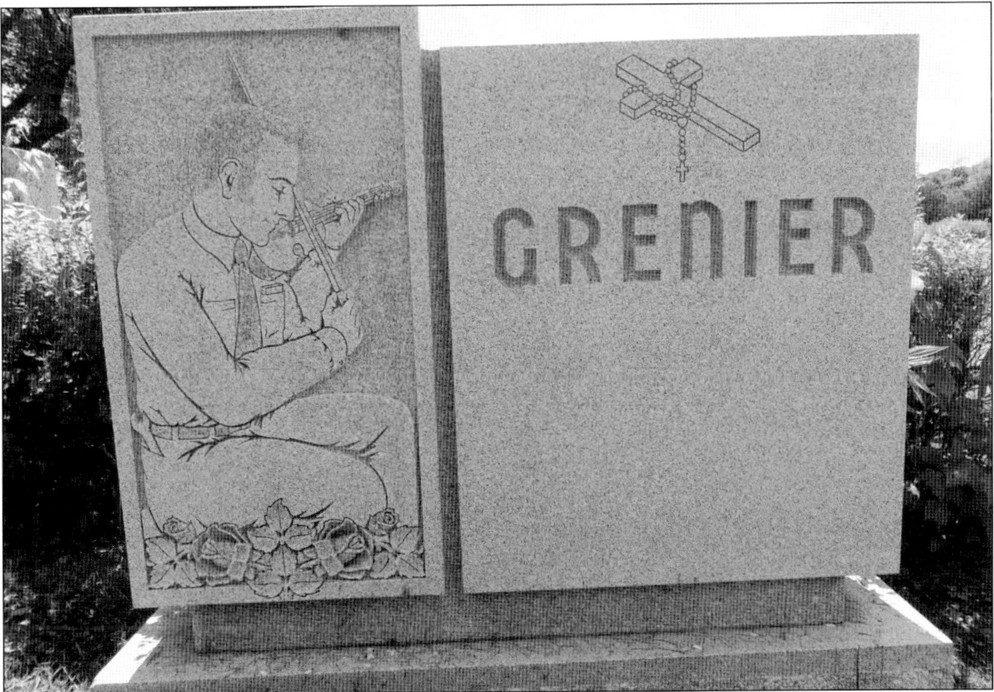

Grenier Family Monument (1974). One of the true passions of this man's life is in clear evidence on this portrait monument. Rodolphe Grenier (1923–1974) was a native of Québec, Canada, who married Florence Duboc in Piopolis, Québec, in 1944. The couple, within a short time, immigrated to Barre and raised a family. Rodolphe was employed in the granite trade as a sawyer.

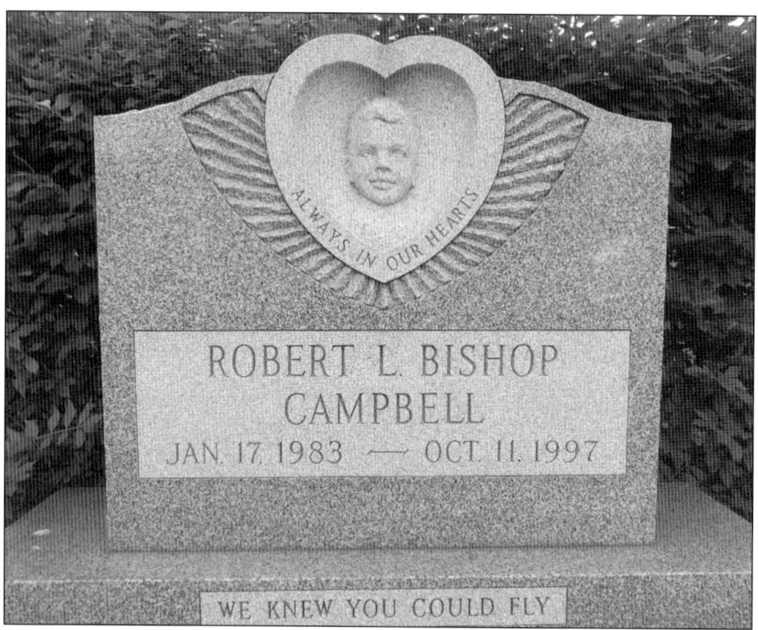

Robert L. Bishop Campbell Monument (1997). Here, the likeness of the beloved son of Darlene Fontaine Campbell and Thomas Bishop is beautifully captured in Barre grey granite in portrait form. The innocence and vitality of youth comes shining through in this comforting work of art.

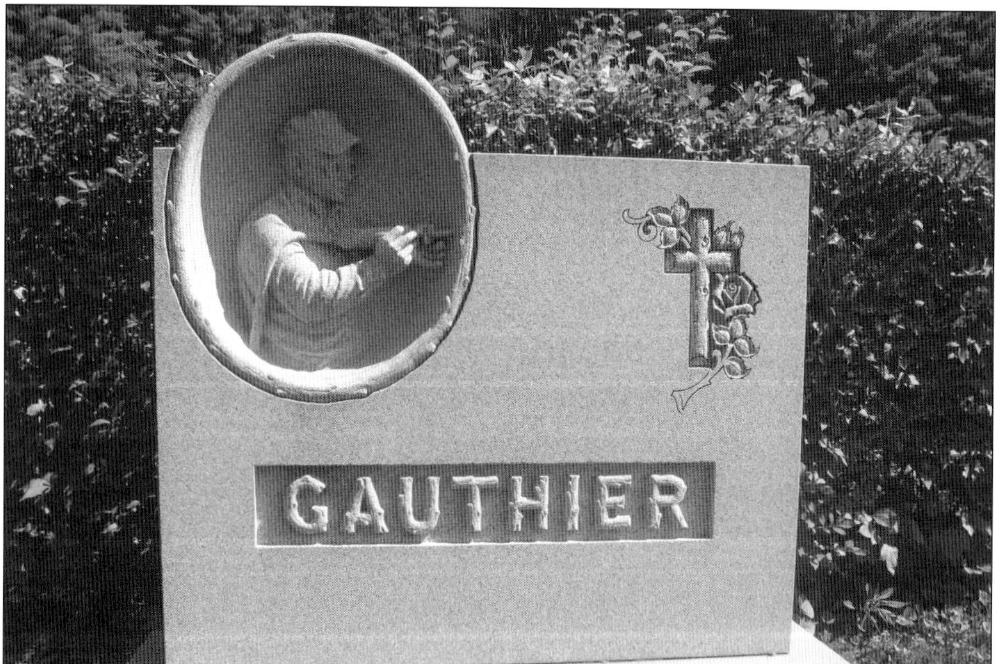

Gauthier Family Monument. Likenesses of Barre's immigrant stonecutters abound in Hope Cemetery, but few show them practicing their trade like this beautiful example. Bernadin Gauthier (1905–1975) was a native of Québec and married Marie Jeanne Lariviere (1913–1984) at St. Zephirant in 1931. He had first arrived in the United States by 1926 and, after his permanent move to Barre, worked as a stonecutter for Zampieri and Buttura Company.

Archie and Lila Buttura Mausoleum (1978). These portraits for members of one of Barre's most distinguished families were carved by Giuliano Cecchinelli. Archie Buttura (1908–1978) worked in the granite business and would be an integral part of their well-known family business, Buttura and Sons, started by his father, John, along with Archie's brothers John and Leo. Archie married Lila Pucci Buttura in 1932.

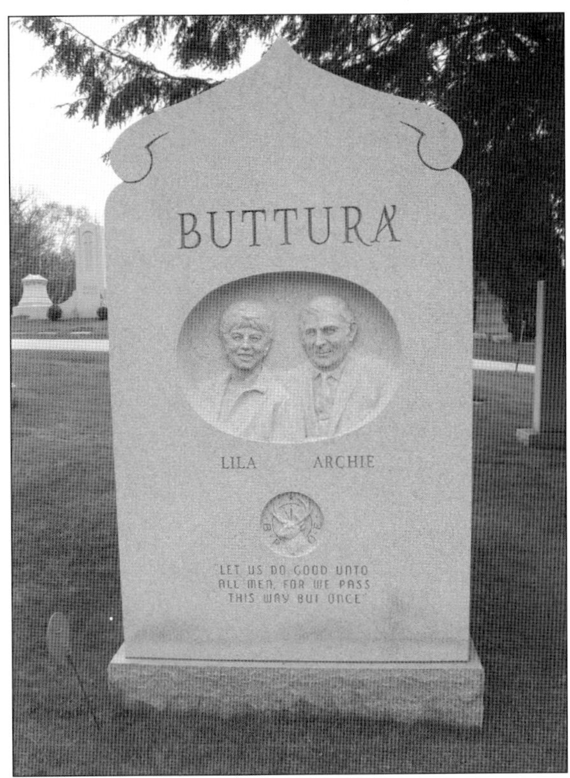

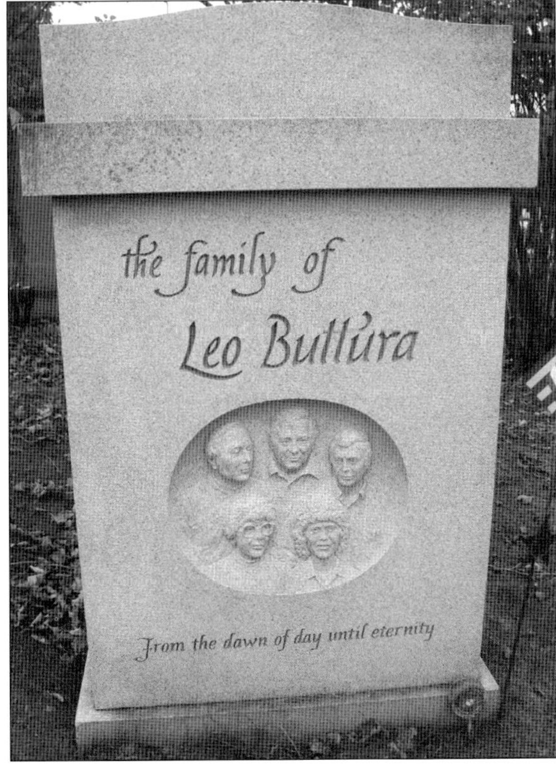

Leo Buttura Family Mausoleum. Located in the Hillside section next to the Archie and Lila Buttura mausoleum, this is the final resting place for Leo Buttura Sr. (1918–1993) and his wife, Pauline Roberts Buttura (1916–2010). The portraits here, also carved by Giuliano Cecchinelli, who has had a longtime association with Buttura and Sons, depict Leo Sr., Pauline, and their children Leo, Michael Brent (1938–2007), and Pamela.

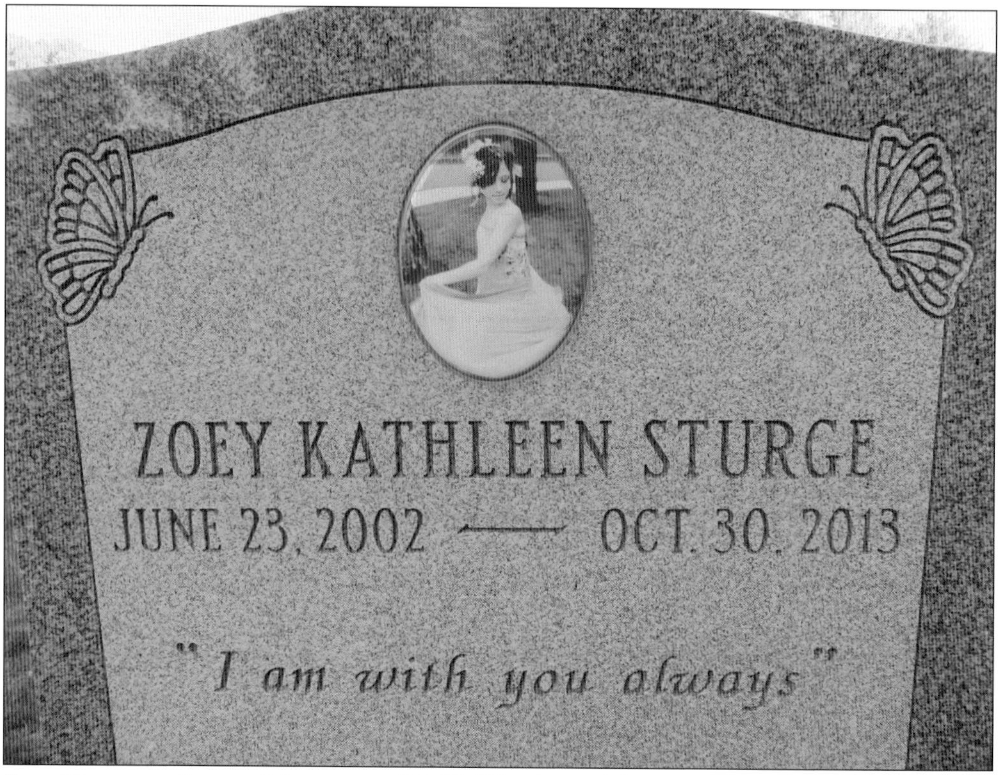

ZOEY KATHLEEN STURGE MONUMENT (2013). This beautiful memorial, with its black-and-white image of Zoey, is an excellent example of modern monumental portraiture. The beloved daughter of Michell and Bryan Sturge, Zoey loved sports and music, and her love of dancing is artfully demonstrated in her chosen portrait.

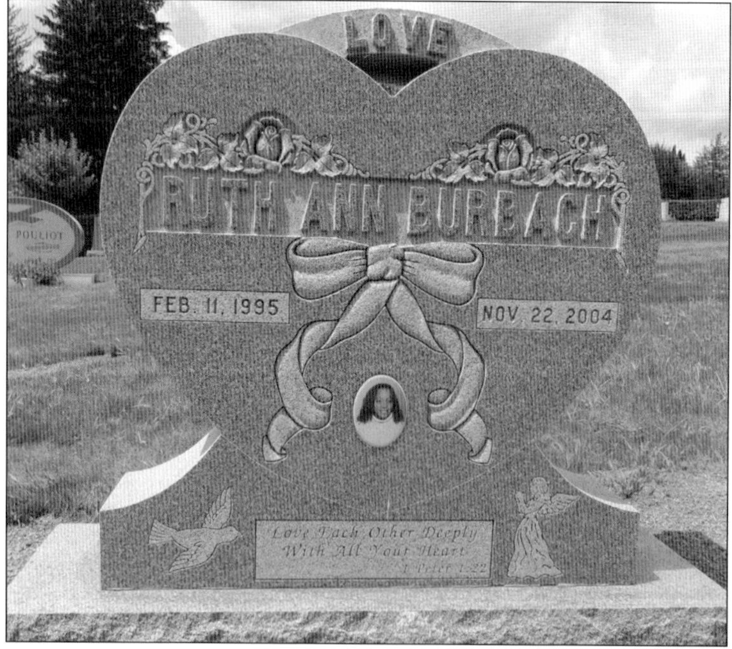

RUTH ANN BURBACH MONUMENT (2004). The beauty of modern monumental portraiture in full-color form is well-demonstrated on this heart-shaped stone. The daughter of John and Lisa Burbach, Ruth was considered by friends and family "an old soul" who "made a lasting impression on all people privileged to meet her." She loved to sing and dance and excelled at such crafts as knitting, sculpting, pottery, and crocheting.

HUTCHINSON FAMILY MONUMENT. This finely sculpted monument for a couple still living is unique in Hope Cemetery. It is the only monument which offers two portrait views, the near-life-sized one carved in stone, as well as a traditional-style ceramic photograph of the couple, dated 1971, showing them in a passionate embrace the year they were married.

GRAIG PETER JOHN MONUMENT (1998). This monument documents the love of athletics by a young man who died in the prime of life. A plaque at the base gives his nickname, "Graiger," and features a football helmet with the initials of Barre's Spaulding High School and the year of Graig's graduation. The sentiment expressed on the stone is one that any parent who has lost a child can relate to.

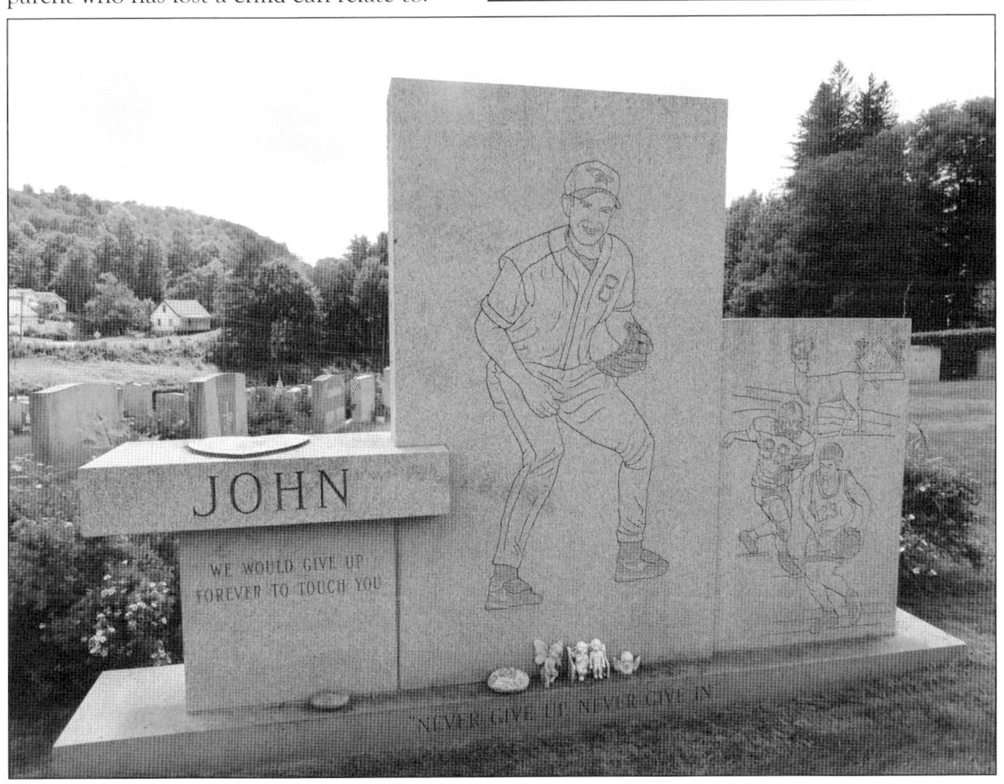

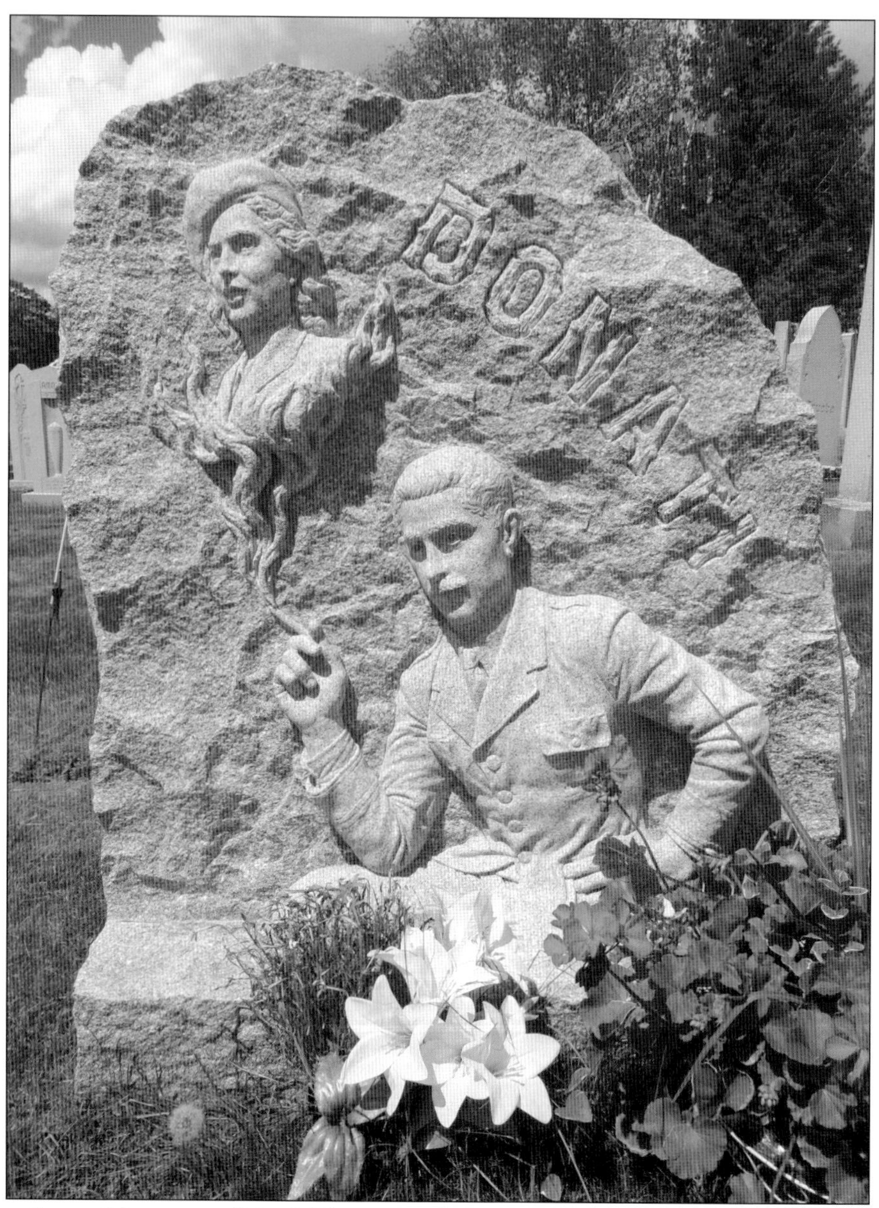

Donati Family Monument (1985). This unusual monument was crafted by Giuliano Cecchinelli in beautiful form, featuring exquisite shell-rock carving and rustic-style lettering in tree-branch style. In addition to marking the graves of the deceased, it is also a personal tribute by its creator, as the Donatis were personal friends of the Cecchinelli family. Giuseppe Donati (1919–1984) immigrated to America from Florence, Italy, and was a noted stonecutter and sculptor in Barre for many years. Among the artists Donati worked with were Alcide Fantoni, with the two even featured on the regional television program *American Trail*, a daily show documenting the rural northeast, in 1980. The depiction of Donati's wife, Orestina (1921–2015), as a young woman within a cloud of cigarette smoke is eye-catching and represents a man thinking about his wife during a time of leisure or contemplation. Giuseppe is commented upon in many online sources as wearing a soldier's uniform, but this is inaccurate. He is instead depicted wearing a typical dress jacket of the kind favored by Italian men from the 1940s, when the young couple first met.

Seven

The Personality of Hope

With its wide range of monuments, Hope Cemetery is renowned as an open-air museum. However, it is also because its stone "collection" tells a story, with the whole being greater than the sum of its parts. The monuments within Hope serve to document, as few cemeteries can, the changes and evolution that have taken place in New England and American mortuary art over the last century. One of the changes that is the most notable, and noticeable, over the years is the increasing degree of personalization found on monuments. In the beginning, the monuments in Hope followed established traditions and only a small amount of personal information about the deceased—such as religious and social affiliations (e.g, the Masons and the Odd Fellows)—was detailed. This would change quickly in the early 20th century, when sculpted likenesses and portraits of the deceased became increasingly prominent features, which added a greater degree of personalization. However, these personal additions to monuments were limited; visitors could know what the deceased looked like but were still offered little insight into the individual's personality and the things that made him or her happy beyond family and religion. Changes would come again to the monuments erected in Hope beginning in the 1950s—not only had the technology in monument making evolved, making more unusual and personal designs possible, but so had the American mind-set evolved after World War II. The increase in personalization for the next 30 years or so was slow, and make no mistake—many customers still preferred monuments that were of a more traditional design. However, with the advent of laser-cutting technology, virtually any design challenge could be met, and it is in the modern portions of Hope, in the Evergreen, Morningside, and Hillcrest sections, that the full personality of Hope Cemetery is revealed. Some of these creative monuments may be viewed as strange, and some are unusual or humorous, but each offers greater insight into the lives of those buried here.

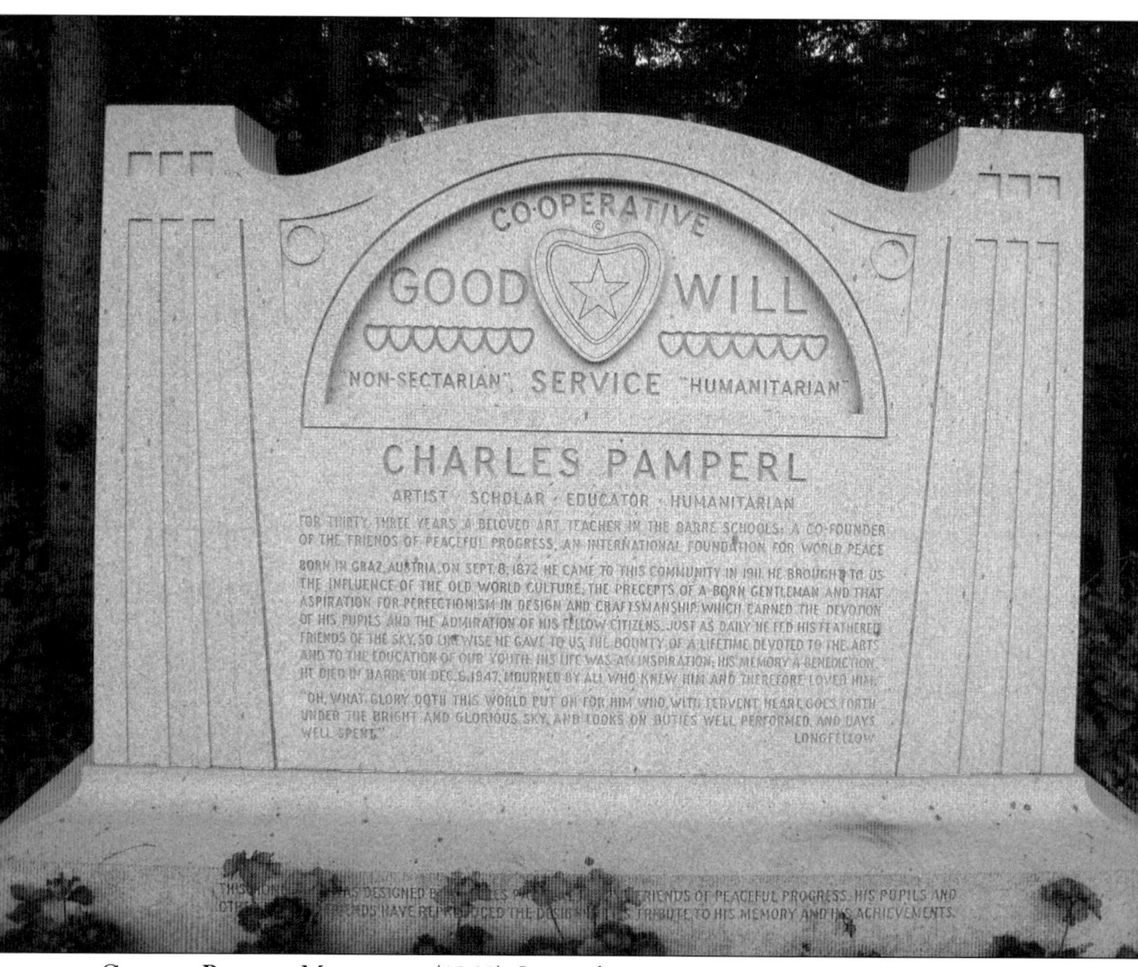

Charles Pamperl Monument (1948). Located on an inexpensive or possibly even a pauper's gravesite at the back of Section D, this monument tells the story of a man committed to the arts, peace, and social justice. Pamperl (1872–1947) came to this country at a young age in 1885 from Graz, Austria, and became a naturalized citizen in 1890. He arrived in Barre in 1911, likely attracted by the active Socialist movement here, and would become a community fixture, teaching drawing and art in the Barre Public Schools for over 30 years. Pamperl never owned his own home and instead worked as a lodger at a boardinghouse on Summer Street for many years. This Art Moderne–style monument was designed and created by his friends, who included many stonecutters and former pupils who learned part of their craft from him.

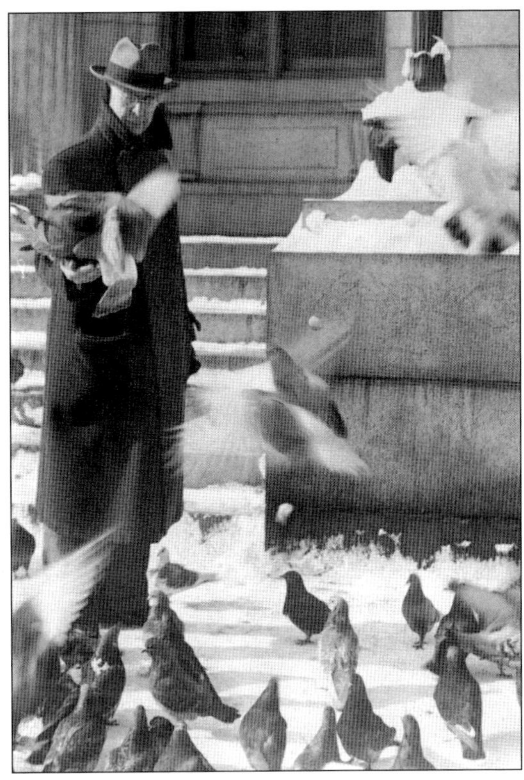

Charles Pamperl. Pamperl is seen here on the steps of the Barre Post Office. As his monument states, "Daily he fed his feathered friends of the sky," an activity for which he was well known. It is likely that Pamperl had few resources when he died, but what he lacked in money, he made up with true friends who ensured that he would not be forgotten. (Courtesy of Aldrich Public Library.)

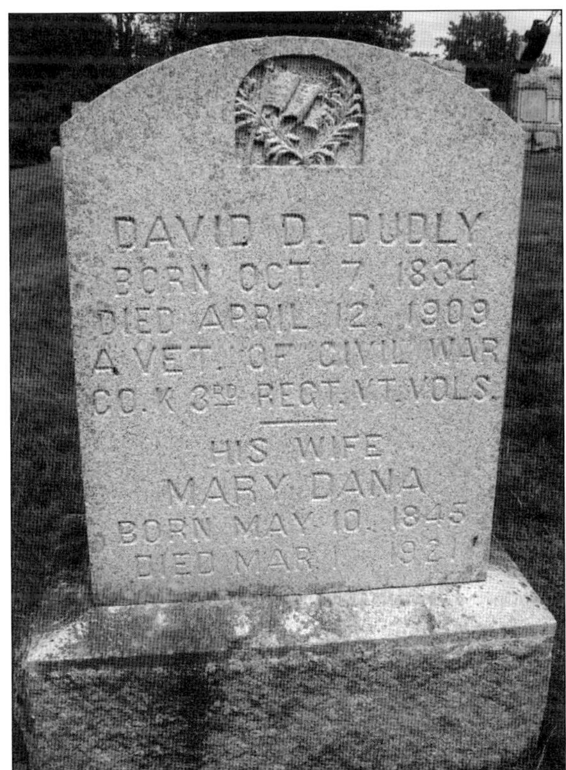

Dudly Family Monument (1909). Military headstones are rare in Hope Cemetery, and this is one of the oldest to be found here. Note the patriotic flag flanked by lilies at the top. Dudly served in the war from July 1861 to July 1865 and took part in the 3rd Vermont's actions in many battles, including Antietam, Fredericksburg, Gettysburg, Cold Harbor, and Petersburg to name a few.

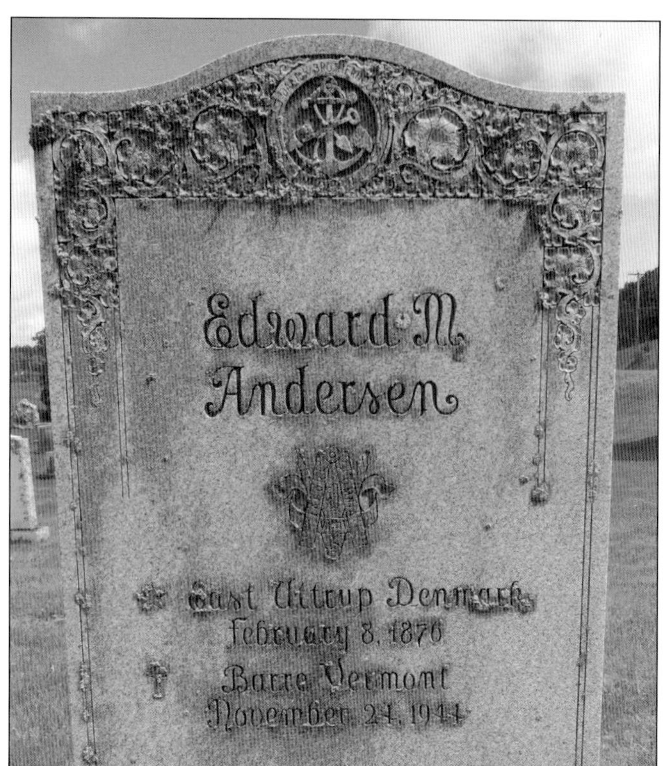

Edward M. Andersen Monument (1944). The social affiliations of this Danish immigrant are readily apparent on this monument. The maritime logo at top is a symbol for the Danish Brotherhood in America, with Andersen belonging to its only Vermont chapter, the Green Mountain Lodge No. 294, established in 1912. Note the logo at center reading "Labor Omnia Vincit," a sign of Andersen's affiliation with the labor union movement.

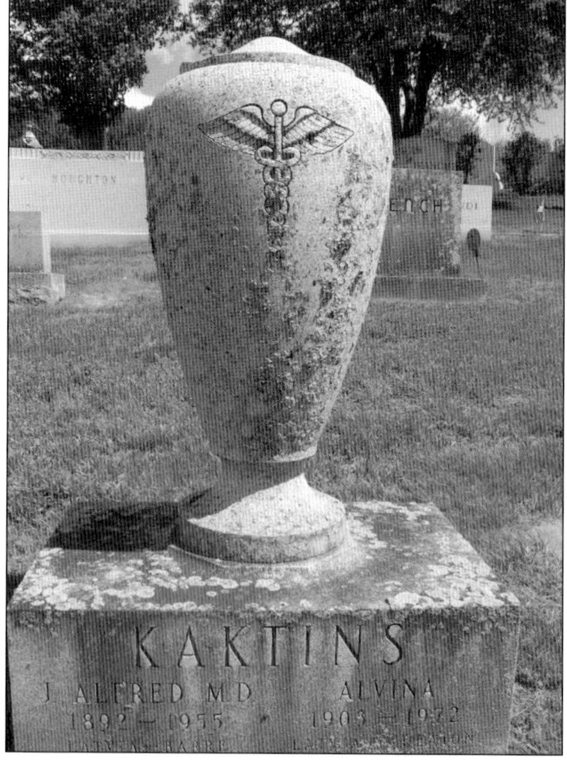

Kaktins Family Monument (1955). The occupation of this immigrant, Dr. Janis Alfred Kaktins (1892–1955), is on display here, with this urn featuring a caduceus, often mistakenly used as the sign of the medical profession. Born in Rujiene, Latvia, he arrived in Boston in 1950 and was employed as a pathologist at Barre City Hospital by 1951 before his untimely death.

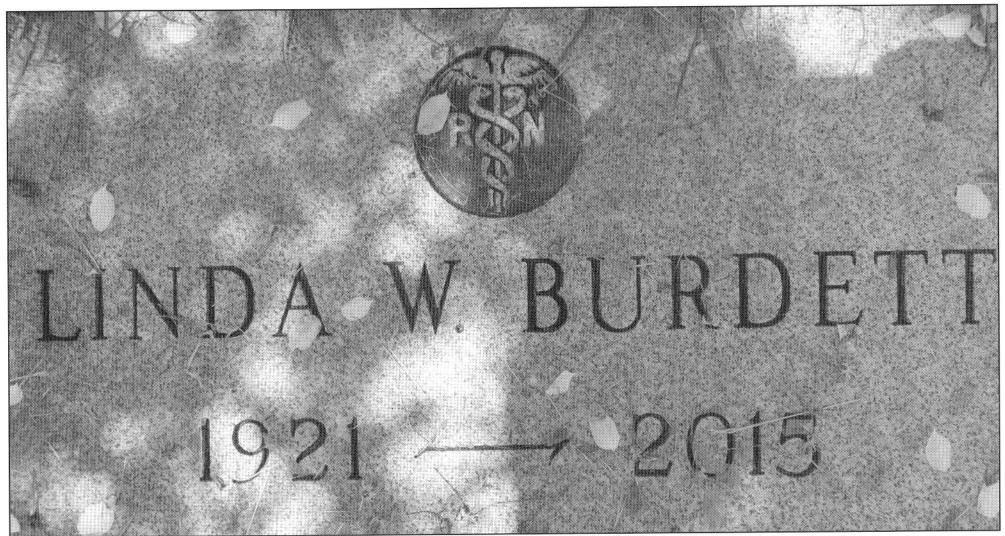

Linda W. Burdett Ground Marker (2015). A native of Minneapolis, Minnesota, and graduate of Wheaton College, Burdett was a distinguished nurse who later attended the Yale University School of Nursing to gain a master's degree and worked at several hospitals throughout New England, including in New Haven, Connecticut, and Huggins Hospital in Wolfeboro, New Hampshire, before her move to Vermont.

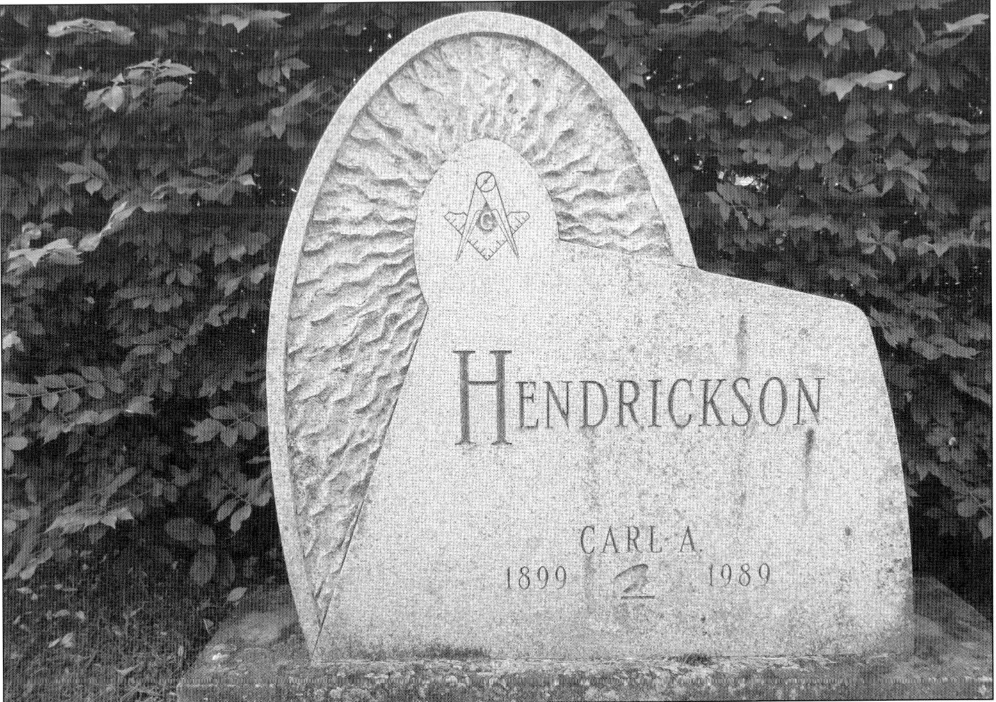

Carl A. Hendrickson Monument (1989). Two lifetime affiliations are visible on this attractive sunburst design monument. The sign of the deceased's membership in the Masons is clearly noted at top with their logo, featuring a set square and compass, but note also the small eagle insignia, the sign of the US Postal Service, below his name. He served as a mail carrier for many years in Barre.

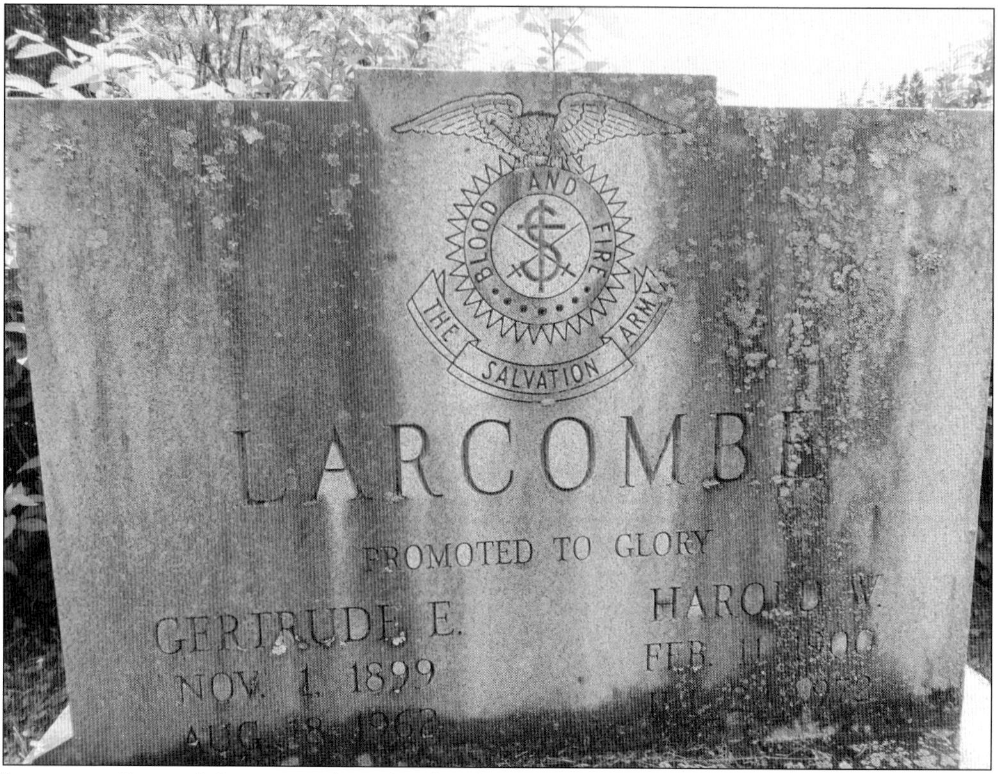

Larcombe Family Monument (1972). The charitable work of this couple is on full display on this unique monument featuring the logo of the Salvation Army. Harold Larcombe (1900–1972) was an immigrant from Somerset, England, who practiced the trade of a tailor and married Gertrude in 1923.

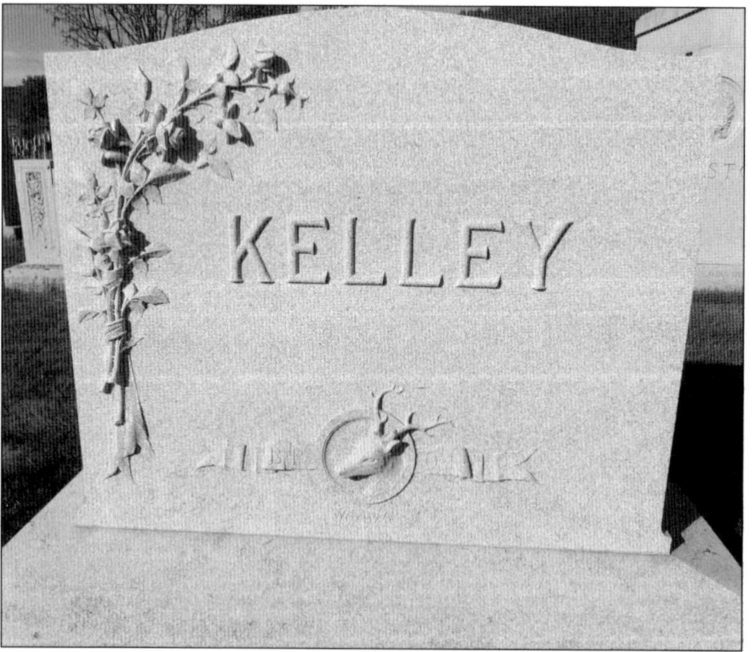

Kelley Family Monument (1925). Their proud membership in the Benevolent and Protective Order of Elks, a well-known social and charitable club very active in Barre for many years, is shown for William Kelley (1850–1925) and his son Harry (1885–1925). Many monuments in Hope bear the distinctive animal logo of the Elks club, but this one sculpted in relief form is perhaps the most finely executed.

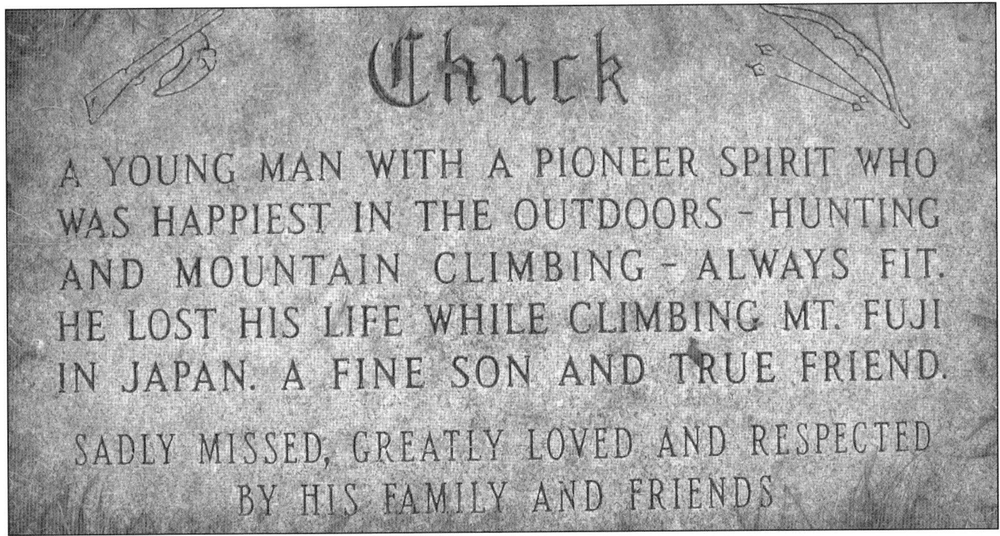

Chuck Chatot Ground Marker. Nearly all of the monuments in Hope Cemetery are accompanied by ground markers, which indicate the individuals buried in each cemetery plot. Often overlooked by visitors, many of these markers provide additional information not found on central monuments, as with that for Charles "Chuck" Chatot (1963–1984), detailed here; these monuments speak to the interests, character, and professions of the deceased, sometimes in a touching and artistic form.

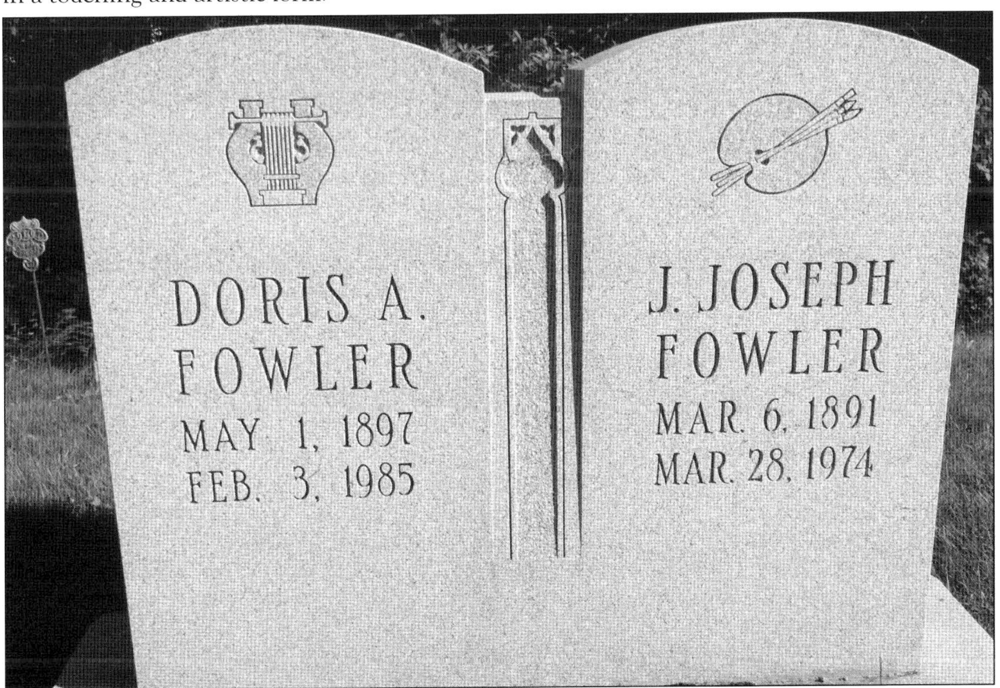

Fowler Family Monument. This elegant monument in dual form shows this couple's love of the arts. The half of the stone for J. Joseph, employed as salesman in the lumber industry, features an artist's palette, while that for Doris features a harp. This harp often has several meanings, with it being a symbol of Christian joy and Irish heritage, but here, it denotes Doris's lifelong career as a private music teacher.

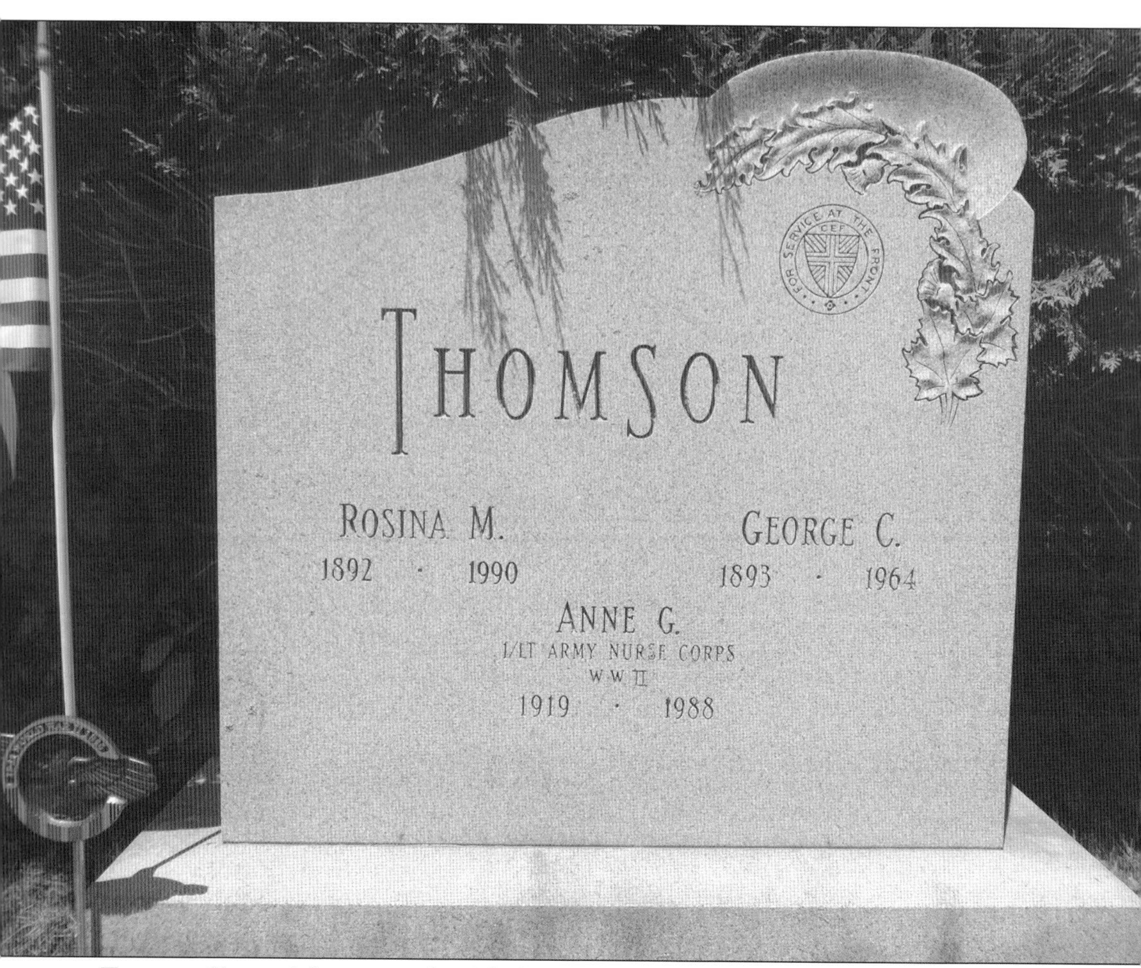

THOMSON FAMILY MONUMENT (1964). Sometimes, even the simplest of monuments in Hope Cemetery, which often get overlooked, offer clues to incredible lives that are both notable and interesting. This family's patriarch, George Thomson (1893–1964), was a native of Canada who served in World War I for his native country, denoted by the insignia at upper right for the Canadian Expeditionary Force, which fought on the battlefields of France. Given his military service, it is perhaps not surprising that his daughter Anne Thompson (1919–1988), born the year after World War I ended, would serve the family's adopted homeland in World War II as an Army nurse and officer.

WING FAMILY MONUMENT (1993). The social and charitable activities of this couple are here displayed in charming fashion. Gordon Wing (1915–2000) was an enthusiastic member of the Shriners, as indicated by the fez at upper right. At the base, Gordon's membership in the Masons is also marked. Florence (1911–1993), whose husband was a Master Mason, was active in the Order of the Eastern Star (as denoted at the base), a group associated with the Masons that was open to their female relatives.

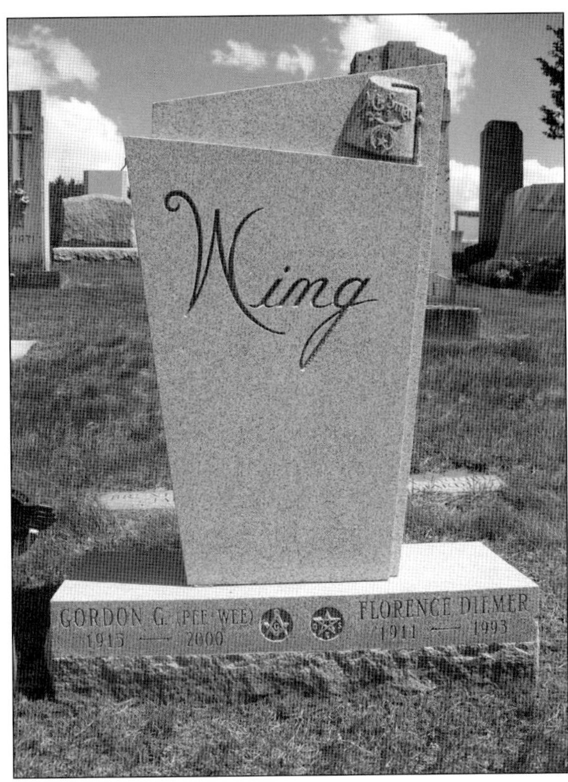

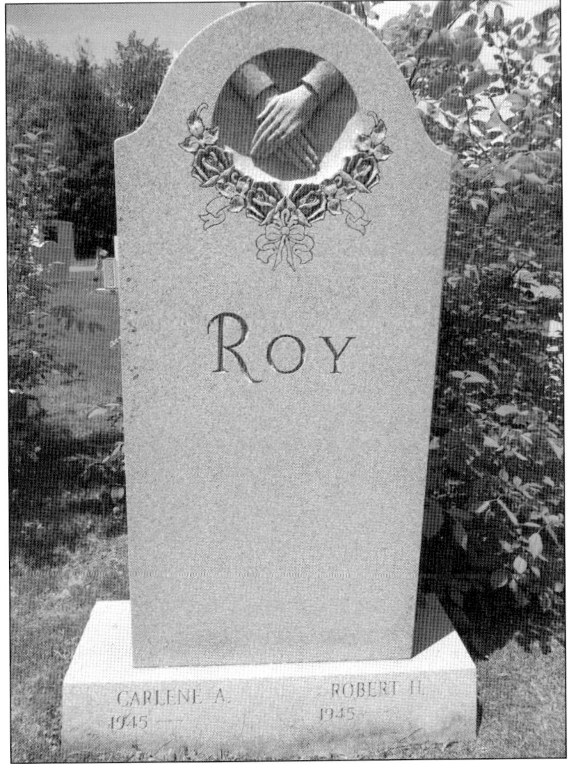

ROY FAMILY MONUMENT. The deep and abiding love that this still-living couple has for one another is here displayed in elegant fashion. The carving of their hands, placed one atop the other above a garland of roses, is exquisitely done and reflects their devotion for one another.

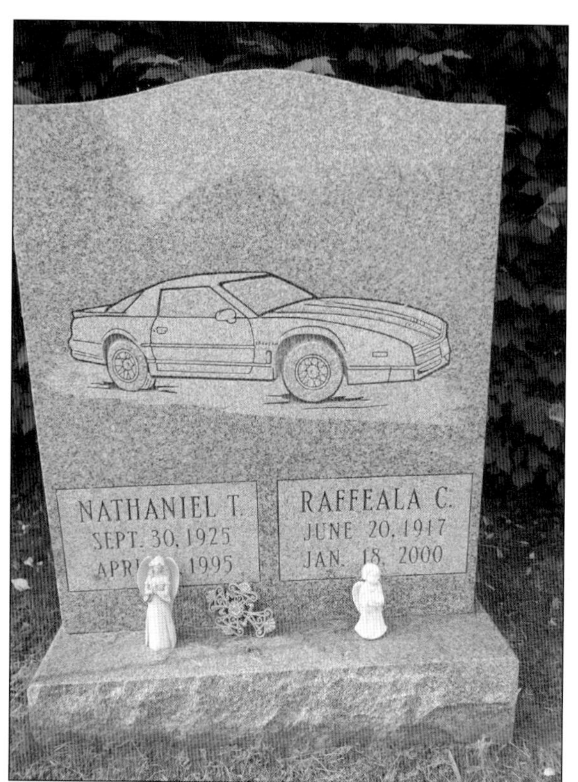

PHILLIPS FAMILY MONUMENT (1995). The love that Americans have for automobiles is amply demonstrated in the form of a Pontiac Trans Am, which was surely Nathaniel Phillips's favorite car—and perhaps his wife Raffeala's too. The advancement in laser technology in the monument business has made personalized stones like this affordable for many.

PIERCE FAMILY MONUMENT (1998). This family's love of cross-country travel in their RV is dramatically shown. One can imagine the travels of Lawrence and Elvira from their Vermont home base, as shown at right as the only state outlined on the map, across the country to the West Coast. Note at the base of the monument the emblems for several of the social organizations to which the couple belonged.

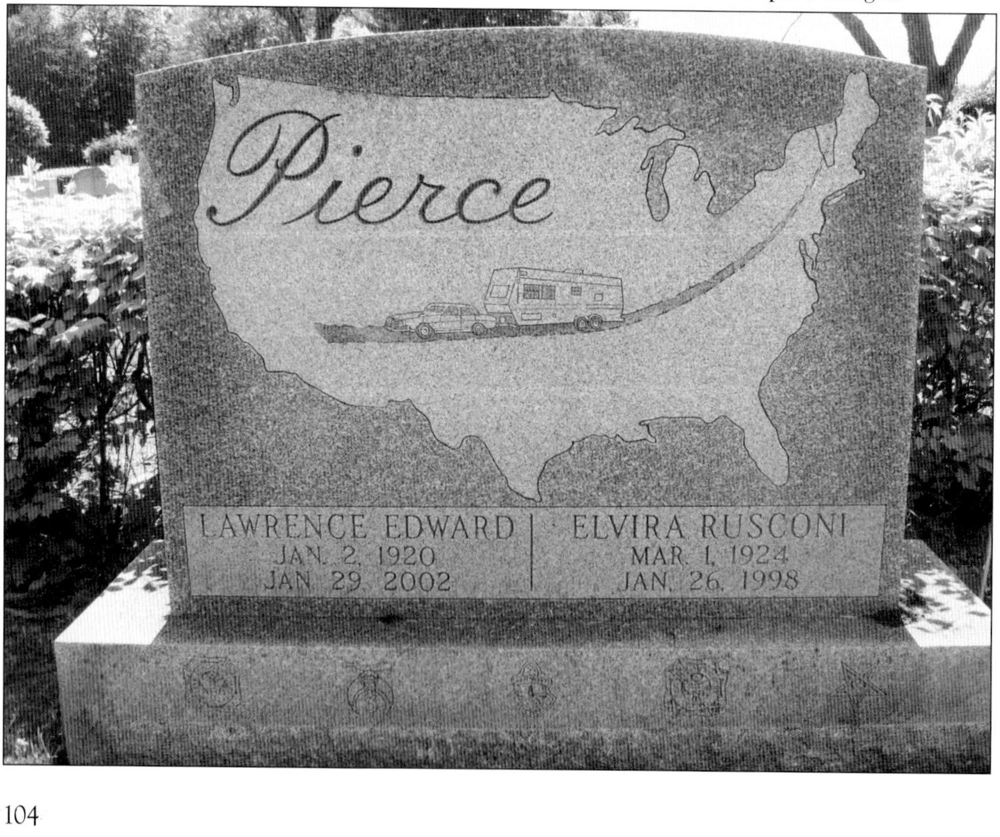

Stuart Family Monument (1983). Monuments in Hope Cemetery featuring semitrucks are, quite surprisingly, more common than those featuring automobiles. This example is one of the most interesting in its detail, featuring Robert Stuart's flatbed hauler with a large sunburst behind, which is perhaps indicative of his final journey in life.

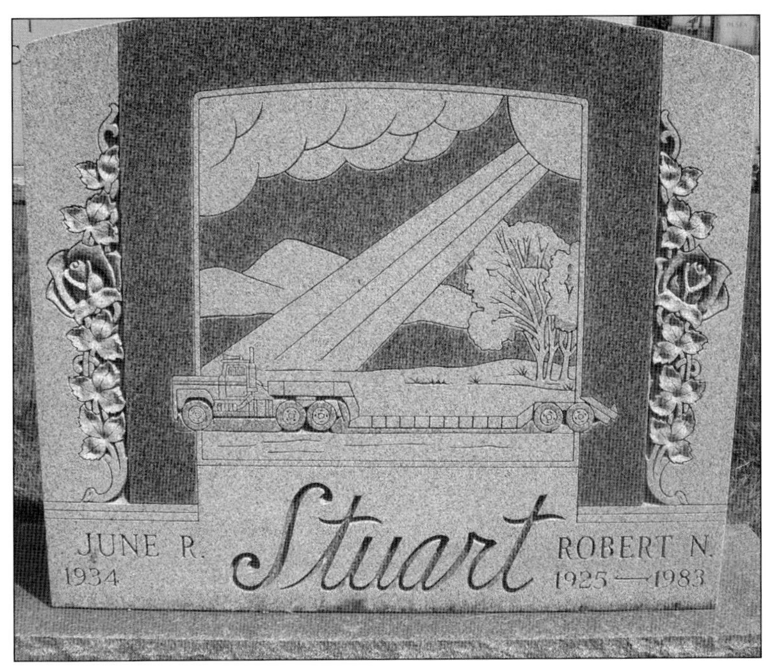

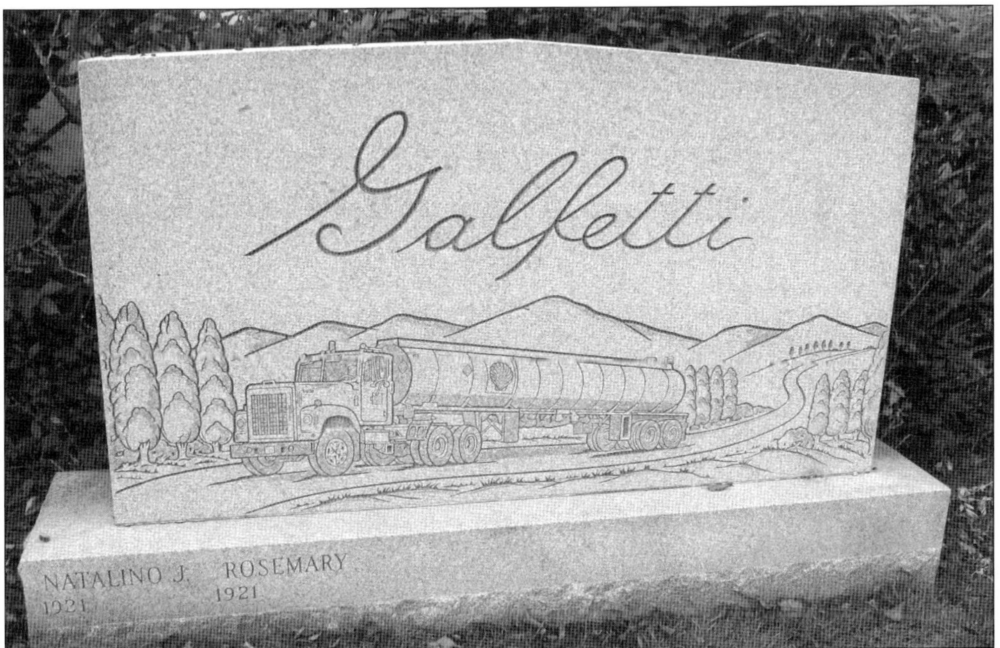

Galfetti Family Monument. Occupational-themed monuments have become increasingly popular in Hope Cemetery. The Shell Oil Company tanker truck, depicted here on the open road, is an indicator of the lifelong occupation of Natalino Galfetti (1921–2017), the son of Swiss Italian immigrants and a World War II Army veteran. He married Rosemary Milo (1921–2013) in 1943.

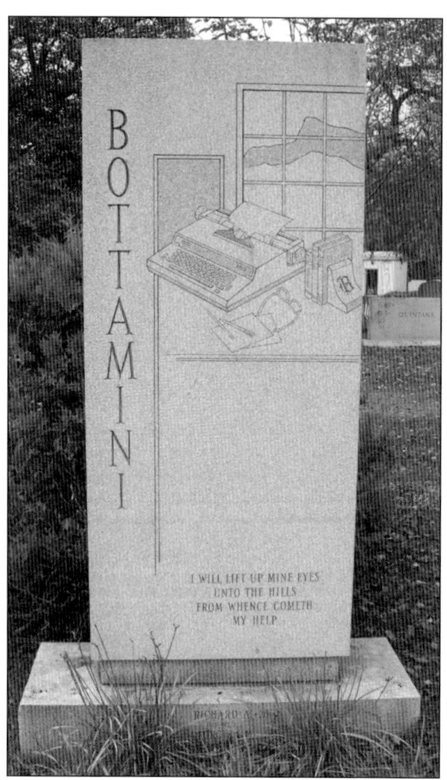

BOTTAMINI FAMILY MONUMENT (2000). The passion of a writer is enshrined here on this monument for Richard (1915–2000) and his wife, Georgina (1919–2011), who was Vermont Mother of the Year in 1972. Richard worked as a newspaper writer for the *Daily Times* early in his career before becoming a public relations director for an insurance company, but he always retained a passion for writing.

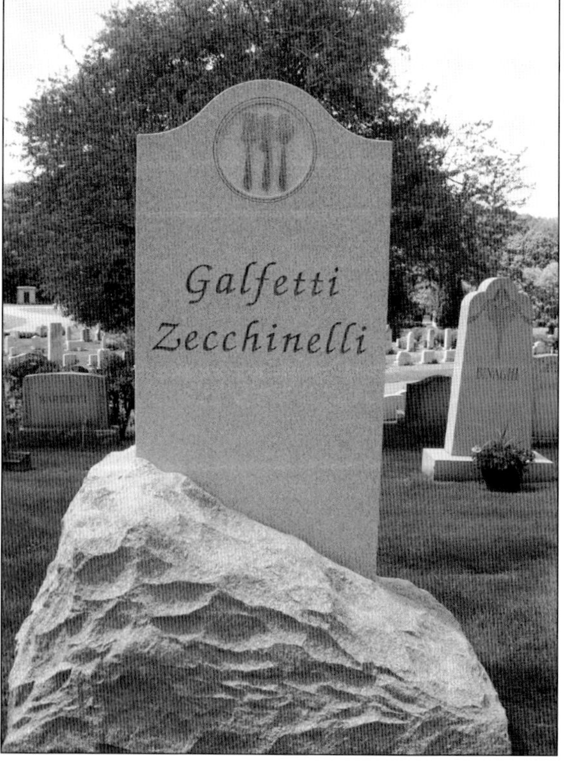

GALFETTI-ZECCHINELLI FAMILY MONUMENT. With its shell-rock-style base, this monument is adorned with a plate and dining utensils, indicative of its owners, Karen Galfetti Zecchinelli and her husband, Bryan, who currently own and operate the famed Wayside Restaurant in nearby Montpelier, a local favorite since 1918. Karen's father, Eugene Galfetti, and her mother, Harriet, operated the restaurant from 1966 to 1998 before passing it on to their daughter and her husband.

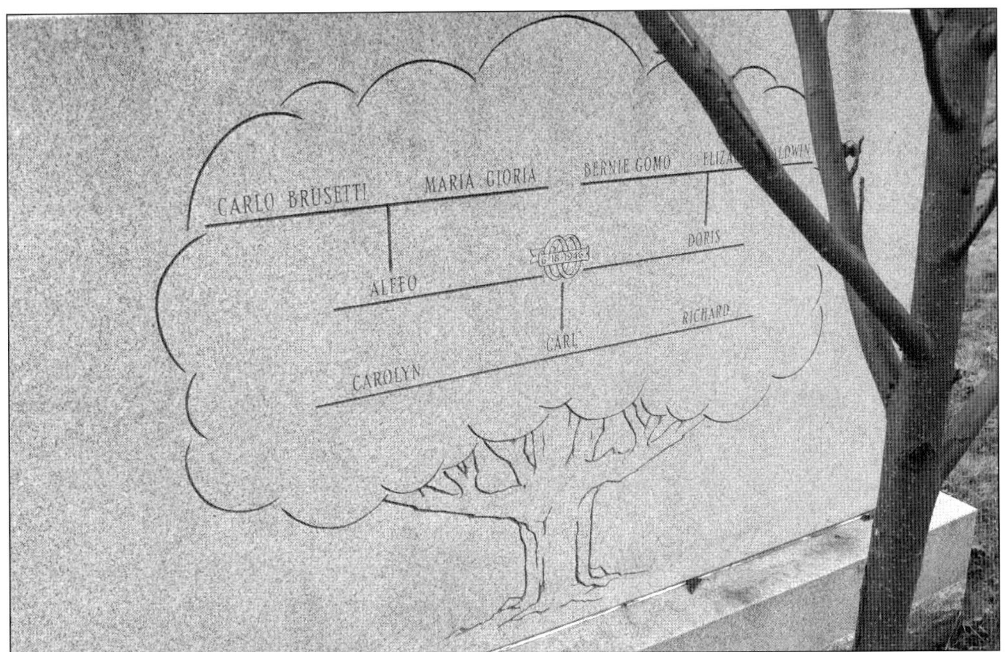

Brusetti Family Monument. Places like Hope Cemetery are often the favored destination of amateur genealogists working to trace a family lineage. On this attractive monument, the Brusetti family has drawn out their own family tree, an indicator of the importance of family ties. Carlo (1887–1979), the Brusetti family patriarch, worked as a stonecutter and became the treasurer of the Modern Granite Company, while his wife, Maria Gloria (1894–1933), was a nurse.

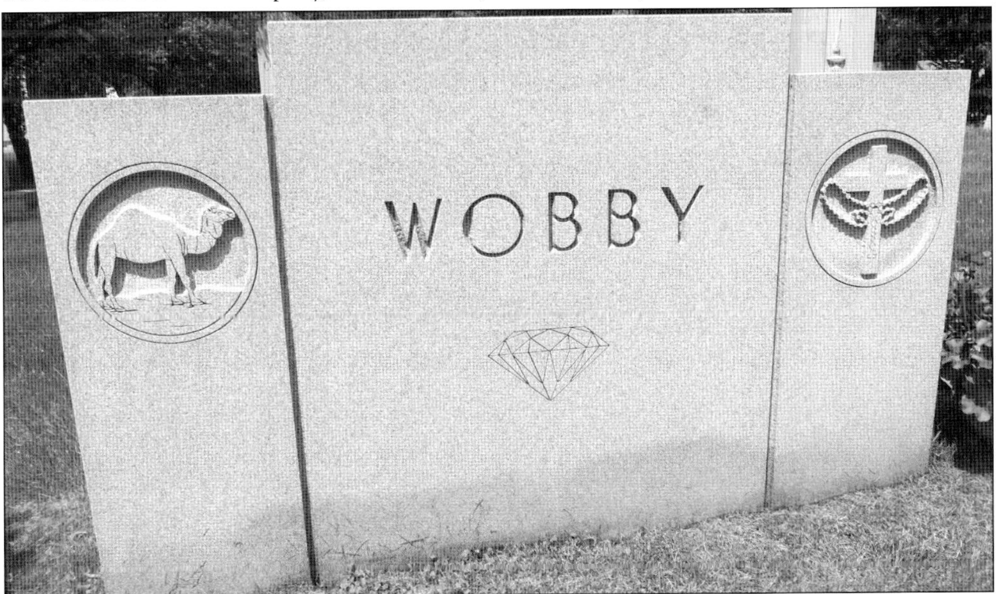

Richard Wobby Family Monument. Several facets of this family's lives are shown here on this monument. Richard Wobby (1931–2004) was the son of immigrants Michael and Lina Wobby (see page 89) and operated a family jewelry store in town for years; it is still in operation in Barre today. The striking camel pays homage to his Middle Eastern heritage, while the cross and rosary beads are indicative of the family's Christian faith.

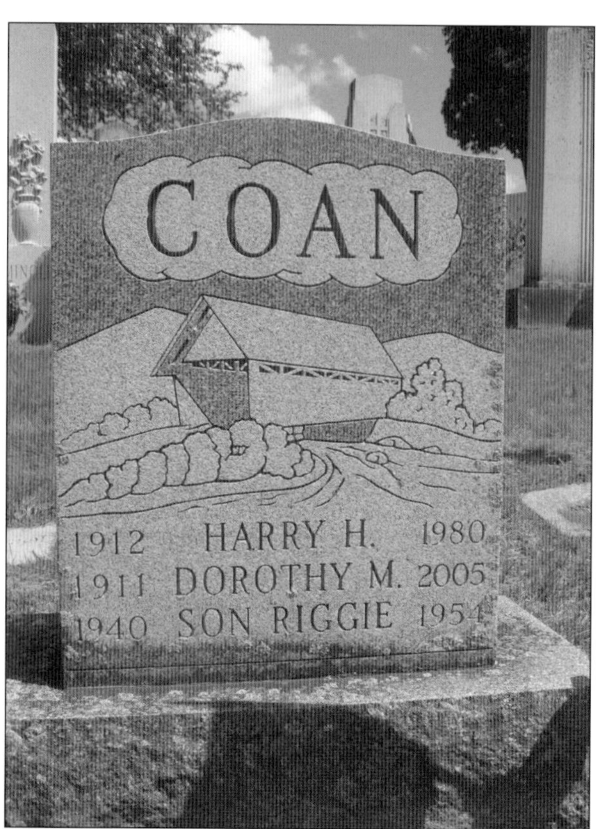

Coan Family Monument. In a state known for its covered bridges, their appearance in Hope Cemetery seems appropriate. The bridge often serves as a symbol for the passage from the mortal to the spiritual world, so perhaps this stone represents a Vermont version of this concept. Whether the Coan family just loved visiting covered bridges, saw them as a spiritual symbol, or chose this imagery for both reasons is unknown.

Gary G. Paquet Monument (1999). A beautifully sculpted sailboat and rustic lettering for the family name make for the tranquil nature of this monument created by Giuliano Cecchinelli. The image is indicative of Paquet's love for sailing and adventure, but it also represents his love for the journey itself. It was designed under the guidance of Mary Paquet as a way of honoring her late husband in a personal way.

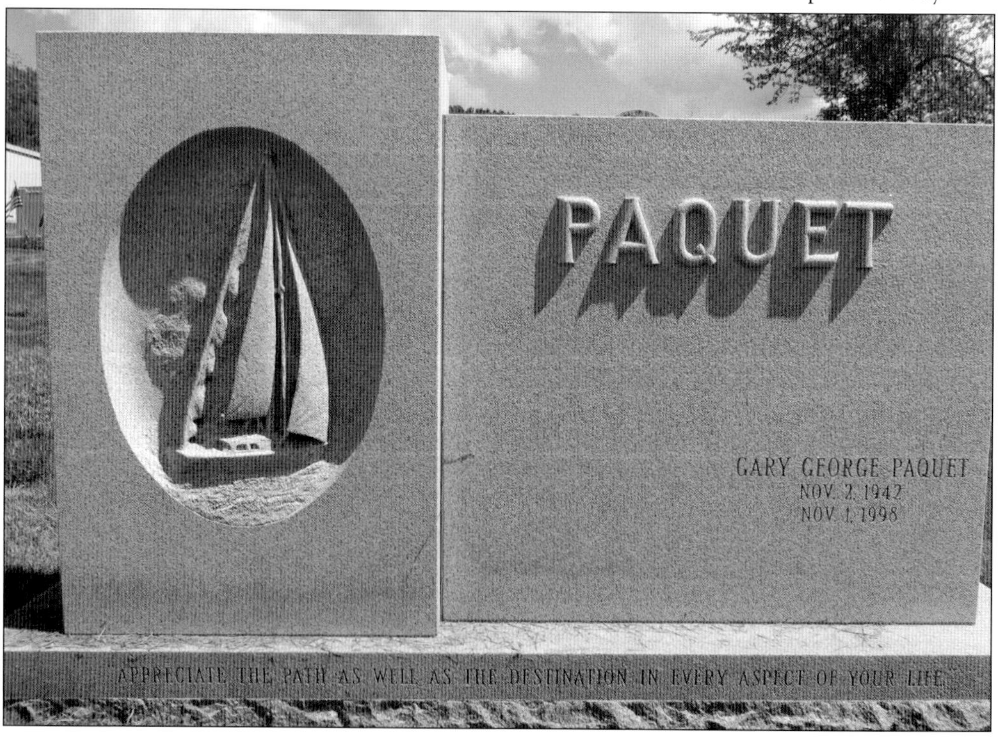

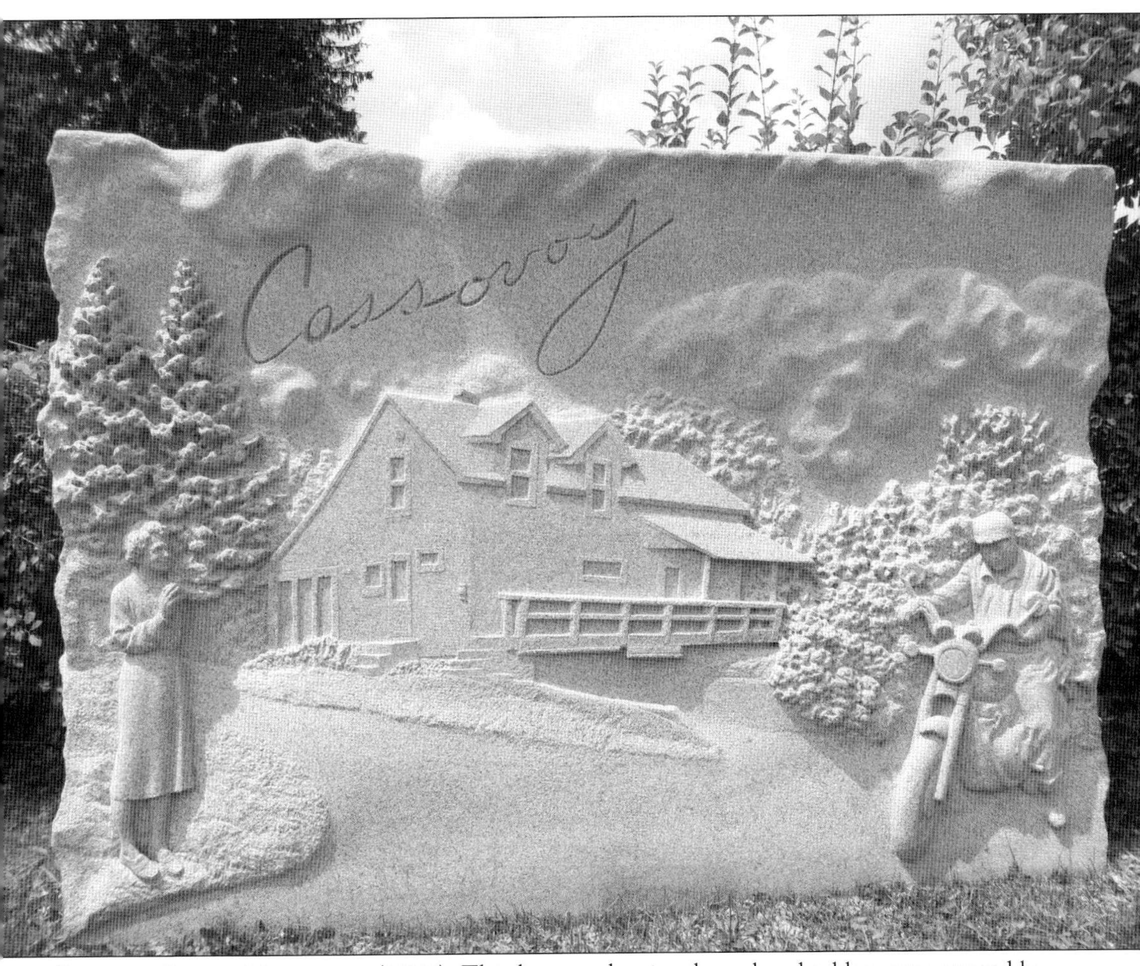

Cassavoy Family Monument (1997). This large and uniquely sculpted tableau was created by Giuliano Cecchinelli and offers a striking view of the couple and their home, with Eva Angelina Cassavoy waving goodbye to her husband, Richard, as he prepares to ride off on his motorcycle. The details on this work of art, especially the trees and the sky, offer a pleasing backdrop to this scene, which is also an allegory for a beloved husband's final journey. Richard Cassavoy (1919–1997), a native of New York, was a stonecutter and plant foreman for Buttura and Sons in Barre for many years. He married Eva Angelina, a native of Barre, in 1940.

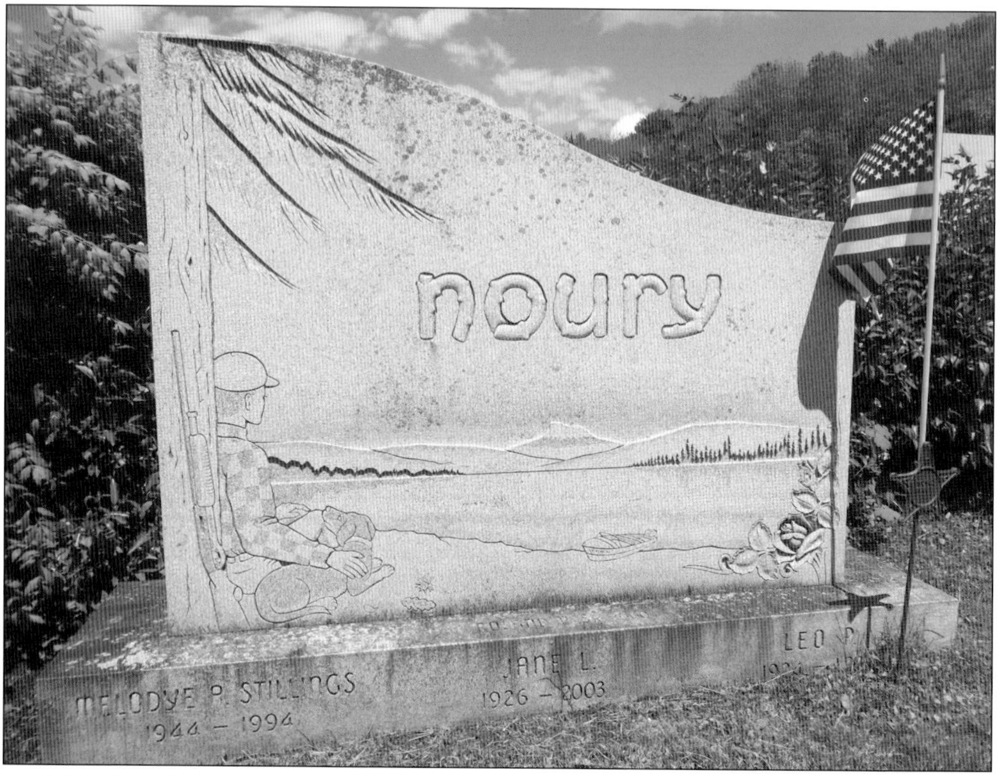

Noury Family Monument. Hunting scenes such as this one may be found elsewhere in Hope Cemetery, which is not surprising due to the rural nature of the area, but this one is perhaps the most interesting. Not only does this scene offer up a realistic view of a favorite pastime for Leo (1924–1971) or Roland Noury (1948–2000), but it also offers up a scene of quiet serenity in the New England wilderness.

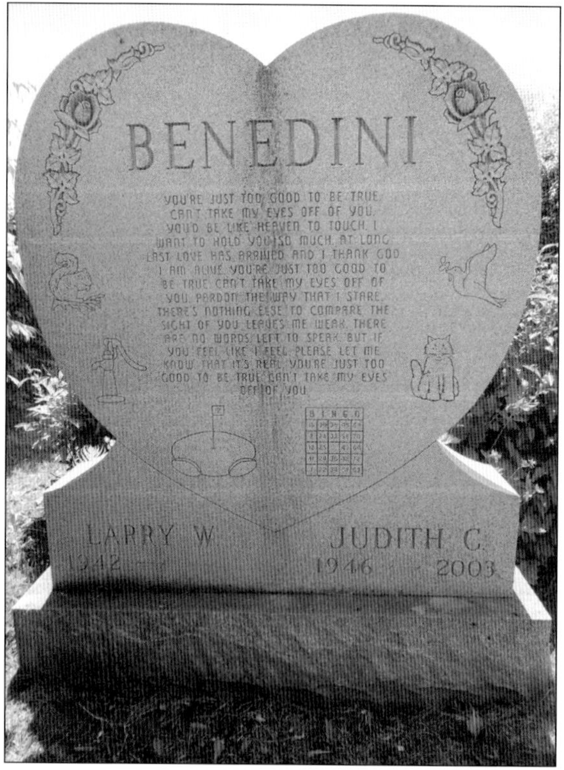

Judith and Larry Benedini Family Monument (2003). A heart-shaped monument with the lyrics from a favorite song serve as the background for the many interests shared by this couple, including bingo, golfing, and a family pet, while the squirrel may represent the animals they fed in their own backyard.

Eight

The Making of Hope

No account of Hope Cemetery would be complete without some discussion of the granite business, which serves as its foundation, making Barre, as the city rightfully claims, the "Granite Capital of the World." The industry got its start in the early 19th century, with Robert Parker and Thomas Courser credited as the first to quarry and manufacture granite. The business would remain small due to transportation constraints until the arrival of the railroad connecting Montpelier to Barre in 1875. With this development, Barre increased in size as the granite industry grew, with its population rising from 1,882 inhabitants in 1870 to over 12,000 by 1910 and including many artisans from Italy, Scotland, and Spain. The granite that has served as the foundation for Barre's industry was hewn from dozens of quarries located in the vicinity, both large and small. Today, the industry still flourishes, with the Rock of Ages Corporation being an industry leader, and many who visit Hope Cemetery also take the famous tour of the Rock of Ages quarry and finishing plant in nearby Graniteville. Some 600 feet deep, the Smith Quarry is thought to be the largest deep-hole quarry in the world and is the source of today's famed Barre grey granite. Once the granite was quarried, it was transported to the many granite processing plants—or granite sheds, as they were called—located in the heart of Barre, where thousands of immigrants were employed in turning the raw granite into monuments and other finished works. Though granite workers were paid a good wage, the working conditions were deadly, as a fine granite dust filled the air inside the sheds and was continually inhaled during the course of an entire eight-hour work shift, five days a week, for years on end. This resulted in a lung disease, termed silicosis, or pulmonary tuberculosis, for which there was no cure; many granite workers would die from this condition. The installation of ventilation systems in the sheds would have solved this problem, but owners resisted, and it would not be until 1937 that they were required.

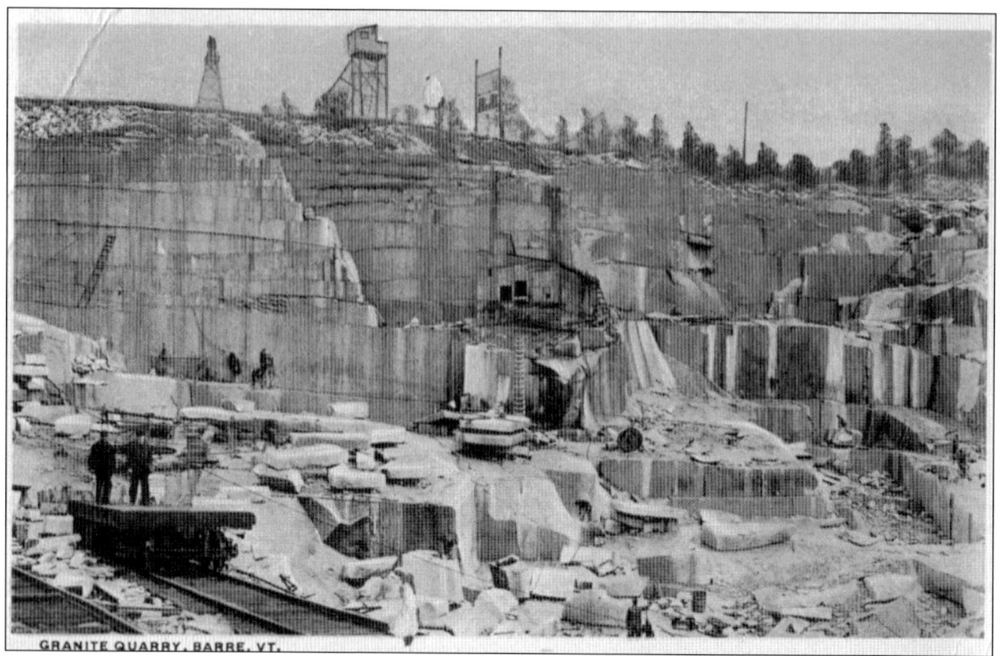

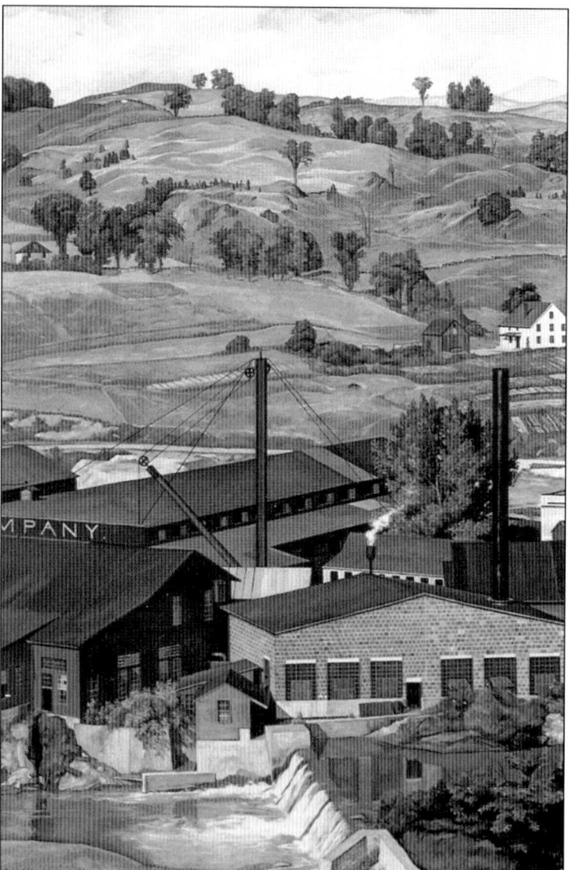

POSTCARD VIEW, GRANITE QUARRY, BARRE, VERMONT (C. 1914). This period postcard offers an idea of the scope of the granite industry. The men at lower left stand on a flatbed railcar that will eventually transport the extracted blocks of granite to one of the many granite sheds around the city, where they will be worked into their final forms.

LUIGI LUCEONI PAINTING (1931). Italian-born painter Luigi Lucioni (1900–1988) started his career as a teenager in New York, but when he received a commission from a Vermont patron in 1930, he fell in love with the state. Over the years, he painted many rural scenes here and was drawn to Barre's Italian community, painting this depiction of one of the city's numerous granite sheds. (Courtesy of the Vermont Granite Museum.)

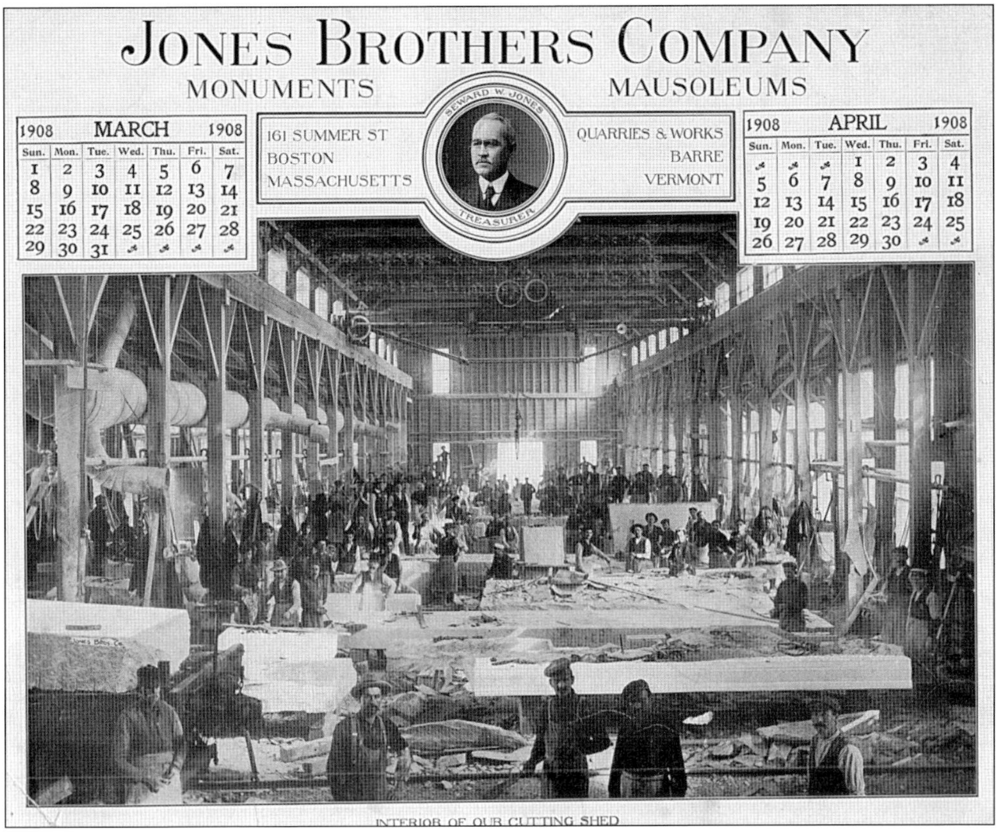

JONES BROTHERS COMPANY

MONUMENTS MAUSOLEUMS

1908			MARCH			1908
Sun.	Mon.	Tue.	Wed.	Thu.	Fri.	Sat.
1	2	3	4	5	6	7
8	9	10	11	12	13	14
15	16	17	18	19	20	21
22	23	24	25	26	27	28
29	30	31				

161 SUMMER ST
BOSTON
MASSACHUSETTS

SEWARD W. JONES
TREASURER

QUARRIES & WORKS
BARRE
VERMONT

1908			APRIL			1908
Sun.	Mon.	Tue.	Wed.	Thu.	Fri.	Sat.
			1	2	3	4
5	6	7	8	9	10	11
12	13	14	15	16	17	18
19	20	21	22	23	24	25
26	27	28	29	30		

INTERIOR OF OUR CUTTING SHED

JONES BROTHERS COMPANY CALENDAR (1908). This granite company was one of the largest and most prosperous in Barre. Seen here is the interior of one of its cutting sheds, where granite blocks were cut into finished form. Note the traveling crane (above center), which carried the granite blocks through the shed in assembly-line fashion, and the many workers involved in doing this work. (Courtesy of the Vermont Granite Museum.)

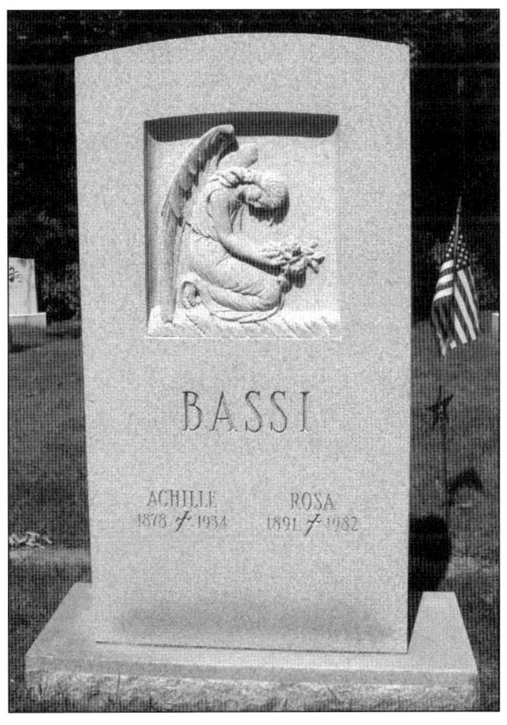

BASSI FAMILY MONUMENT (1934). Buried here is stonecutter Achille Bassi (1878–1934). He arrived from Italy in 1909 and is, perhaps, typical of the thousands of unheralded immigrant artisans who made their way to Barre. He probably helped create hundreds, if not thousands, of monuments during his decades-long career, but like most stonecutters, his work is undocumented.

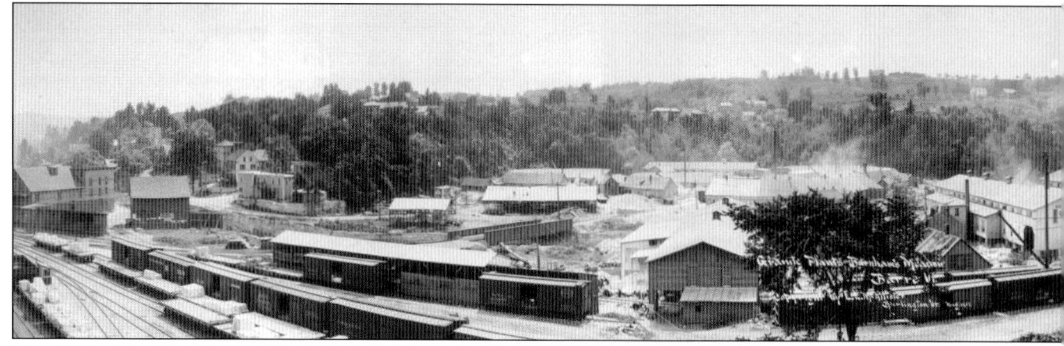

The North End Granite Plants, Barre, Vermont (1917). This panoramic photograph view by L.L. McAllister illustrates just how sizeable the granite industry was in Barre, contributing to

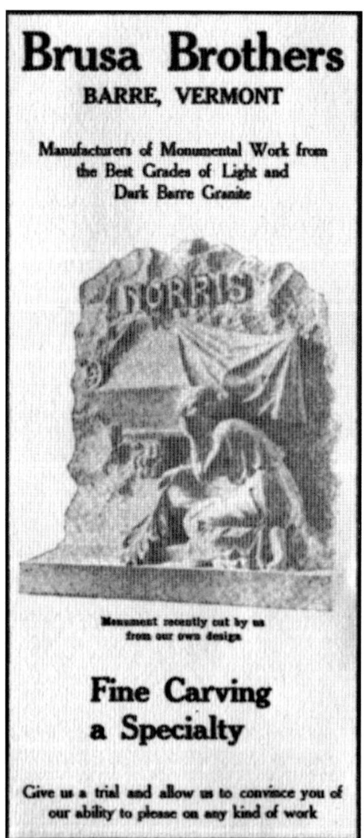

Brusa Brothers Advertisement (1909). Louis and John Brusa formerly worked in the granite trade as stonecutters for other firms, with Louis employed by Jones Brothers; however, in 1908, Louis and John formed their own company, which would be one of the most renowned in all of Barre for its fine work.

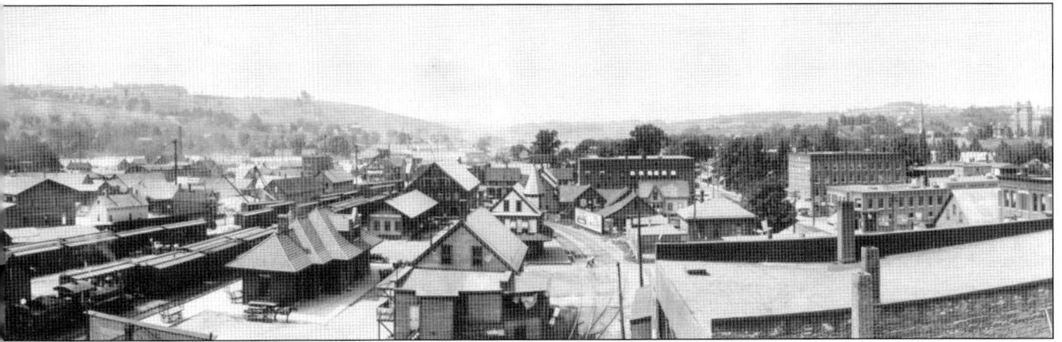

its incredible growth. (Courtesy of the Library of Congress.)

Induni-Malnati Monument. Giuseppe "Joseph" Induni (1880–1917) was an immigrant stonecutter from Switzerland who operated his own granite company known for its fine carving. After his death due to tuberculosis, his wife, Anna Maria (1886–1959), married another stonecutter, Ernesto Malnati, who also ran his own business. This stone is notable for its carvings depicting the tools of the stonecutter's trade.

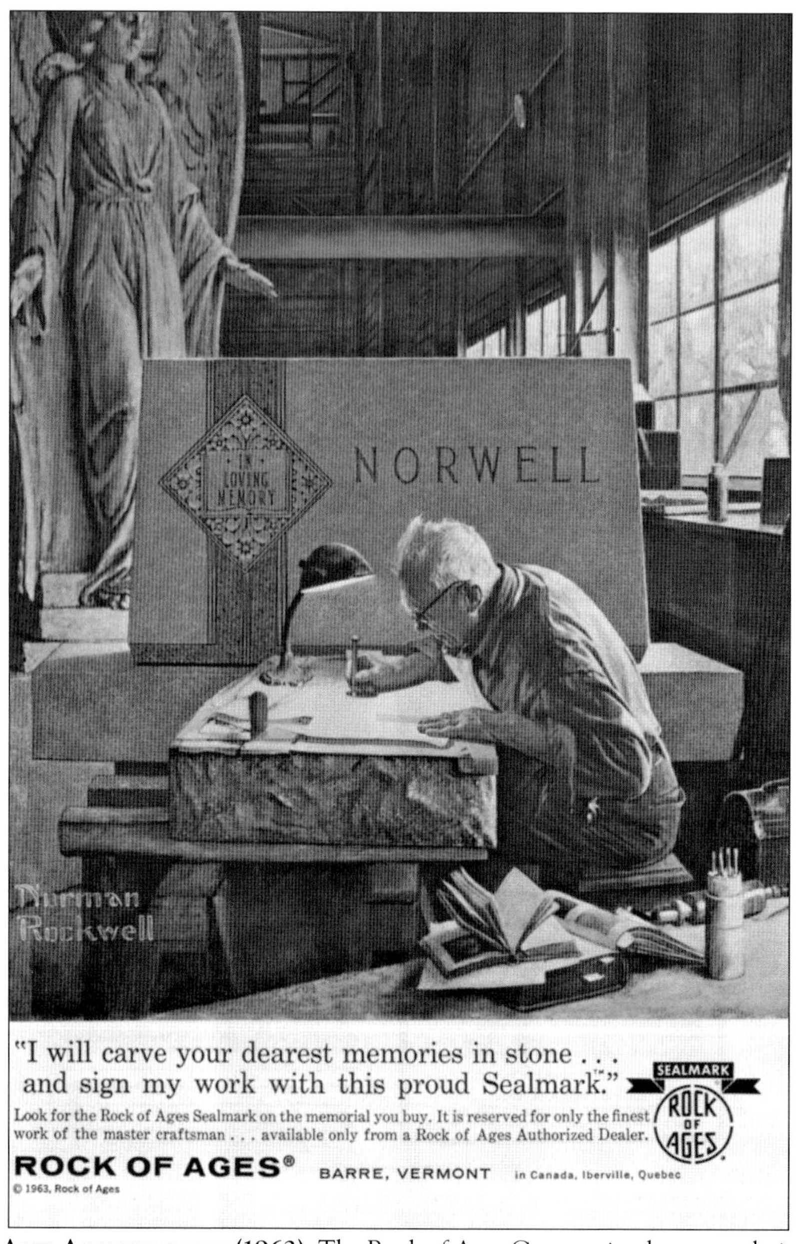

Rock of Ages Advertisement (1963). The Rock of Ages Corporation has roots dating back to 1885, when George Milne established his own granite company. It expanded in 1905, when Milne went into business with two quarry owners, James Boutwell and Harvey Varnum, and operated under the name Boutwell, Milne, and Varnum until 1914, when the brand name Rock of Ages was adopted for its finished products. In 1925, because of its success, Rock of Ages became the official name of the company, which has been a leader ever since in the monument business. In 1955, Rock of Ages hired the distinguished artist Norman Rockwell to do several paintings for its ad campaign, which was a big success. For this painting, Rockwell chose Rock of Ages artisan George Seivwright (1887–1966) as the model for his work. Seivwright was a Scottish immigrant stonecutter who worked for Rock of Ages for over three decades, rising from plant manager to a board director position. (Courtesy of Rock of Ages.)

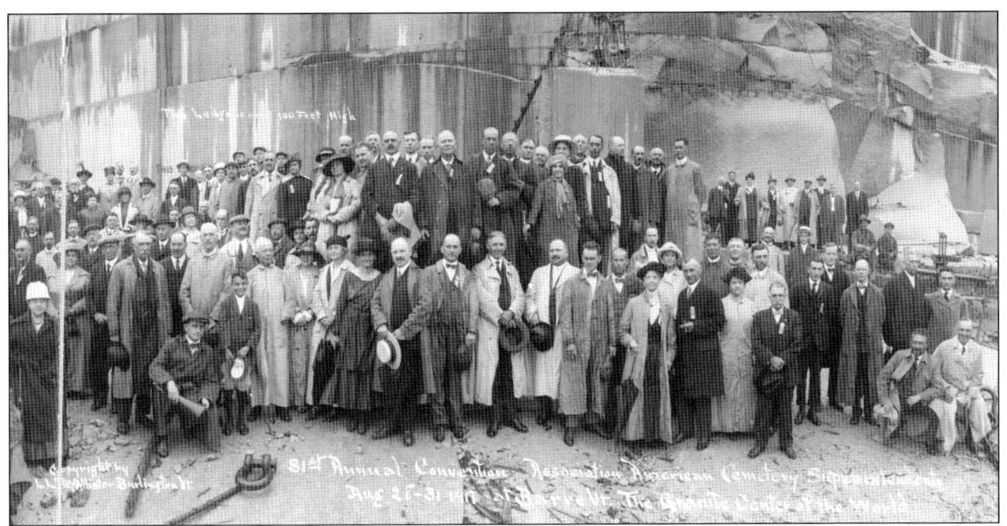

ASSOCIATION OF AMERICAN CEMETERY SUPERINTENDENTS GROUP PHOTOGRAPH (1917). As it is the leading center of granite production and the monument business in America, it was only fitting that members of this group would pay a visit to Barre for their annual convention. Not only did they visit several of the noted granite quarries, as shown here, during their four-day stay, but they also toured Hope Cemetery. (Courtesy of the Library of Congress.)

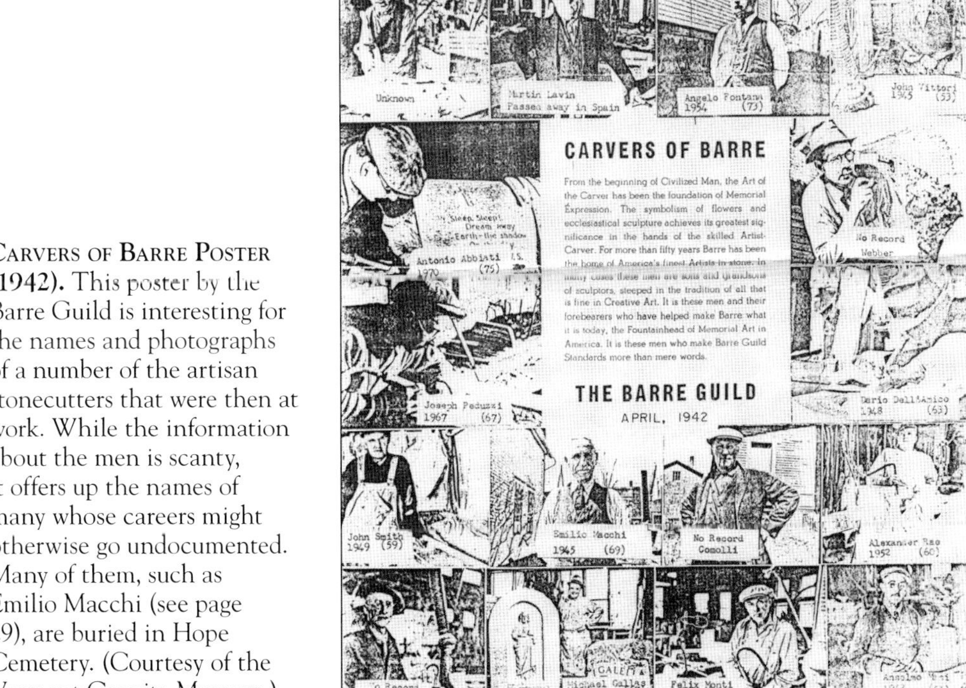

CARVERS OF BARRE POSTER (1942). This poster by the Barre Guild is interesting for the names and photographs of a number of the artisan stonecutters that were then at work. While the information about the men is scanty, it offers up the names of many whose careers might otherwise go undocumented. Many of them, such as Emilio Macchi (see page 29), are buried in Hope Cemetery. (Courtesy of the Vermont Granite Museum.)

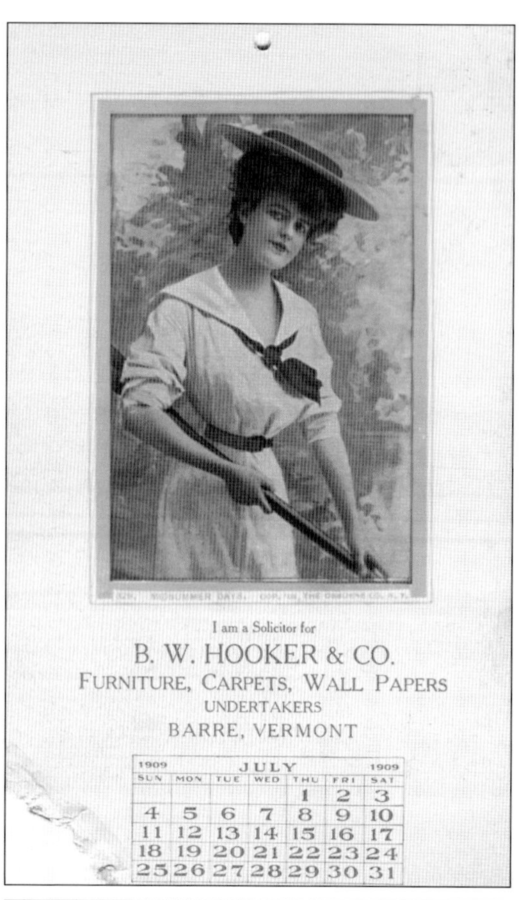

B.W. Hooker & Company Advertisement (1909). Along with the quarrying and stonecutting trades, funeral homes have also been a part of Hope Cemetery's history from the beginning. This company was one of the first of its kind in Barre, and it eventually merged with the Whitcomb Funeral Home in 1957 to form today's Hooker and Whitcomb. Note that in the early years, funeral home establishments also sold a variety of other products.

Cecchini Family Monument (1966). Silvio Cecchini (1885–1966) was born in Veneto, Italy, and arrived in the United States in 1906. He worked as a blacksmith in the granite industry, and his monument features images of the tools of his trade, along with the word *fabbro*, Italian for "blacksmith." Blacksmiths were important in the granite industry, as they were tasked with making and sharpening the tools of the granite cutter and other tasks.

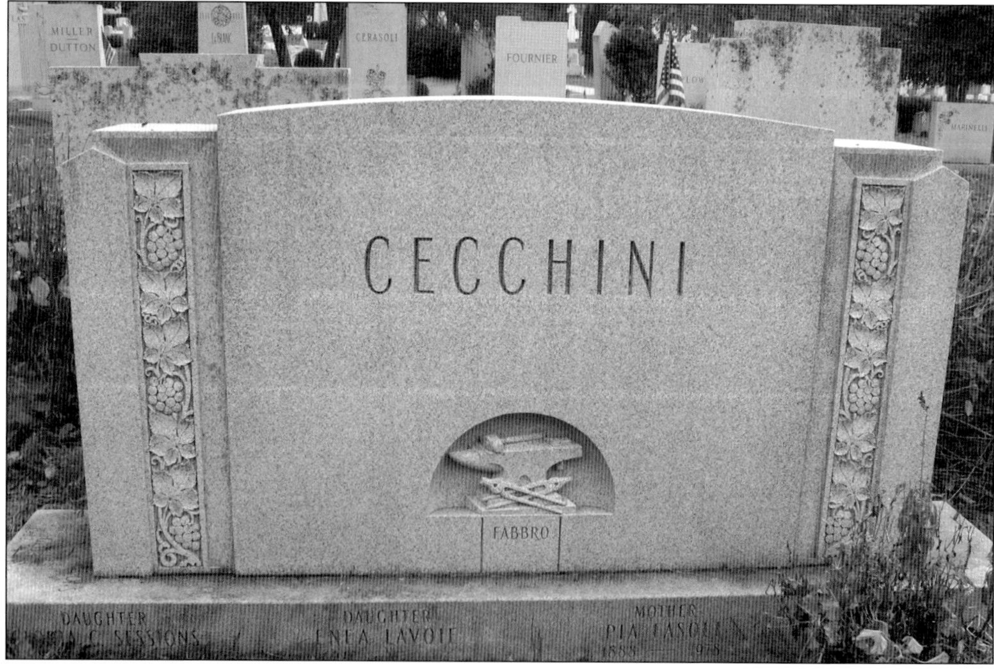

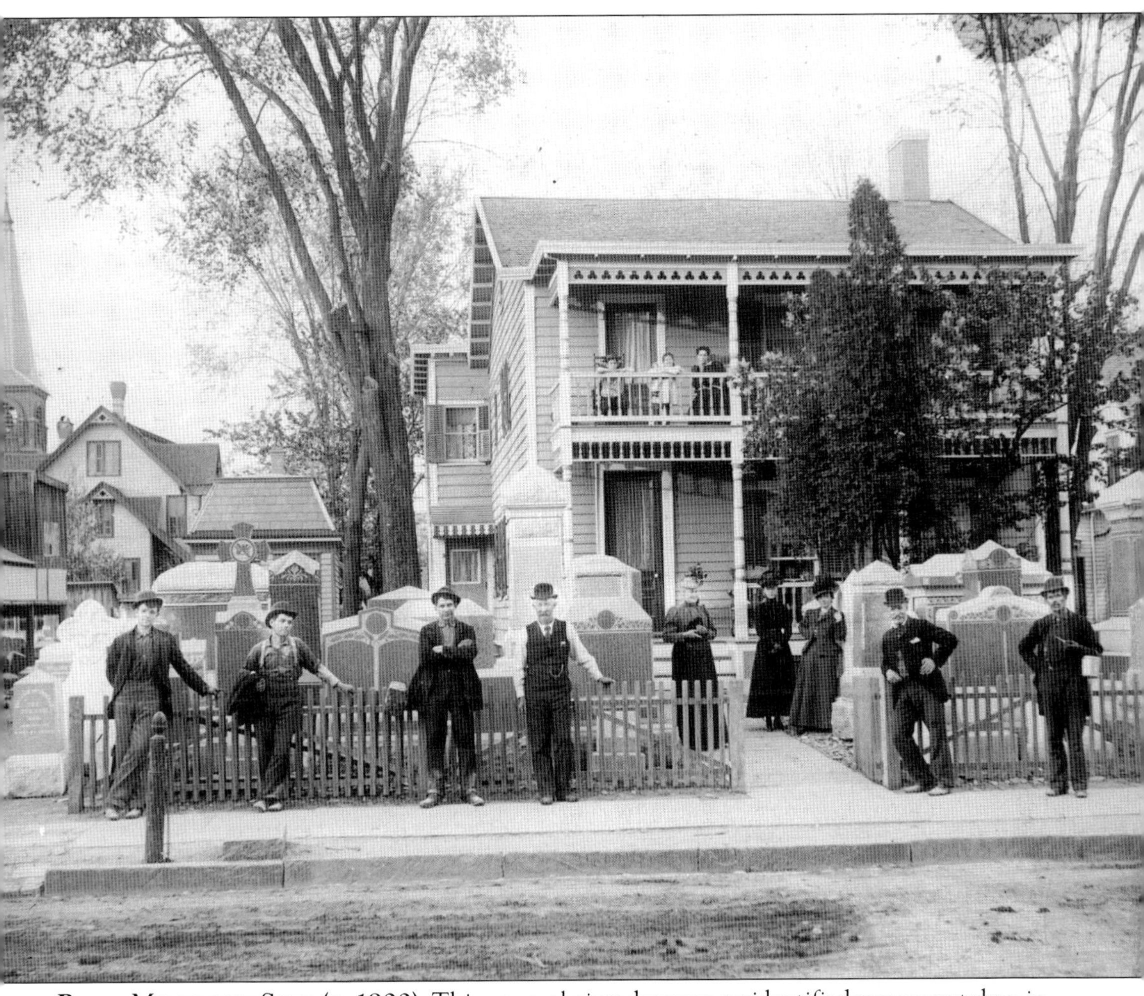

Barre Monument Shop (c. 1900). This unusual view shows an unidentified monument shop in Barre. As with today's monument dealers, shops like this served as the middleman between customers who needed a monument and the stonecutters who made them. Note that the "showroom" is in the dealer's front yard in a residential section of town. (Courtesy of the University of Vermont, Bailey-Howe Library, No. BHSC058.)

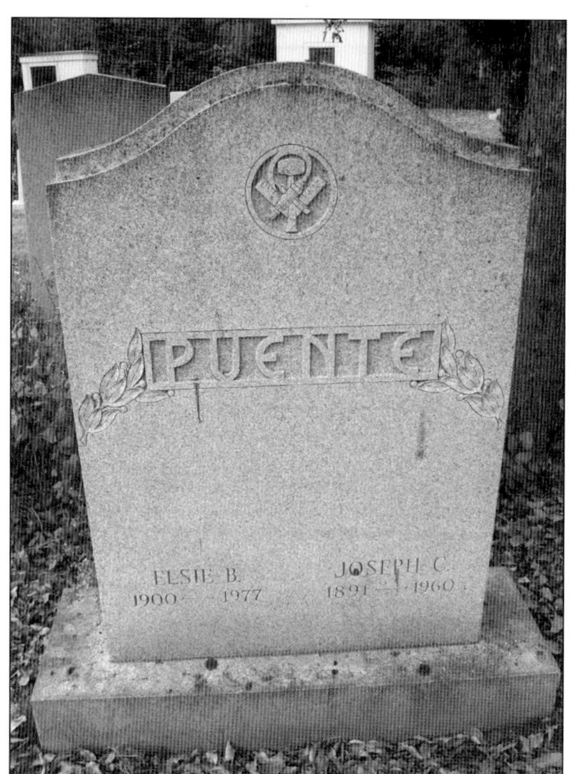

PUENTE FAMILY MONUMENT (1960). While Italian and Scottish carvers made up the bulk of Barre's granite artisans, a number of men from Santander, Spain, including Jose "Joseph" Puente (1891–1960), also made their way here. Puente arrived in America in 1912 and, in 1922, married Elsie Brusa. The tools of the stonecutter's trade adorn their monument.

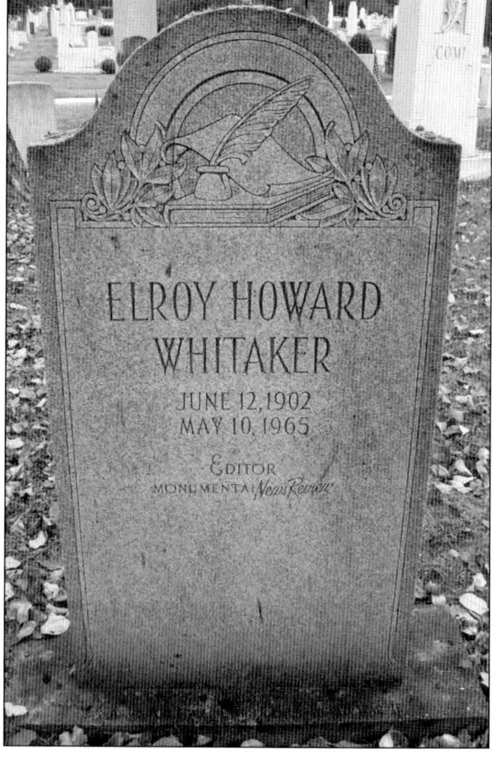

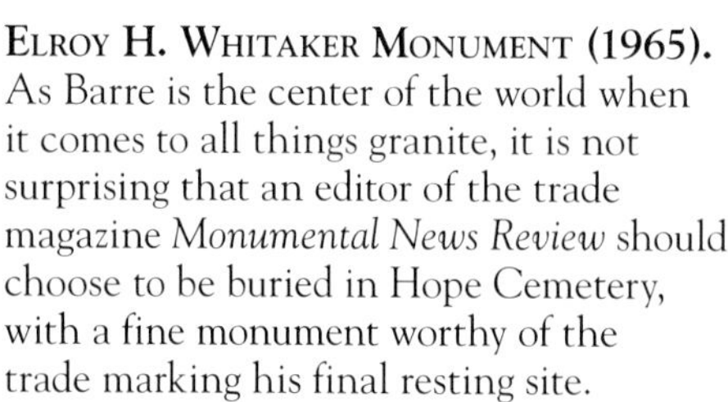

ELROY H. WHITAKER MONUMENT (1965). As Barre is the center of the world when it comes to all things granite, it is not surprising that an editor of the trade magazine *Monumental News Review* should choose to be buried in Hope Cemetery, with a fine monument worthy of the trade marking his final resting site.

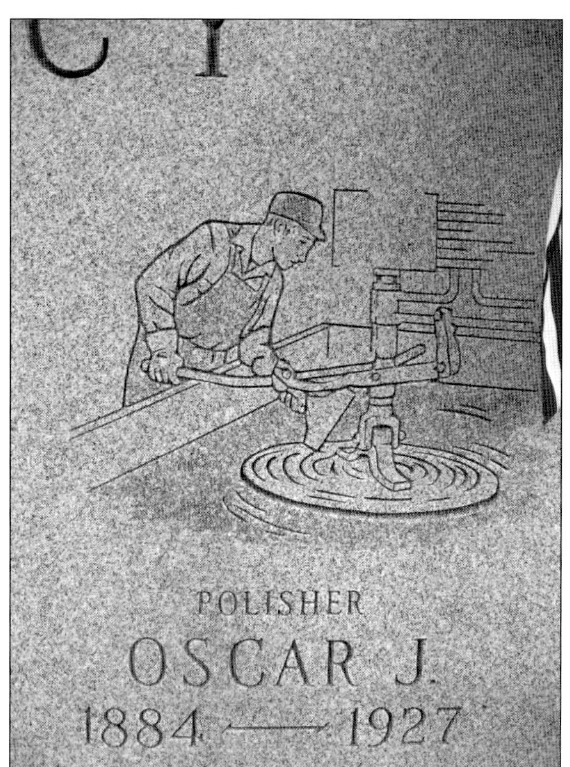

Stacy Family Monument Details (1990). This modern stone highlights the granite industry careers of a father and his son. Oscar Stacy (1884–1927) worked as a polisher (right) in the granite trade, marrying Louise Mills in Barre in 1924. The same year that his son Clayton Stacy (1927–1990) was born, he died suddenly. Still, Clayton followed his father in the granite trade to become a stonecutter (below).

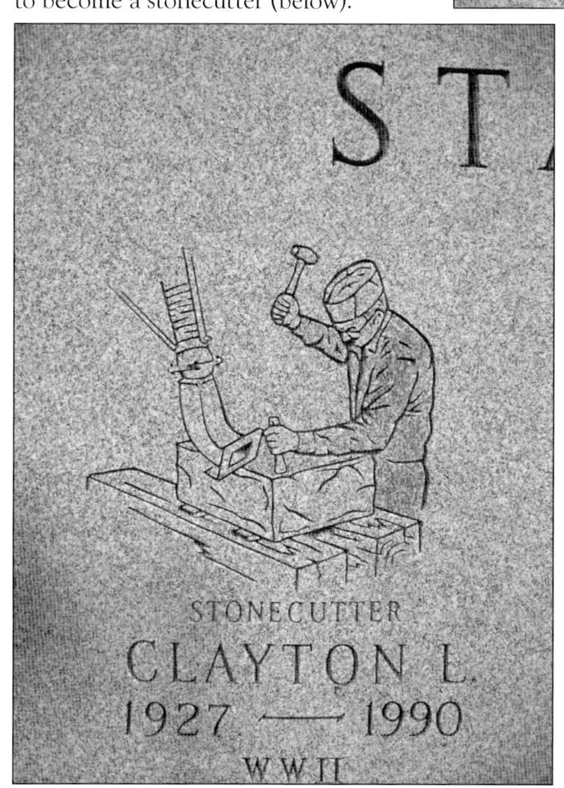

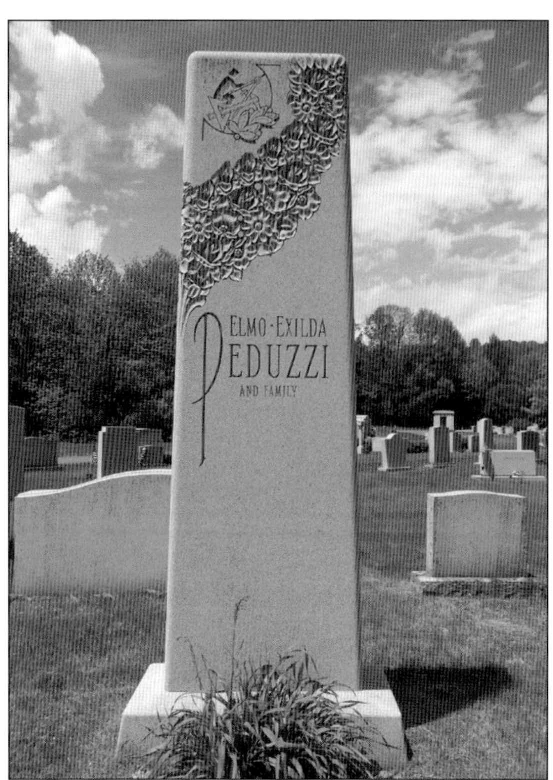

PEDUZZI FAMILY MONUMENT (1988). Elmo Peduzzi (1924–1988) was the son of a grocery store owner who became a draftsman, working in the monument business for the South Barre Granite Company. The tools of his trade and a cutout of him sitting at his drafting table (below) are shown at the top of the monument for him, his wife, Exilda, and their family. Though he designed many monuments in Hope, he is best known as the designer of the Italian American monument in Barre.

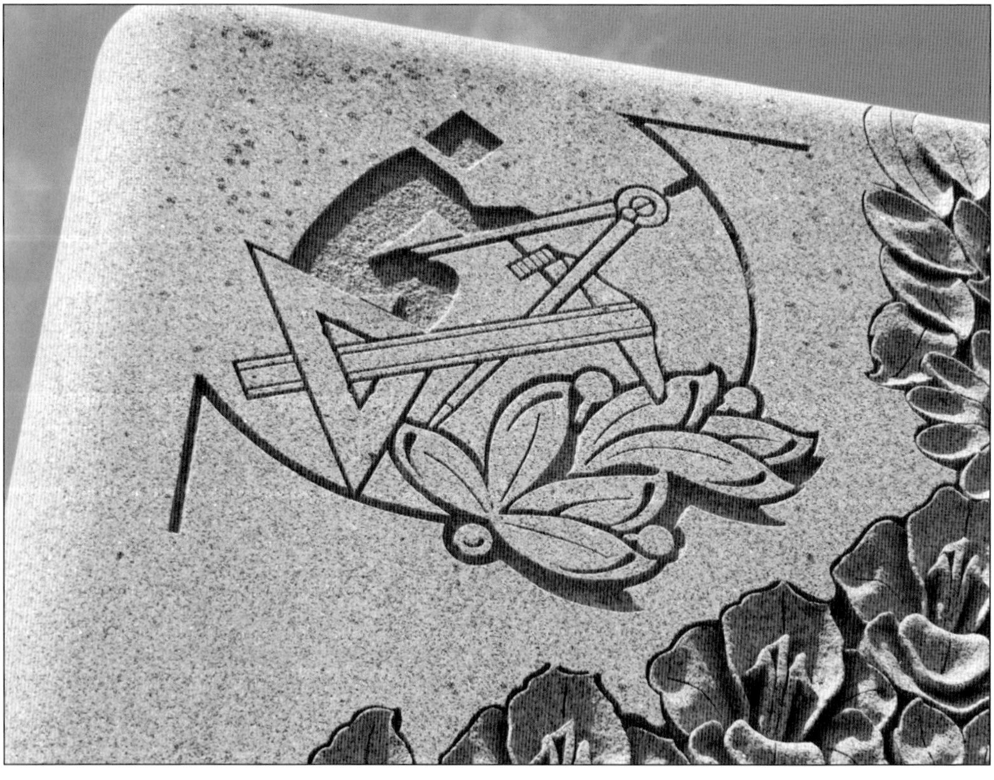

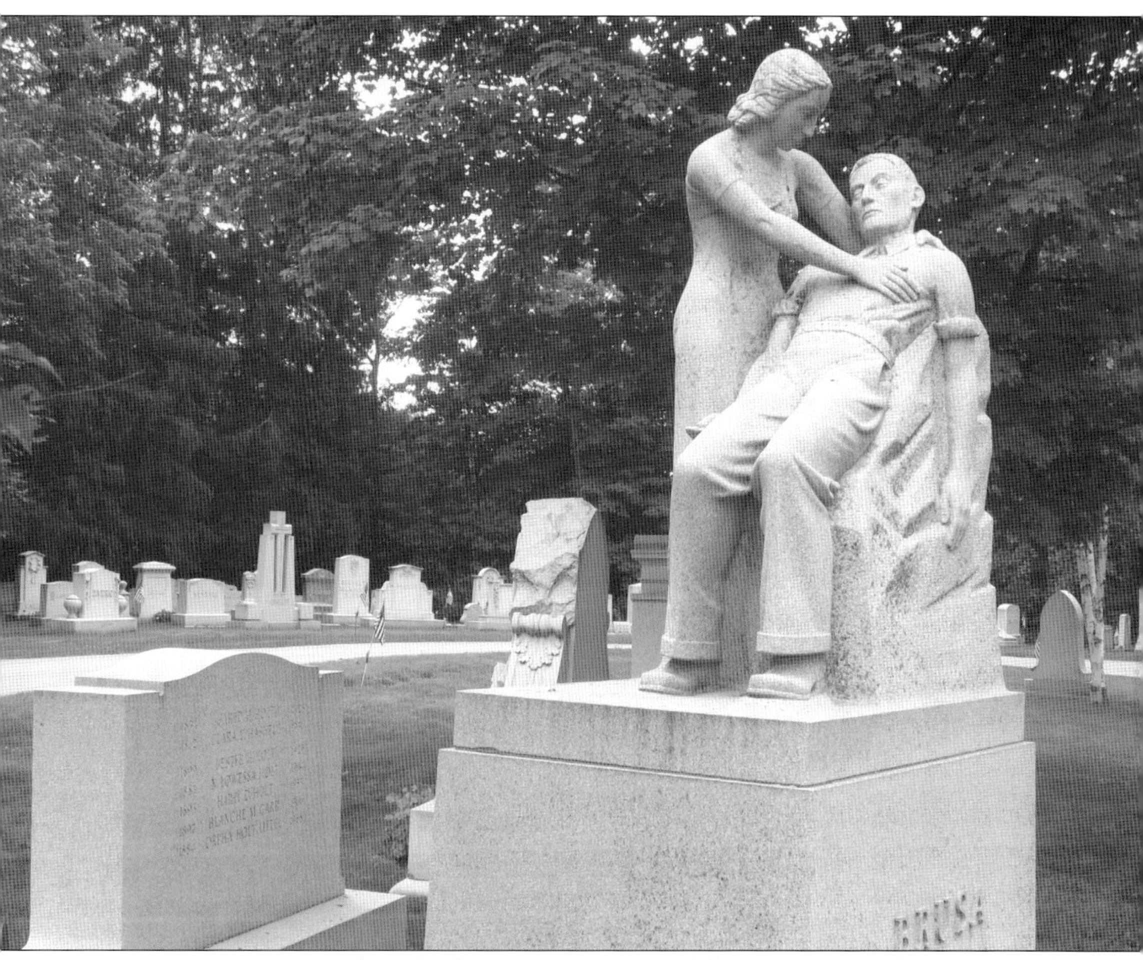

Louis G. Brusa Monument (1937). This monument is one of the most iconic and important of all the monuments in Hope Cemetery. Louis (1886–1937), along with his brother John, was the owner of Brusa Brothers and a skilled and successful granite artist. He was also a local activist in the fight for better working conditions, pushing granite shed owners to install ventilation systems so that stonecutters would not inhale the fine granite dust that resulted in the stonecutter's lung disease, silicosis, often termed pulmonary tuberculosis. Louis was dying from this disease when he designed this monument, and the depiction of him and his wife, Maria (1890–1957), serving as the models for a dying stonecutter being cared for by an attentive wife, was carved by Donato Coletti. The monument was not just controversial for its advocacy, but also for the shapely form of the woman (rumored to be Brusa's mistress). The same year that Brusa died, the Vermont legislature passed the safety laws he had fought for.

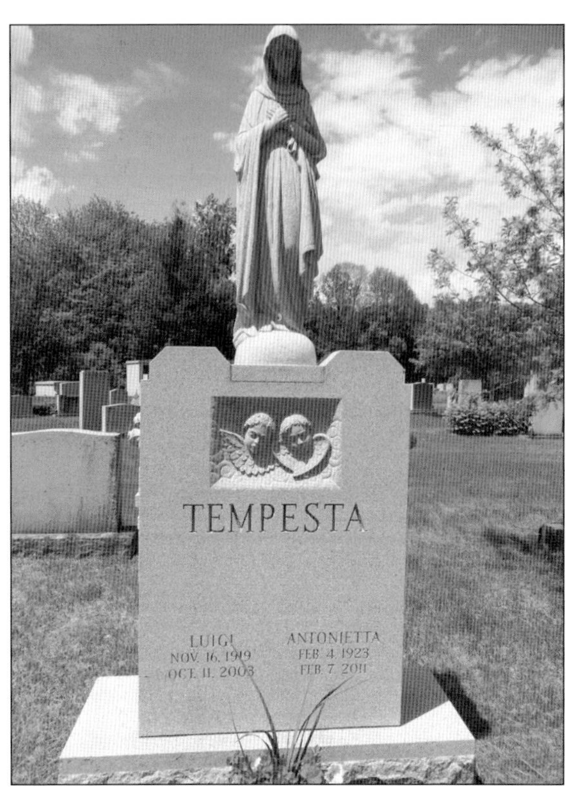

TEMPESTA FAMILY MONUMENT (2003). Luigi Tempesta was a sculptor from Italy who arrived in America in 1954 and, by 1957, was in Barre, employed as a sculptor by the Peerless Granite Company. The stone is said to have been carved by Tempesta himself, including the fine relief carving of the two cherubs (below), which were said to be one of his specialties.

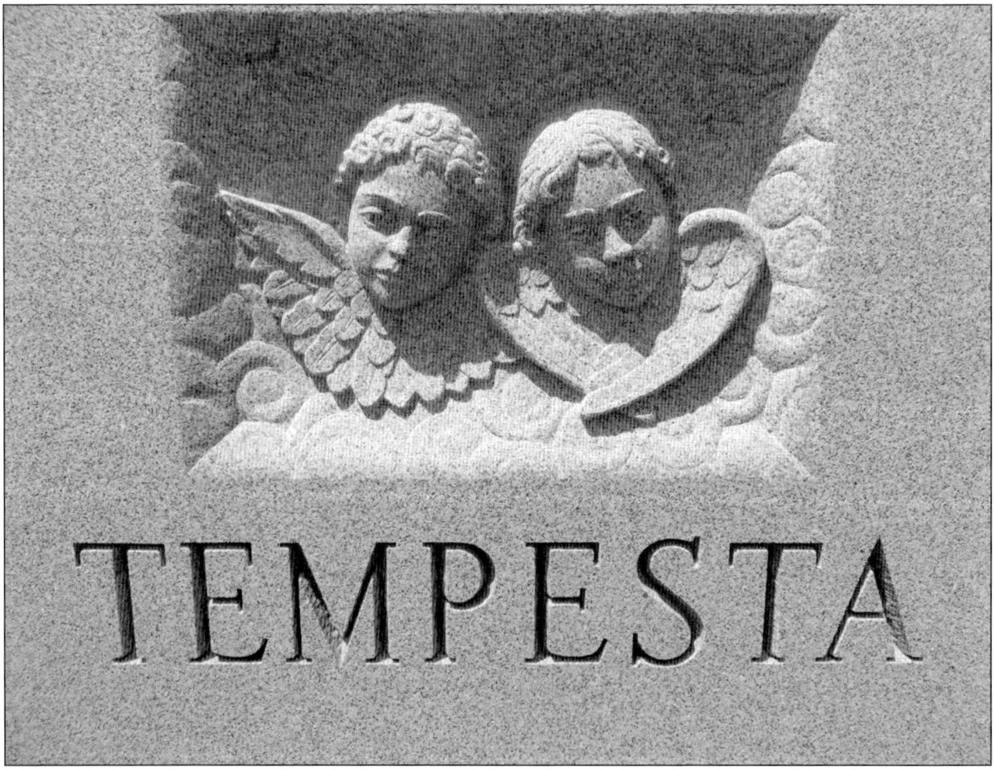

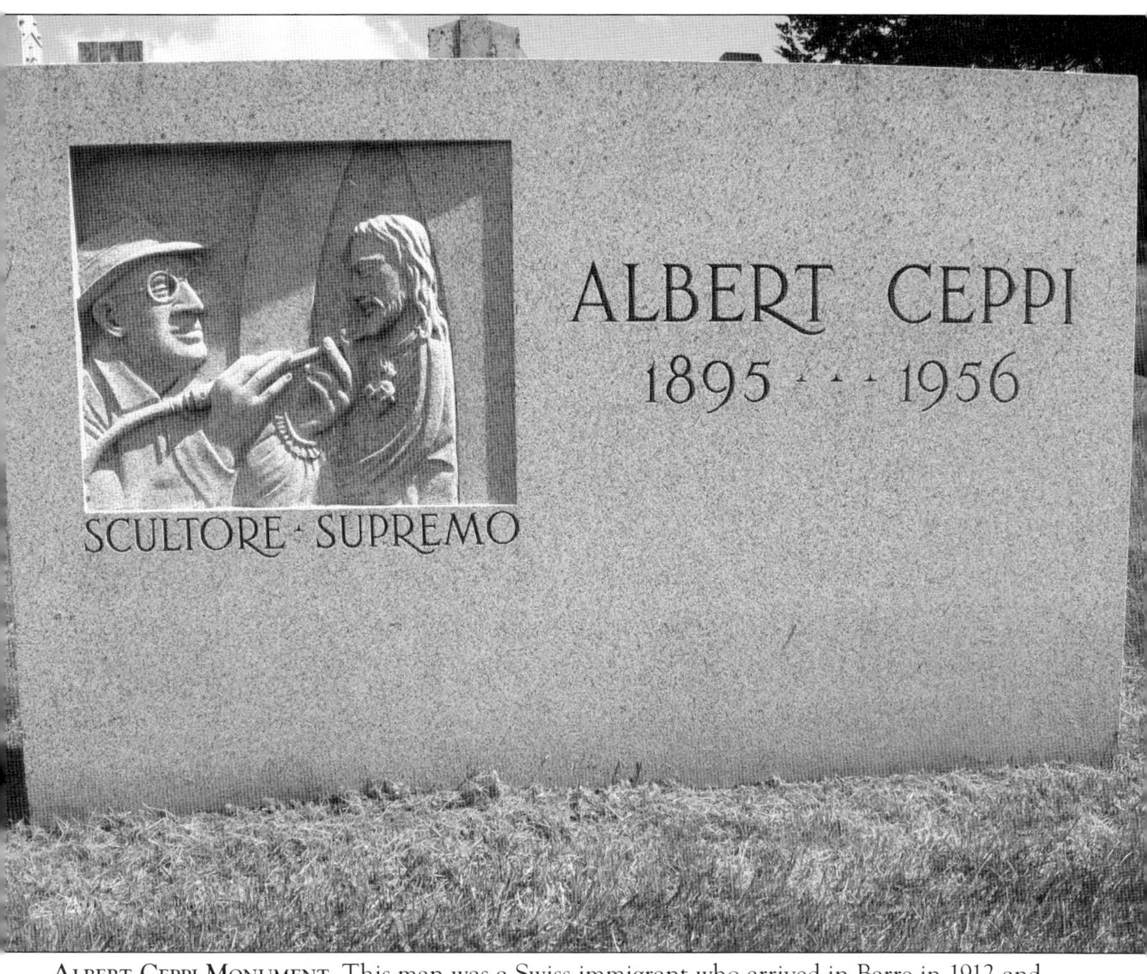

Albert Ceppi Monument. This man was a Swiss immigrant who arrived in Barre in 1912 and worked as a stonecutter for many years for the Chioldi Granite Company. The monument offers a pleasing view of the stonecutter at work, but it is unknown if this *scultore supremo*, Italian for "supreme sculptor," created his own monument.

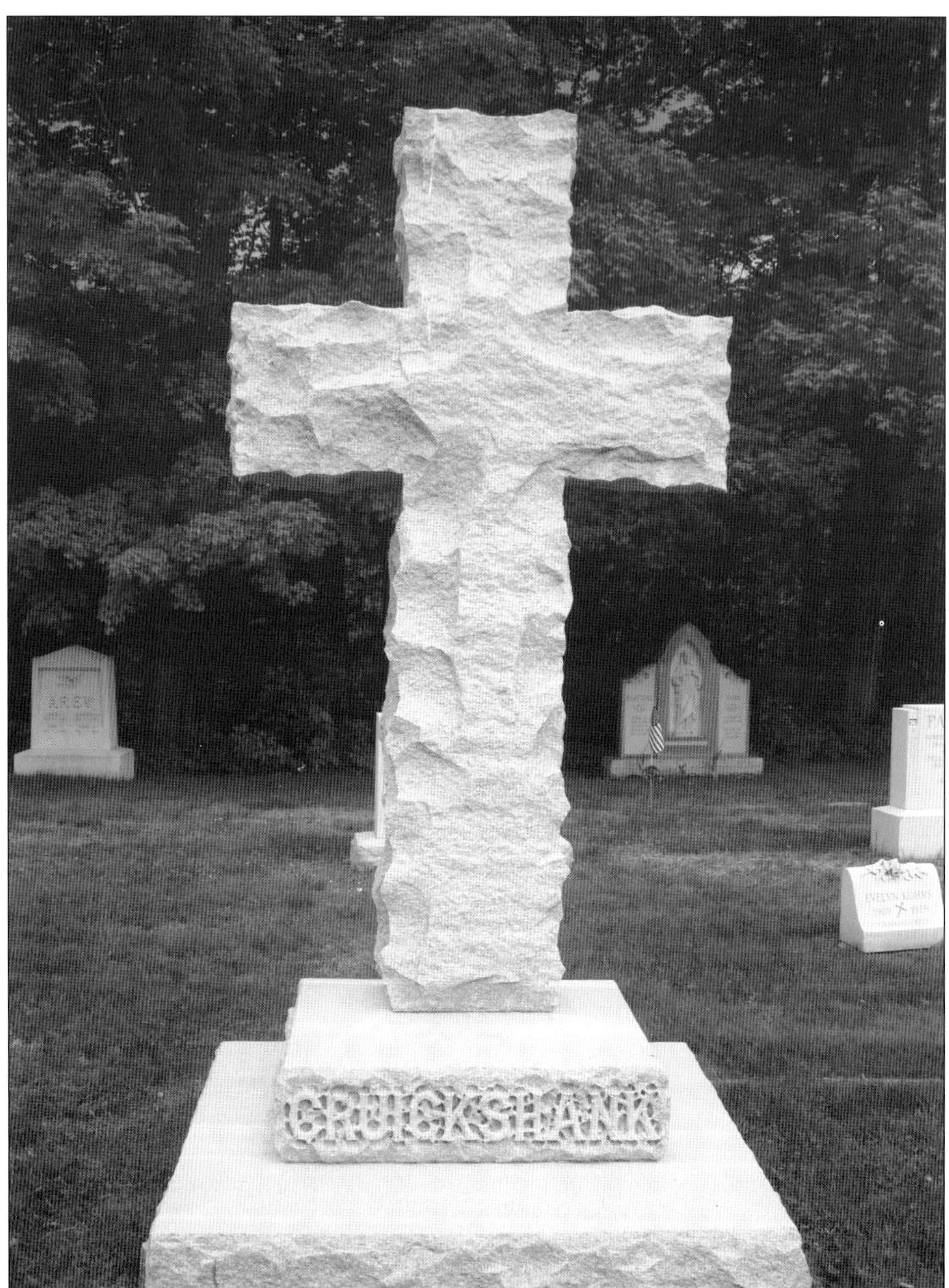

Cruickshank Family Monument (1915). This large cross, cut in shell-rock style, is an excellent example of the work of the firm Innes and Cruickshank, a form in which it specialized. Alexander Cruickshank (1858–1915) was a native of Banffshire, Scotland, who arrived in Barre in the 1870s at the beginning of the growth of the granite business. He would eventually die from pulmonary tuberculosis.

Monument Index